Usk Castle, Priory and Town

Usk Castle, Priory and Town

Edited by

Jeremy K. Knight & Andy Johnson

Logaston Press

LOGASTON PRESS
Little Logaston Woonton Almeley
Herefordshire HR3 6QH
logastonpress.co.uk

First published by Logaston Press 2008

ISBN 978 1 906663 02 5 (paperback)
978 1 906663 01 8 (hardback)

Set in Times New Roman by Logaston Press
and printed in Great Britain by
Bell & Bain Ltd., Glasgow

Front cover: A view across the town and St. Mary's church from the castle

Contents

Geoffrey Mein, 1922-2008

Geoffrey Mein, the foremost authority on the history of Usk, and intended co-editor of this book, died suddenly in February 2008, immediately after completing work on his chapters but before he was able to participate in the work of editing the remaining chapters. We hope that we have now brought his work to a satisfactory fruition.

Geoff was born in Nottingham on 23 July 1922. Educated in the University of Nottingham, he took a law degree and joined the National Coal Board as a solicitor in 1947. He was active in the county archaeological society, the Thoroton Society, and took part in a number of excavations. Transfer to the Durham coalfield enabled him to carry out fieldwork and excavation on Hadrian's Wall and other prehistoric and Roman sites in Northumberland.

In 1972 he settled in Usk with his second wife, Patricia, and his two sons. He became very active in the Usk Civic Society and in a range of other local bodies, including the Gwent County History Association, the Gwent Local History Council and the Glamorgan Gwent Archaeological Trust, of which he became Chairman. In 1986, shortly after his retirement, he published *Norman Usk: The Birth of a Town*. He was a skilful fieldworker, and hopefully his long running excavations at Trostrey Castle will be brought to publication.

It is hoped that his contributions to this book will be not only a fitting memorial to his work, but also a legacy on which future Usk historians and archaeologists can build.

Jeremy K. Knight and Andy Johnson

Preface and Acknowledgements

Usk Castle Friends were created in 2000 to support the castle and to promote it as a place of education and inspiration for visitors. This has been done by financial assistance to improve the facilities and assist in conserving the fabric and through a range of events in the grounds making use of the evocative surroundings which are so much a part of the castle's unique atmosphere. Through these activities and their support for the hugely successful pageant commemorating the battle of Pwll Melin between the forces of Glyndŵr and those of the English crown in 1405 (one of a number of such events staged within the castle), the castle and the community have been drawn together in what is the latest chapter in the history of Usk.

The Friends have also organized a highly successful series of lectures by distinguished invited speakers, exploring many aspects of the history of the castle, priory and town. In 2006 the Friends suggested that some of the lectures might be printed as a valuable and permanent record of the town's history. They approached Logaston Press and the present editors with this in mind. Most of the present chapters originated from this lecture series, but for a variety of reasons, some of the lectures given to the Friends were not available for publication. Several other writers then kindly agreed to contribute chapters to complete the story of Usk's remarkable past, from its origins in prehistoric and Roman times to the present day.

Usk Castle Friends owe a debt of gratitude to Andy Johnson of Logaston Press, whose histories of Chepstow, Ludlow and elsewhere provided the inspiration for the present volume and whose wise and relaxed editorial guidance and experience brought it together. We are also very grateful to the individual authors who so readily agreed to contribute to the volume, and to our editors.

Virginia Hoselitz
Usk Castle Friends

Notes on Contributors

Jan Barrow is a well regarded local historian, whose books are characterized by solid archival research and the use of oral history. Born and brought up in the Midlands, she qualified as a librarian and spent all her working life among books, firstly in Birmingham Reference Library, then as BBC Midland Region librarian and later Staffordshire schools librarian. After raising a family, she returned to librarianship at Corpus Christi College, Oxford. She retired to Llanbadoc in 1987. *From Dawn to Dusk: Usk: the story of its markets, trades and occupations* was published in 2004 and *Usk at War*, an account of Usk and its people during two world wars, including the memories of many local people, in 2006. She is married to John Barrow.

John Barrow. After graduating in the University of Birmingham and gaining a diploma in Town and Country Planning at the University of Manchester, John Barrow's professional life was spent in the English counties, culminating in Oxfordshire, where he was Director of Planning and Property Services. After four years retirement pursuing his hobbies — notably calligraphy and fly fishing — he joined the Planning Inspectorate as a Local Plans Inspector, charged with considering and making recommendations to five local planning authorities on statutory objections to their Local Plans. In addition, after studying expressions of concern, he advised one District Council on the changes they should make to their planning service in order to restore public confidence. On leaving the Inspectorate, he became involved with Usk Civic Society, of which he has been Honorary Secretary for five years. All opinions expressed in his chapter are his own however, and do not reflect the views of the Society.

Professor Chris Given Wilson is Professor of Late Medieval History at the University of St Andrews. His main area of research is centred on English social and political history in the later middle ages, particularly historiography and chronicles. His other research interest is the Inca Civilization. His many publications include *The Chronicle of Adam Usk 1377-1421* (Oxford Medieval Texts 1997), *Chronicles: The Writing of History in Medieval England* (2004), *The English Nobility in the Late Middle Ages (1987)* and *The Royal Household and the King's Affinity: Service, Politics and Finance in England 1360-1413* (Yale 1986). He has also edited 16 volumes of Medieval Parliament Rolls. In 1987 he was awarded the Alexander Prize of the Royal Historical Society.

Madeleine Gray is a Senior Lecturer in History at the University of Wales, Newport and one of the editors of the Gwent County History. A specialist in medieval religion and culture (and a highly popular speaker on those topics), her *Images of Piety,* studying the iconography of late medieval religion in Wales, was published in 2000. Recent publications include *The Protestant Religion: Beliefs and Practices* (2003) and a chapter on the pre-Reformation Church in *Gwent County History* vol II (2007).

Henry Humphreys. A farmer and forester, Henry Humphreys was born in Usk Castle, where his family have now lived for exactly one hundred years. He formed the Garrison Troop society aged 7 with his friends to man the castle. After Cirencester Agricultural College 1973-4, with holidays spent on restoration projects at the castle, he set off for America to meet his sister. He then worked his way around the world, returning three years later with a love of travel particularly in the Far East, India and Nepal. He started farming near Usk in 1977, taking over the management of the woods from his father, working on the care and conservation of the castle and carrying out garden schemes in stone and ironwork to entertain and astonish visitors.

Rosemary Humphreys, née Trant, was born in Montgomeryshire and educated at Dartington Hall and at the University of East Anglia, where she read art history. She came to Monmouthshire in the 1970s to work on the first version of Pevsner's *Buildings of England: Gwent/Monmouthshire.* Later she worked for Laura Ashley at Carno, returning to Monmouthshire in 1978 to farm on the Sugar Loaf mountain before swapping her farm for 70 acres near Usk, a husband and a child allowance, which have kept her in the style to which she is accustomed — an old house with dodgy heating and a large garden. She now works full time from home as Usk Castle *châtelaine*, events organiser, gardener, groom, scullery maid and mother of three.

Jeremy Knight F.S.A. Born and brought up in Caerleon, he read archaeology in University College, Cardiff before becoming an Inspector of Ancient Monuments in what is now English Heritage and then in Cadw, where his area of responsibility included Monmouthshire. He has excavated on Roman and Medieval sites, particularly Montgomery Castle, and published many guidebooks and articles on Welsh castles and other sites, including Usk. His books include *The End of Antiquity* (1999, new edition 2007); *Roman France, an Archaeological Field Guide* (2001) and *Civil War and Restoration in Monmouthshire* (2005). He is Chairman of the Monmouthshire Antiquarian Association and Past President of the Cambrian Archaeological Association. He has been the recipient of two festschrifts: *Essays in Honour of Jeremy K. Knight (Monmouthshire Antiquary* XII 1996) and *The Medieval Castle in Ireland and Wales* (Dublin 2003).

Professor William Manning F.S.A. is Emeritus Professor of Roman Archaeology at Cardiff University, where he was a member of the Archaeology Department from 1964 until 2000. Before that, he had worked in Reading Museum and The British Museum. He has directed excavations at a number of sites in England and Wales of which the most important was the series of large scale excavations at Usk between 1965 and 1976. He has published widely on aspects of Roman Wales, including a series of volumes on the results of the Usk excavations (University of Wales Press) and *Roman Wales: A Pocket Guide* (Cardiff 2001). He has also worked extensively on Roman iron artefacts, his most notable publication in this field being the *Catalogue of the Romano-British Tools, Fittings and Weapons in the British Museum* (London 1985).

Geoffrey Mein. Born in Nottingham, Geoffrey Mein qualified as a solicitor in 1946. His Scottish ancestors having been involved in mining or quarrying since 1500, he joined the National Coal Board in 1947 and moved south in 1972 as the Board's legal advisor in south Wales, retiring in 1984 to devote his time to historical research. An active field archaeologist since before the war, he always found himself helping in its organization and encouraging others to take part. Many volunteer helpers later read the subject at University. For some years Field Research Secretary of the Monmouthshire Antiquarian Association and Trustee of the Glamorgan-Gwent Archaeological Trust, he chaired the Gwent Local History Council, Raglan Local History Society and Usk Civic Society. A founding Trustee of Gwent County History Association, he continued to excavate, research and publish to the end. His other interests included natural history and music, both classical and jazz. His publications include *Usk: The Birth of a Town* (1986).

Frank Olding was for many years curator of Abergavenny Museum. Sometime Inspector of Ancient Monuments with Cadw (Welsh Historic Monuments) he is now Heritage Officer of Blaenau Gwent County Borough Council. His published works include *Vanished Abergavenny: from the collections of Abergavenny Museum* (1994), *Folklore of Blaenau Gwent* (1995) and *The Prehistoric Landscapes of the Eastern Black Mountains* (2000).

Sian Rees F.S.A. An Inspector of Ancient Monuments with Cadw (Welsh Historic Monuments), she read archaeology at Birmingham University, where she was awarded her doctorate for research on ancient agriculture. She then joined the Inspectorate of Ancient Monuments in England before moving to Wales, where she excavated Carreg Coetan burial chamber and Haverfordwest Priory. She has worked on the study and conservation of many castles and abbeys, including Cwmhir Abbey, Ewenny Priory and Monmouth Priory. She lives in Raglan.

Peter Rennie. A native of Usk, Peter Rennie practised for many years as an agricultural surveyor and valuer, a partner, then senior partner, of Rennie, Taylor and Till. This gave him a detailed knowledge of the Monmouthshire countryside and its agricultural scene. His brother was patrol leader of the Usk Auxiliary Unit and his brother-in-law patrol leader of the Chepstow unit. He has researched the Auxiliary Units for many years and knows the locations of six of their eight bunkers.

Keith Underwood (who has provided the heraldic drawings and associated information) was educated at Monmouth School, Newport College of Art and the Western England College of Art in Bristol. After army service in the Education Corps he spent a year in France on a Leverhulme scholarship before becoming a teacher. He settled in Chepstow in 1972. A painter and calligrapher, his interest in heraldic art was aroused when he painted the arms of the Colonel of Beachley army camp for the Colonel's elderly relative. This began an interest, both scholarly and artistic, in heraldry. His work can be seen in a number of places in Chepstow, including the mural frieze of historic Chepstow figures in the Drill Hall. As Brother Thomas, a Cistercian monk, he also conducts visitors around Tintern Abbey for Cadw, sometimes to the confusion of foreign tourists.

List of Figures and Plates

Foreword

Usk – the word corresponds to the ancient British *iska* or Celtic *uisge* which is found compounded in various forms in many place names around Britain, such as Exeter, and in far-flung places on the Continent. Unsurprisingly, it means water. So Usk town acquired its name from the river alongside. Set between the river – fordable at this point for most of the year – and the Olway brook, this was a useful defensive location in which the Romans could build a fortress before creating a permanent base serviceable directly from the Severn, a few miles to the south at Caerleon.

Whether the Romans had a bridge at Usk is not known, but as their main purpose was military they might not have been looking to attract regular trade from across the river. The Normans, on the other hand, under whose aegis the town took shape, needed to ensure its commercial viability, for which a bridge would have been a necessity, together with a castle from which to protect it. Certainly it is impossible to imagine modern Usk without its bridge, and its importance is underlined by the main street's being named Bridge Street.

Usk developed slowly during the long and unruly rule of the marcher lords, a semi-autonomous nobility put in place by William I and ousted by Henry VIII, the first king to feel powerful enough to do so. When order eventually descended, the town did not grow like others in the county for it did not attract much industry. But it remained important as a river crossing and junction, so that publicans were a well represented trade; and there are still quite a number of pubs in relation to the size of the town.

Throughout the centuries when to move goods by road was a struggle, the river was highly important in the life of the town, such that until fairly recently the mayor was known as the Portreeve. The river would flood into the town sometimes, though it was probably not so prone to do so when the uplands were more wooded than they are now. Occasional flooding was looked upon as part of life in lower-lying areas until electric wiring, fitted carpets and other aids to modern living made the state of affairs unacceptable. The necessary embanking has reduced the picturesque appearance of the riverscape but has of course enhanced property values. The embankments themselves have not affected the river's famous salmon fishing, which has diminished somewhat for other reasons as elsewhere. Usk's own Town Water remains an attractive asset, nevertheless.

The town has unfortunately become something of a victim of the success of the motor vehicle; traffic which used to be welcomed for its 'passing trade' has grown to a volume which threatens to overwhelm the ancient streets. In spite of that it is a most agreeable place to live in, having the intimacy of a small rural town with convenient access to employment and amenities in larger neighbouring ones, and good communications to places beyond.

Every town has a past full of interest if one can discover it, but our knowledge of history depends very largely on what contemporary written evidence happens to have survived, and the further back the date the less there usually is. Such records of Usk's story are not abundant, but the authors of the essays in this volume have used those that are to hand, supplemented by what archaeology can tell us, with some discourse on the early architecture. The result is a sort of historical collage with which one can gain a picture of the town's character and how it has developed throughout the centuries. There are also some thoughts about the future. It provides informative reading even if one is familiar with the town, and undoubtedly it will be greatly appreciated by the visitor.

Lord Raglan
Cefntilla

CHAPTER I

Usk in Prehistory
by Frank Olding

The Mesolithic Period

The earliest evidence for human activity at Usk dates to the Mesolithic period or Middle Stone Age (*c*.10,000-4,500 BC) when small groups of hunter-gatherers made regular use of favourable places to intercept the seasonal movements of reindeer, wild oxen, horse and red deer. During the winter, the hunters and their families settled in base-camps on the coast or in the valley bottoms and the River Usk, teeming with fish, wildfowl and other game, would have been a valuable source of extra food. During the summer, smaller groups would have moved into the higher hunting grounds in the uplands. Scatters of small flint flakes and tools (known as microliths) indicate their patterns of movement through the landscape and may also represent the remains of their camps or hunting stands.

Prehistorians divide the Mesolithic into two periods — the early and later Mesolithic. This is on the basis of a distinct change in the style of flint tools used that took place between about 7,900 BC and 7,600 BC. This saw a change from the use of broader microlithic blades to much smaller and narrower blades and points. A flint scatter found during the excavations of the Roman fortress at Usk dated to the early Mesolithic (*c*.10,000-7,900 BC) and included two 'backed points' and two smaller fragments (Fig. 1.1).[1] These could have been lost during hunting — possibly embedded in game.

Finds of the later Mesolithic are much more numerous and scatters from Usk and the Black Mountains show that inland settlement was growing in this period.[2] The largest group of later Mesolithic objects yet found in Gwent were also discovered during the excavation of the Usk fortress. A discrete scatter of 729 flint artefacts included burins (engraving tools for working bone and antler), scrapers, and a variety of blades. Blade cores and debitage (waste flakes and fragments) showed that flint had been worked on the spot and many of the artefacts had been damaged by use. The fact that the early tools mentioned above were also found here suggests that Usk was a spot favoured by Mesolithic hunters for many generations — for centuries in fact. Other Mesolithic scatters have been found at Trostrey and Llanmelin Wood.

The Neolithic Period

The Neolithic period or New Stone Age (*c*.4,500-2,500 BC) saw the introduction of farming and a more settled lifestyle to these valleys. Small fields and clearances were hacked out of the dense woodland using polished axes of flint and stone. Excavations at Gwernvale, near Crickhowell, clearly illustrated the establishment of small farming communities in the Usk Valley by about 3900 BC. Cereals were grown locally and processed for consumption on site, and cattle, sheep and pigs also played a part in the farming economy.

Finds of Neolithic axes go some way to indicating the extent of the new clearances and settlements. They also indicate the existence of widespread trading networks as stone axes from a variety of sources are found widely scattered across Britain. The products of different quarries and axe 'factories' have been assigned by specialists to distinct groups (e.g. Group I axes from Cornwall). In the Usk area there have been finds of axes from as far afield as Cornwall, north Wales (Group VII) and Pembrokeshire (Group VIII). One of the most unusual of the Neolithic artefacts from the area is a fine flint sickle blade, found somewhere near Usk (though the exact provenance is unknown), now in the collections of the National Museum and Gallery of Wales (Fig. 1.2).[3] Its edge shows a distinctive 'corn gloss', showing that it was used in the harvesting of cereal crops.

The Neolithic period also saw the first use of pottery in the British Isles. Typical of the earliest period are plain, round-bottomed bowls probably used for cooking or storing foodstuffs. These sometimes have a distinct shoulder or 'carination' in the profile of the bowl. From about 3,400 BC onwards, more decorated styles of pottery (known as Peterborough ware) evolved. Excavations at Trostrey have produced sherds

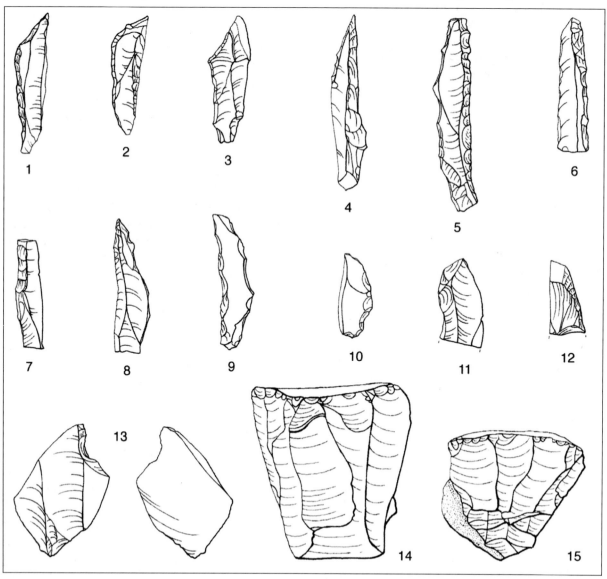

Fig. 1.1 Finds from the Late Mesolithic flint scatter at Usk

2

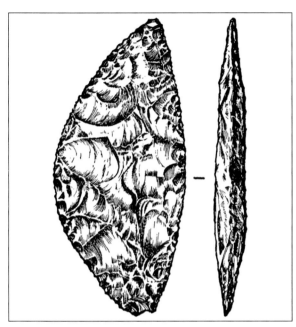

*Fig. 1.2 Neolithic flint sickle blade
with corn gloss from Usk*

of both styles, indicating activity on the site throughout the Neolithic period (see below). The fortress excavations at Usk produced parts of at least eight vessels including early plain and carinated bowls, a Peterborough ware bowl and part of a vessel that may be Grooved Ware.[4] This highly decorated style of pottery is closely associated with the massive henge monuments of southern England like Avebury, Stonehenge and Durrington Walls.

As in the preceding Mesolithic period, scatters of flint tools also offer an important insight into the patterns of Neolithic activity and settlement in the landscape. Large scatters of Neolithic material have been found at Trostrey, Llanmelin Wood and at the Rhadyr, just north of Usk. The fortress excavations again contributed to the overall picture with the discovery of scrapers, knives, awls, blades, leaf-shaped arrowheads and fragments of polished axes. It was obvious that flint tools had been manufactured on site and the scatter probably represents part of an extensive area of occupation along both banks of the Usk.[5]

The remains of wooden Neolithic houses have been found in other parts of Wales, but there are no fully published examples from Gwent.

Excavated examples indicate a wide variety of house types. The earliest are rectangular halls with internal partitions and hearths and a doorway into the gable end. The best example so far has been found at Llandygai, Gwynedd, and dated to 4,400-3,700 BC.[6] At Gwernvale, near Crickhowell, a similar structure has been dated to 4,000-3,700 BC, but it is possible that this was a ritual platform associated with the nearby chambered tomb (see below).

Excavations at Trostrey have uncovered a series of rectangular Neolithic structures constructed of wattle panels supported by posts. At least two had internal hearths and an entrance in the south-eastern corner. Calibrated radiocarbon dates from one of the corner posts give a date range of 4780-4500 BC.[7] These structures are interpreted by the excavator as a sequence of small Neolithic houses associated with cereal farming and sheep rearing on a favoured and regularly reoccupied site. Although the remains of up to ten structures have been found, these represent a long sequence of rebuilding and only three may have been occupied at any one time.[8] In Usk itself, six roughly circular post and stake-built structures were discovered beneath the Roman layers in Old Market Street. These are undated, though Neolithic and Early Bronze Age flintwork was found on the site.[9]

It was also during the Neolithic period that the people of south-east Wales began to build the first large scale ritual monuments — the famous chambered tombs that cluster around the Black Mountains. These are long, wedge-shaped cairns of stones with one or more burial chambers built into the broad end or the sides. These chambers were the communal burial places of the communities that built them. In them were placed the mixed bones of many people rather than the body of a single individual. Excavations at Gwernvale found evidence of a six-post structure in the forecourt of the tomb[10] and it has been suggested that the bodies of the dead were first exposed on high wooden platforms in a sort of 'sky burial'. Once the flesh had rotted away, the bones were gathered up and deposited in the chambers of the long cairns.

Similar activities may have taken place at Trostrey where excavations have uncovered a ritual site dating to the early Neolithic period (3980-3710 BC).[11] The site comprised an oval excarnation mound used for the exposure of bodies to allow them to be reduced to bare bones. This mound had a double setting of boulders, a timber façade, two cremation pyres and five deposits of cremated bone, pottery and flint debris. Each of these deposits had been topped by a stone cairn and they are dated 3785-3647 BC.[12]

Excavations at Mynydd Troed, near Cwm Du, showed that when they were built, the tombs were set in clearings in open, dry oak forests in areas which would have served as summer pastures.[13] Worshipping and venerating the ancestors at these sacred sites forged strong bonds between Neolithic people and particular places in their landscapes. The construction and use of the chambered tombs may well have contributed to the development of a fixed sense of place, a feeling of home. To this tradition belongs the much-disturbed chambered tomb at Gaer Lwyd (originally Garn Lwyd), Shirenewton (ST 448 967) (Fig. 1.3). Five large uprights still support a large capstone that has slipped from its original position and split. Two of these stones probably originally flanked the entrance to the chamber.[14] Two others that now lie flat may also have been uprights.[15] The jumble of stones that can be seen today once formed a stone burial chamber at the east end of an impressive long cairn, and may well have been similar to the portal dolmens of south-west Wales.[16]

Another phase of ritual activity at Trostrey saw the construction of a timber circle surrounding a rectangular setting of stakes and a standing stone. The circle was some 9.5m in diameter with an opening to the north-west. The whole complex seems to have been centred on a tree that may have been the object of special veneration.[17] Radiocarbon evidence dates this structure to 3100-2580 BC — the very end of the Neolithic period.[18]

Fig. 1.3 The much disturbed Neolithic chambered tomb at Gaer Lwyd

The Bronze Age

The Early Bronze Age (*c*.2500 BC-1200 BC) saw the introduction of the first metal tools — first of copper and then of bronze itself. Bronze Age farmers and shepherds began widespread upland forest clearances in search of cultivable soil. Territories that had kept mainly to the lower ground during the Neolithic expanded onto the adjoining hills. The high ridges of the uplands became summer grazing grounds for herds of cattle and flocks of sheep, and it is on these high ridges that the most striking remains of Bronze Age people and their religious beliefs are to be found.

The Early Bronze Age sees a radical shift from the ritual and burial traditions of the preceding Neolithic period. In place of long barrows and cairns housing communal burials, the Early Bronze Age sees the introduction of round barrows and cairns containing the burials and grave goods of individuals — often accompanied by the new pottery vessels known as Beakers. Two fine examples of these burial mounds are to be found on the top of Wentwood ridge. When the mounds were built, the ridge upon which they stand may have been less densely wooded than today — the barrows and, perhaps, those buried in them, would have enjoyed spectacular views out over the Usk valley to the west.[19]

Standing stones remain enigmatic and difficult to classify — some were certainly erected with a ritual intention, while many have acted as waymarkers or boundary stones in recent times. Elsewhere in Wales excavations suggest two basic types — large stones which appear to be central to ritual or burial activities, and smaller stones which were erected to mark the site of small burial pits. Standing stones are traditionally dated to the Early Bronze Age and the evidence from the handful of excavated examples in Wales does indeed suggest that the period of their erection and use ranged from about 1870 BC to 1050 BC.[20]

The most striking examples of this type of monument in the Usk area are those at Llangybi and Grey Hill. The solitary stone at Llangybi, about 4km south of Usk, is a pointed slab of conglomerate sandstone some 1.8m high (Fig. 1.4). Its position in the low-lying fields adjacent to the river Usk is similar to many others in central and southern Monmouthshire.[21] The stones on Grey Hill form part of a much more complex monument that probably represents a long history of construction and adaptation. A large, D-shaped

Fig. 1.4 The standing stone at Llangybi

Fig. 1.5 Part of the stone circle on Grey Hill

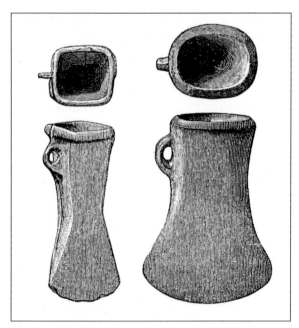

Fig. 1.6 Late Bronze Age bag-shaped socketed axe found at Castle Hill, Usk

enclosure surrounding the summit of the hill may date to the Neolithic. Near its southern boundary is the Grey Hill stone circle consisting of 13 stones up to 0.5m in height, some of which are laid flat, others set on their edges (Fig. 1.5). East of the circle is a standing stone some 1.8m high, and a further three standing stones run in a line to the north-west. Beyond them and further north is another standing stone about 2m high. The two largest stones are set in line with the mid-winter sunrise.[22] Several round barrows are located on the summit of Grey Hill to the north and it has been suggested that the standing stones mark the route of a ceremonial processional way linking the barrow cemetery with the stone circle.[23]

At Trostrey, this period saw the construction of a wooden, four-post structure surmounted by upper cross-members with carved, horn-like terminals. Carbon dating places its construction between 1910-1530 BC[24] and it has been likened to the Early Bronze Age 'shrine' from Bargeroosterveld in the Netherlands.[25] Another phase of activity consisted of a ring cairn (a circular rubble bank enclosing an open central area) built around this shrine and yet another phase saw the construction of a stone circle.[26]

The middle of the Bronze Age, the period around 1200 BC, saw a catastrophic change in the climate. The weather became colder and wetter. The summer grazing grounds on the high ridges became overgrazed and waterlogged and soon peat bogs began to cover the once lush pastures. The uplands had to be abandoned and a larger population struggled for survival. As the Late Bronze Age (*c.*1200-750 BC) progressed, conflict between groups led to warfare. Finds of Late Bronze Age weaponry such as the spears from Raglan Castle and Llantilio Crossenny and hoards of swords, spears and axes from Raglan, Glascoed, Llanfihangel Gobion and Trostrey give ample evidence of troubled times.[27]

The Iron Age
The need for defence continued into the Iron Age (*c.*750 BC – AD 43) — the period marked by the emergence of a distinctively Celtic culture and way of life. Brittonic, the ancient language spoken by Iron Age peoples, is the mother of modern Welsh. The Iron Age also saw the growth of separate tribes, each with their distinct territory. In Gwent and Glamorgan lay the homeland of the Silures; to the east, in what is now Herefordshire and Gloucestershire, a tribe called the Dobunni held sway. Their respective territories may have met at the eastern edge of the Black Mountains and defended villages and hillforts were erected at strategic points to protect territory and control movement. Formidable fortifications at sites like Llancayo Camp (Usk), Great House Camp at Llansoy and Gaer Fawr, Llangwm, still retain an air of threat and challenge.

The impressive hillfort with its multiple ramparts and ditches on Clytha Hill at Coed y Bwnydd is one of only a handful of Iron Age sites that have been excavated in the county (Figs. 1.7 and 1.8). The excavations demonstrated that the innermost of the multiple ramparts on the eastern side of the hillfort was a complex structure revetted on the outside by turf walls on stone footings and on the inside by a substantial, post-built timber wall. It is also likely to have had wooden defences on top of the rampart itself. These were impressive structures, surely with a deadly purpose.[28] Just behind the defences were a sequence of large roundhouses with wattle and daub walls built on stone and clay footings. The overall impression was of dense settlement over a long period. One house had been rebuilt *in situ* with its second phase radiocarbon dated to about 400 BC. Comparable evidence at Twyn y Gaer, in the Black Mountains some ten miles to the north, points to an initial phase of construction *c.*470 BC and it may well be that the 5th century BC sees the major period of hillfort building in south-east Wales.

The excavations also showed that the occupation of the hillfort had been ended by systematic destruction of its defences in the period around 200 BC. This phase of destruction ties in with the evidence from Twyn y Gaer. Here, the period around 200 BC saw a distinct shift in the cultural affinities of the hillfort. The pottery in use in the earlier phases was the duck-stamped ware made in the Malvern Hills and widely used by the inhabitants of Iron Age Herefordshire at sites like Croft Ambrey and Midsummer Hill. From about 200 BC onwards, the pottery is similar to that found

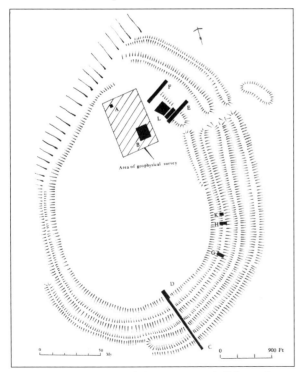

Fig. 1.7 Plan of the Iron Age hillfort of Coed y Bwnydd

at Llanmelin and Sudbrook — the heartland of the Silures of south-east Wales.[29]

This evidence clearly points to the extension of Silurian power into the eastern Black Mountains in the period around 200 BC. The evidence for the destruction of Coed y Bwnydd in the same period may well indicate that the disruption caused by this process was not confined to the Black Mountains alone. Did inter-tribal warfare sweep across central Monmouthshire? Was Coed y Bwnydd one of the victims of shifting power patterns in Iron Age Wales?

Although only published in interim reports, the excavations at Twyn y Gaer threw considerable light on the daily lives of the Iron Age inhabitants of south-east Wales. Finds of pottery, quern stones, sickles, hammers, saws, knives and jewellery suggest that the hillforts were self-contained, defended villages housing communities of farmers, artisans and craftsmen. Other finds — of weapons and sling-shots — speak of more warlike episodes.[30]

As we have seen, the excavator of Coed y Bwnydd argued that the evidence for rebuilding new houses on their old footings implied that the interior of the hillfort would have been densely occupied, with a considerable population and high levels of social organisation. The presence of structures interpreted as cattle pounds also indicates a strong pastoral element to the local economy. Coed y Bwnydd may well represent a defended village acting as a focus for a mixed-farming landscape in the surrounding area.

In fact, the best evidence for Iron Age settlement outside hillforts comes from this central area of Monmouthshire. At Camp Hill, Bryngwyn, a roughly circular enclosure some 90m in diameter with a possible entrance to the east was partially excavated in 1962.[31] The excavations traced a deep ditch and found pottery dating to the 1st and 2nd centuries AD. This shows that the traditional pattern of native settlement in central Monmouthshire continued through the Roman period and probably beyond. Prior to the excavations, the enclosure bank stood to a height of 1.2m from the bottom of the ditch. The site is now completely ploughed out and is a telling

Fig. 1.8 The ramparts of Coed y Bwnydd

example of the alarming rate of destruction of such sites in the area.

At White Castle Farm, Llantilio Crossenny, aerial photographs show a possible Iron Age or Romano-British farmstead consisting of a roughly circular enclosure some 75m in diameter with an entrance again to the east. The remains of adjacent field systems and roadways have also been identified together with possible hut circles within the enclosure itself.[32] In addition, the circular enclosure surrounding Tregaer churchyard and comprising a bank and ditch with a marked outer counterscarp is similar in size, aspect and elevation to Camp Hill and is probably of similar date.[33] These sites may well be the remains of defended farmsteads containing one or two houses for an extended family, together with outbuildings and other structures necessary for a mixed farming economy growing crops such as wheat and barley and raising sheep, cattle and pigs.[34] It is likely that a modern visitor to Iron Age Monmouthshire would have seen a largely familiar farming landscape.

CHAPTER II

The Legionary Fortress
by William Manning

The existence of a Roman site at Usk has been suspected since the late 16th century when William Camden suggested that *Burrium*, one of the posting stations listed in the Antonine Itinerary, had been situated at the town.[1] A century later John Horsley concluded that *Burrium* must be the same place as *Bulleum*, the only *polis* or settlement listed by the geographer Ptolemy in the territory of the Silures.[2] The meaning of the name is somewhat uncertain, but it is probably derived from a personal name, either *Burros* or *Bullos*.[3] In either case it suggests that Usk was an identifiable place before the arrival of the Roman army, although there is no archaeological evidence for an Iron Age settlement in the immediate area.

Despite these early identifications, the first significant discovery of Roman material in the town did not come until 1846 when the new County Gaol was built. Unfortunately these discoveries were ill-recorded, and it was only when the Courthouse was built by the side of the gaol in 1876 that a record was made of some of the finds. These were sufficiently impressive to encourage A.D. Berrington to undertake some excavations in the area around the Courthouse. The results of this work were published two years later by W. Thompson Watkin in a paper which remained the only serious, if, with hindsight, rather misleading, study of Roman Usk until the 1960s.[4]

Most of the pottery from Berrington's work was lost, but in 1962 George Boon published a reassessment of the small amount of pottery which had survived.[5] Before his work the evidence had usually been interpreted as indicating the existence at Usk of one of the forts which were built throughout Wales in the years after AD 75.[6] What he found, however, was that some of the samian ware from the site actually dated from the mid-50s, suggesting a significantly earlier date for the beginning of the Roman occupation at Usk. Historically the existence of such a site could be linked with the series of campaigns against the Silures in the years after AD 47 which were recorded by the Roman historian Tacitus,[7] and as such it was the first archaeological evidence for this phase of the history of Roman Wales. The opportunity to test this theory was offered three years later in 1965 by the decision to build houses on the Priory Orchard field next to the Courthouse where Berrington had sited one of his trenches. The result was a hastily organised rescue excavation directed by the writer for the Department of the Environment (now Cadw). Although the restrictions imposed — that no excavation was allowed in areas where houses or roads were to be built — severely limited the scope of the work, it did produce a number of important results, confirming the existence of a large Roman site which had been founded in the mid-50s and which probably continued to be occupied until at least the end of the 4th century.[8]

In 1967 this initial work was followed by trial trenching in the field to the east of the gaol which

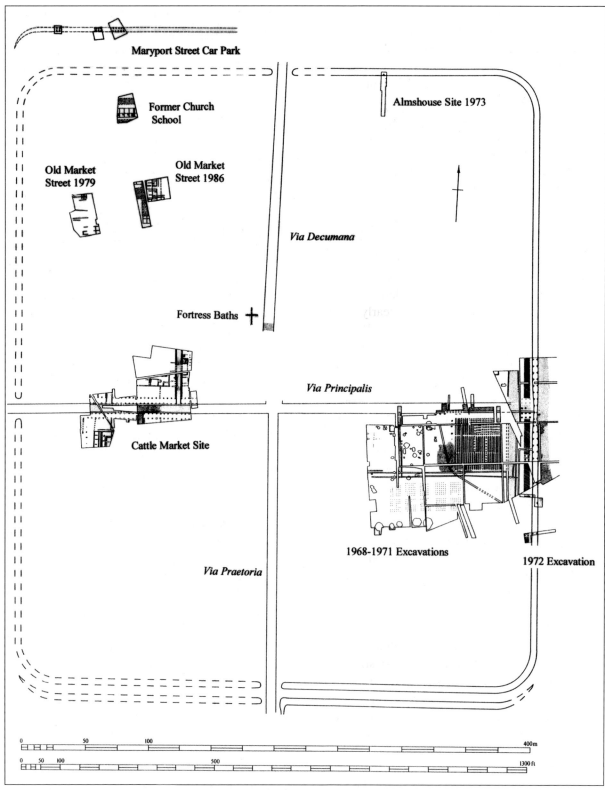

*Fig. 2.1 Plan of the legionary fortress showing the excavated areas
(after Manning 1981 and Marvell 1996)*

revealed that the whole of that area also contained signs of Roman occupation, a discovery which raised a number of questions about the nature and size of the site, which now appeared to be far too large to be a normal auxiliary fort of around 2 ha. It also made it clear that far larger open area excavations were needed if the structures, which had been built of timber, were to be elucidated. As a result a series of large excavations were undertaken in the area to the east of the gaol between 1968 and 1971, to be followed in 1973-4 by the excavation of most of the site of the former cattle market on the western side of Maryport Street opposite the gaol. In all a total of some 1.8 ha of the fortress was almost completely excavated. This work, together with smaller excavations in various parts of the town, revealed a significant part of the plan of what was clearly a full size legionary fortress covering some 19.5 ha, as well as greatly increasing our knowledge of later Roman and medieval Usk.[9] Later work by the Glamorgan-Gwent Archaeological Trust in the north-western sector of the town produced important information on the buildings in that part of the fortress (Fig. 2.1).

The historical context of the fortress is provided by Tacitus, amplified by archaeological work in the west of England and the Welsh Marches. Tacitus records that the second governor of Britain, Ostorius Scapula, undertook a series of campaigns against the tribes of Wales, of whom the Silures proved to be so obdurate that he was forced to move a legion from *Camulodunum* (Colchester) to a new base in or near Siluria.[10] This was in AD 49 or at latest AD 50 and the legion involved was almost certainly Legio XX Valeria. As the fortress at Usk was not founded until the mid-50s the legion was probably first stationed at Kingsholm, now a suburb of Gloucester and a key crossing point on the River Severn. From there it will have been able to strike into Wales, almost certainly following a route to the north of the Forest of Dean and along the Wye Valley towards Monmouth and thence to Usk and the coastal plain of south-east Wales.[11] Once this area had been brought under control it was possible, indeed logical, for the legion to be moved forward

in preparation for the next stage of the conquest of south Wales. A legionary fortress did not stand in isolation but was the centrepiece of a system of forts housing smaller units of auxiliary infantry and cavalry, sometimes brigaded with legionaries, and this was the case with the fortress at Usk. In addition to various forts to the north of the Forest of Dean others are now known to exist at Monmouth, Abergavenny, which was a key point for the control of the uplands of Breconshire, and Cardiff, a site which commanded the coastal plain and the Taff valley, an important route into the hills of Glamorgan.[12] Work elsewhere in Britain has shown that the fortress at Usk was one of a series built in the middle years of the 1st century, the others being at Exeter, Wroxeter and Lincoln. Taken as a whole they reflect a major reassessment of the military situation in Britain undertaken at the end of the first stage in the conquest, probably by Didius Gallus who was the governor of Britain between 52 and 57.[13] Had the conquest continued at the pace of its first phase most of these fortresses and their attendant forts would have been replaced within a few years. However, a series of problems within the province, including the Boudiccan revolt of 60-61, together with the demands of military campaigns elsewhere in the empire, prevented the Romans from completing the conquest of Wales until the mid-70s, with the result that the system of forts centred on Usk continued in use until then.[14]

In the 1st century Roman forts and fortresses almost always had wooden internal buildings with earth and turf ramparts, only the bath house being built of stone, and Usk was no exception. A series of excavations established the line of the eastern and northern defences and a geophysical survey traced those on the southern side.[15] Only the western defences remain to be located, but their course can be established with a high degree of probability since the position of the south gate, which will have lain on the midline of the fortress, is known. The length of the fortress from north to south was *c*.475m (1558 feet) and from east to west *c*.410m (1345ft), giving an internal area of *c*.19.48 ha or 48 acres, slightly less than its successor fortress at Caerleon. The defences

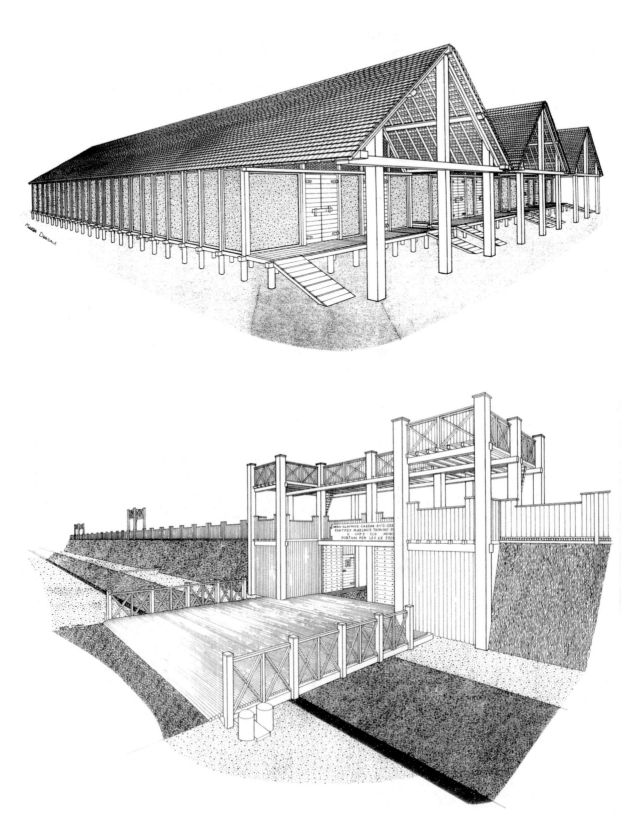

Fig. 2.2 Reconstruction drawings of (top) the large granaries and (bottom) the east gate of the fortress (Drawing by Martin Dugdale)

consisted of a single V-sectioned ditch between 4m and 4.5m wide and around 2m deep, set in front of a turf-faced earthen rampart *c*.4.3m wide which is thought to have stood around 3m high; a berm between the two was 1.8m wide. On the south side a second ditch lay some 7m in front of the first, no doubt to strengthen the defences where they faced level ground. There is also a second ditch on the north side, but this was 30m beyond the main ditch and may have defined a dead zone around the fortress.[16] A smaller ditch 40m from the main ditch on the eastern side is thought to have had a similar function.[17] The position of the east gate is known from excavation, while that of the south gate was located in the geophysical survey, which also revealed the causeway across the ditch in front of it. By contrast, the ditch in front of the east gate had been crossed by a timber bridge. The gate itself was of the type normal in forts of this period with two deep towers, each carried on three pairs of large posts, flanking a double carriageway (Fig. 2.2). Between the gates the defences were strengthened with a series of timber towers set within the bank at intervals of 30m (100 Roman feet); each was 3m (10 Roman feet) square carried on four massive posts. A wide but lightly metalled road was found to run on the outer side of the fortress ditch on its eastern side and this probably continued around the entire perimeter of the fortress.[18] Immediately inside the defences a narrow strip separated the steeply sloping back of the rampart from the *intervallum* road which ran around the fortress to give unimpeded access to all parts of the defences.[19] A number of bread ovens were found behind the rampart, a traditional position for such ovens, well away from the timber buildings which dominated the interior of the fortress.[20]

As with all such forts the interior was divided up by a grid of roads of which the main one, the *via praetoria*, was that running from the main gate, in this case the south gate, to the centre where the headquarters building or *principia* stood; an area now unfortunately under the Courthouse. The north end of this road was located by excavation within the gaol in 1968.[21] In front of the *principia* was the second major road, the *via principalis*, which at Usk ran between the east and west gates (Fig. 2.3).[22] A third road, the *via decumana* running from the back of the *principia* to the north gate,

Fig. 2.3 Section through the via principalis *showing the original road consisting of stone blocks at the base of the road with later Roman metalling*

was found in the Priory Orchard excavations and identified as the road trenched by Berrington in 1876.[23] The eastern arm of the *via principalis* had continued in use into modern times where it ran along the edge of the field behind the gaol; in the 19th century it was still known as Pook or Puck's Lane (Fig. 2.1). The excavations revealed that the metalling of almost all of the minor roads, as well as the western section of the *via principalis*, had been completely robbed away, probably in the Middle Ages. Where they did survive the major roads were extremely solid structures with a core of large stones, some clearly quarried, covered with compact gravel. The fact that quarried stones were used is significant for it shows that although almost all of the internal buildings were built of timber the army must have opened quarries, probably on the western side of the River Usk, to obtain this stone.

The excavations of 1968-71 lay in the area to the south of the eastern end of the *via principalis*, a part of the fortress which had been dominated by two groups of granaries separated by a road flanked by square-cut drains, running parallel with and to the south of the *via principalis*. The main group consisted of three very large buildings, each consisting of a series of 25 parallel trenches 12.8m or 40 Roman feet in length.[24] These had held a series of round-sectioned posts set at intervals of 1.5m (5 Roman feet) with each row 1.5m from the posts in the trenches on either side, giving each granary a total length of 36m or 120 Roman feet (Fig. 2.4). The function of these posts was to support a raised floor designed to protect the contents from damp and vermin. Above this the building probably had a strong timber framework clad with planks or panels of wattle and daub. The absence of fragments of tiles from this part of the site suggests that they were roofed with wooden shingles; thatch would have been far too inflammable. A covered loading bay had stood at the western end of each

Fig. 2.4 The large granaries under excavation in 1969

granary opening onto a large gravelled area (Fig. 2.2). It was not by chance that these granaries stood near the east gate, for such buildings were normally placed close to one of the main gates of forts and fortresses, no doubt to reduce the problems created by moving large and heavily laden wagons within the fortress. The granaries were separated from the adjacent *via principalis* by a fence carried on posts set at intervals of 3m (10 Roman feet).[25]

The area to the west of the granaries was devoid of major buildings, although the presence of a latrine suggests that it was in regular use.[26] It was bounded on its western side by a road running from the *via principalis* to the secondary road between the two groups of granaries.[27] The area on the western side of the north/south road was equally devoid of buildings, but a second latrine building and a line of post-holes, probably part of a fence, confirms that it was actively used, perhaps for storing items such as timber or wagons which could have been kept in the open.[28] Late in the life of the fortress large rubbish pits were dug in both of these areas.

A second group of granaries on the southern side of the minor east/west road had taken a somewhat different form to those on its northern side.[29] They consisted of ten identical buildings, arranged in five pairs with a gap of 3m (10 Roman feet) between the buildings of each pair. As with the large granaries they were defined by a grid of posts set at intervals of 1.5m or 5 Roman feet, in this case with six rows of seven posts each covering an area of 7.5m x 9m. Unusually the posts were not set in trenches or individual post-holes but were pointed and had been driven into the ground, almost certainly with a pile-driver. Various reconstructions are possible but the one preferred by the excavators would see them as five double granaries with covered loading bays in the centre of each pair.

The historian Tacitus in his eulogistic life of his father-in-law Agricola tells us that Agricola ensured that each fort he built held sufficient grain to supply its garrison for a year, and presumably this ideal also applied to legionary fortresses.[30] Although certainty is impossible, it has been calculated that between them the two groups of granaries at Usk could have held enough grain to feed 4,450 men for a year, and, as will be pointed out below, there were more granaries elsewhere in the fortress.[31]

Although a number of trenches were dug in 1967 in the south-eastern part of the gaol, they failed to produce much evidence for buildings in that area.[32] Unfortunately, as later work showed, it is extremely difficult to detect the ephemeral remains of the timber buildings at Usk in relatively small, deep trenches, and the failure to find buildings in this area does not preclude their existence. Indeed the discovery of a bread oven in this area may confirm that buildings had existed there, for it is very similar to the oven associated with the final phase of the officer's house near the west gate. The exact number of officers' houses in a legionary fortress is slightly uncertain, but it could have been as many as eight.[33] Although they were usually placed on the opposite side of the *via principalis* to the headquarters' building, the presence of granaries at each end of this zone at Usk means that some must have been placed elsewhere and the most probable place will have been behind the front row on line with the smaller granaries. If so one will have lain under this part of the gaol.

The excavations of 1973-4, which were on the site of the former Cattle Market on the west side of Maryport Street, opposite the Courthouse, lay on either side of the *via principalis* where it approached the west gate of the fortress.[34] As well as the road, fragments of five *insulae*, or blocks, and their defining roads, fell within the excavated area (Fig. 2.5). This part of the road, which had been almost totally robbed of its metalling, had been flanked by well-built stone drains which must originally have been covered with stone slabs; these were probably removed and shipped to Caerleon when the fortress was demolished.[35] Beyond the drains were colonnades 4.3m wide (15 Roman feet) on the north side of the road, and 4m wide on the south side, all being defined by two rows of posts set at intervals of 3.1m (Fig. 2.6).[36] Covered walks of this type were a feature of legionary fortresses and are probably

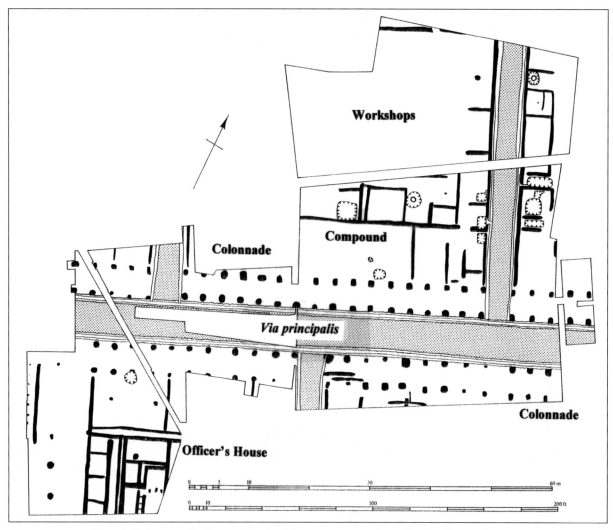

*Fig. 2.5 Restored plans of the buildings excavated on the Cattle Market site
(after Manning and Scott 1989)*

derived from similar colonnades seen in Roman cities in the Mediterranean world. The three side roads which ran north/south between the *insulae* had slight side ditches but had lost most of their metalling.[37] Behind the colonnades was a series of compounds probably separated from the colonnades by panels of fencing supported by the inner posts of the colonnades.[38] Although the fence at the back of these compounds was probably continuous, there were internal subdivisions which would have allowed areas within them to be used for different purposes. Too little of most of them fell within the excavated area for any internal structures to be found, but the

most complete, which fronted a works complex or *fabrica* on the north side of the *via principalis*, had a small shed at one end, as well as a latrine and a well.[39] The compounds on the opposite side of the road will have fronted the range of officers' houses to which they were probably linked.[40]

Of the three *insulae* which lay to the north of the main road, the southern and eastern ranges of the middle one fell within the excavated area, together with the western range of the eastern one.[41] Both had a large central courtyard surrounded by ranges of rooms or halls some of which contained large pits, latrines and possible cisterns. In all cases the walls had been carried on posts set in trenches. There was a notable absence of evidence for smithing or any other metallurgical process, but they could have served as stores, buildings or carpenters' shops.

On the southern side of the main road the excavations only extended beyond the colonnade at its western end.[42] Here again compounds separated the main buildings from the colonnades, although only one fell within the excavated area. The colonnade on this side of the road, but not on the other, ended in line with the western edge of the officer's house which was the main building in this area. Examples from other sites, such as the fortress at Inchtuthil in Scotland,[43] suggest that this house will have had ranges of rooms around a central courtyard, but unfortunately only the north-western part of the Usk house could be excavated (Fig. 2.7). Interestingly it was possible to show that its plan had been changed during its construction to enlarge some of the rooms.[44] Along its western side were a series of small rooms separated from the main house by a narrow corridor, rooms which could have had a number of functions including offices for the tribune's staff, or slaves' quarters or stores. Late in the history of the fortress these rooms were demolished and a bread oven built on the site, one of a number of changes made in the fortress at this time. The compound in front of this house had originally contained two wells and was probably linked to the house itself; late in the life of the fortress it had been filled with rubbish pits.[45]

Most of the area to the west of the house was devoid of buildings, but on its edge was a single trench with regularly spaced posts behind which was a row of posts mirroring those in the trench.[46] The length of this trench was very similar to those of the large granaries near the east gate, and the fact that this building stood quite close to the west gate suggests that it too was a granary. On the

Fig. 2.6 The drain alongside the via principalis *on the Cattle Market site. The posts of the flanking colonnades are marked with ranging rods*

other hand there are arguments against this explanation and the identification cannot be regarded as certain. If it was a granary it stood on its own rather than forming part of a group.

The only building which has been located by excavation in the central part of the fortress to the north of the *via principalis* is the legionary baths.[47] A solidly built, cold plunge bath found in 1965 on the western edge of the Priory Orchard site was a tiny fragment of what would have been a huge complex, probably the only stone building within the fortress. Unfortunately the bulk of it lies under Maryport Street.

In the years between 1979 and 1988 a number of excavations were undertaken by the Glamorgan-Gwent Archaeological Trust in the north-western corner of the fortress, the area where, on the analogy of other fortresses, barrack buildings should have stood (Fig. 2.1). Two of these excavations were on the northern side of Old Market Street. The first in 1979 revealed the side ditches of a possible east/west road with parallel gullies to the north of it which the excavators tentatively identified as a fragment of a possible barrack building.[48] To the south of the road were a number of trenches which, although probably part of a building, were too fragmentary for its function to be identified. The second excavation in Old Market Street, in 1986, was some 30m to the east of the first. A narrow road ran from north to south across the middle of the site with a wider road running in from the west to meet it. On the eastern side of the north/south road was a fragmentary building, possibly a barrack block although other explanations are possible, which had been abandoned before completion. In the north-eastern angle between the roads a fragment of another building can also be identified as a barracks.[49] The third excavation, on the site of the former Church Voluntary Primary School, lay

Fig. 2.7 The officer's house on the Cattle Market site under excavation

18

near the northern edge of the fortress some 40m to the north of the others. It revealed part of the *intervallum* road, here rather narrower than on the eastern side of the fortress; on its southern side were the ends of two barrack blocks with a second street, also running east/west, beyond them. Although the barracks had the usual arrangement of smaller rooms at the front with larger ones behind, there was no sign of the veranda which normally fronted barrack blocks, although there was certainly room for one.[50]

The Boudiccan revolt of 60-61 brought an abrupt end to the Roman conquest of Wales which had been moving apace in the years after 57. The foundation of the fortress at Usk and its associated forts in the southern Marches and as far east as Cardiff had been mirrored in the northern Marches with the establishment of a fortress for Legio XIV at *Viroconium*, the modern village of Wroxeter.[51] The north of England was dominated by the Brigantes, a large and powerful tribe ruled by their strongly pro-Roman queen, Cartimandua, although, as time was to show, there was a strong anti-Roman element within the tribe. For that reason alone it was necessary to maintain a strong military presence in the area of the southern Pennines and this, together with controlling north Wales, was the responsibility of the legion at Wroxeter. But in 66 or 67 Nero decided to move Legio XIV to the Continent, a decision which unbalanced the careful arrangements which had maintained peace in Britain in the years after the Boudiccan revolt. Until 67 there had been legions based at Exeter, Usk, Wroxeter and Lincoln, but, as a result the change, one fortress and its associated forts had to be closed. To denude the north of Wales and the southern Pennines of their garrison by closing Wroxeter was clearly judged to be impossible at a time when anti-Roman forces were increasing their influence in Brigantia, and the same argument applied to Legio IX at Lincoln which guarded the eastern end of the Brigantian frontier. On the other hand the south of Wales and south-western England had been under Roman control for almost 20 years, and the evidence suggests that it was felt that while the complete removal of Roman forces from the area

was impossible, they could be reduced. The result was that Legio XX was transferred from Usk to Wroxeter and Legio II moved north from Exeter to a new fortress at Gloucester, from where it could strike either west into Wales or south into the Dumnonian peninsula.[52]

Despite these changes it is clear that the fortresses at Usk and Exeter were not actually demolished until the mid-70s, and we must assume that both fortresses were held by a reduced garrison in the ten years between the removal of the legions and their final demolition.[53] The complete abandonment of Usk would have left a major gap in the chain of forts in the Usk valley and severely reduced the Roman army's ability to control the area. Such a change should have left tangible traces in the archaeological record at Usk and indeed there are several strands of evidence to support this scenario. It is clear that at a relatively late stage in the history of the fortress rubbish large pits were being dug in various parts of the site, including in the *fabricae* and the compound associated with the officer's house on the Cattle Market site. Before that rubbish had not been buried within the fortress, but a reduced garrison might well have felt justified in using some of the large empty plots for this purpose. Similarly the range of rooms at the back of the officer's house was demolished and a bread oven built on the site, suggesting that while the house itself was retained it had changed its function (Fig. 2.5). A detailed study of the coins from the site would also support the idea that it had housed a reduced garrison in its final years.[54]

The excavations in the north-western corner of the fortress produced even more dramatic evidence of change. The possible barrack block on the 1979 excavations of the Old Market Street site had been replaced by a granary,[55] while during the 1986 excavations in Old Market Street it was found that the unfinished barrack block had been demolished and replaced with a new block which combined both barracks and stables, probably for auxiliary troopers, similar to others known from some auxiliary forts.[56] At much the same time the barracks on the northern edge of the fortress on the site of the former school were modified to create still more combined barracks and stables.[57] All of these changes can be explained if we assume that when Legio XX was removed it was replaced by an auxiliary cavalry unit which effectively created a fort for itself in the northwestern corner of the great fortress. Whether a detachment of legionaries remained to supplement the cavalry is an open question, but is not inherently unlikely. However, it is possible that for a short time in 69 to 70 the fortress may have housed a full legion once again when Legio XIV, which had backed one of the losers in the Civil War which followed Nero's death, was returned to Britain and presumably stationed in one or other of the largely empty fortresses at Usk and Exeter.

We know relatively little of the area outside the fortress although the excavations of 1971 and 1972 did extend beyond the fortress defences. The area immediately beyond the fortress ditch had been kept clear save for a few minor roads,[58] but one of the more interesting discoveries was a series of plough furrows, which were contemporary with the fortress, some 140m from its eastern side.[59] That legionary fortresses were to some extent self-sufficient is well known but rarely do we have such explicit evidence as this for agriculture associated with a fortress. We know nothing of the *vicus* in which the traders and camp followers lived, although we must assume that it existed, nor do we know the location of the legionary kilns which produced most of the coarse ware used by the garrison.

CHAPTER III

Later Roman Usk
by William Manning

The victory of Vespasian which ended the chaos of the civil war of 69 was soon followed by a resumption of the conquest of Britain, initially with campaigns in the north of England and then, with the arrival of Julius Frontinus as governor in 74, against the Silures of south Wales. The existing system of forts and fortresses, all old and no doubt in need of refurbishment, reflected the situation as it had been 20 years before, and Frontinus had no hesitation in sweeping most of them away. A few such as Cardiff and Abergavenny which were in positions of strategic importance were rebuilt, but in the main he created a new system centred on a fortress for Legio II Augusta at Caerleon, a site which had the great advantage over Usk of being accessible to sea-going ships, and also perhaps of being less liable to flooding.[1]

The demolition of the fortress at *Burrium* was undertaken with characteristic thoroughness. Rubbish was buried in pits which were carefully sealed with the clay dug from them, the cover slabs were removed from the drains alongside the *via principalis*,[2] the lead from the bath-house was cut up and removed, although one small bundle was overlooked,[3] the panels of wattle and daub which had clad hundreds of buildings were burned, and the massive timbers which formed the framework of the east gate were lifted bodily from their settings, no doubt with a crane, probably to be floated down the Usk to the new fortress at Caerleon there to join the other reusable material salvaged from the old fortress.[4] The demolition

crews, themselves almost certainly soldiers from Legio II, left few traces but one discovery must be attributed to them — a row of bread ovens cut into the outer edge of the fortress ditch near the south gate, a position where no ovens would ever have been allowed in a functioning fortress, but which was a suitably sheltered spot for the demolition crew.[5] Nor was their work wholly destructive, for in the area of the demolished east gate they carefully refilled the deep post-holes of the gate-house and the ditch in front of it with large stones to form a solid foundation over which they laid a new length of road to link the former *via principalis* of the fortress with the road to Monmouth.[6]

The existence of a legionary fortress no more than 8 miles (13km) from Usk would have made it unnecessary for an auxiliary fort to have been placed there. Roman forts were normally around 20 miles apart and, in any event, Usk lay in an area which will have been completely pacified by 75, so the discovery of a Flavian fort (i.e. dating from the Flavian dynasty 69-96 AD) within the area of the former fortress is somewhat surprising.[7] It is known only from the defensive ditches on the south and east sides (Fig. 3.1) and a fragment of a rampart, which can probably be associated with it, on its western side;[8] all by unfortunate coincidence lying on the edges of the excavated areas with the result that no part of the interior has ever been examined. Its precise area remains uncertain, but the north side must lie between the Old Market Street 1986 excavations, which produced

Fig. 3.1 Section through the ditch of the Flavian fort on the Cattle Market site

the evidence for the western rampart, and the former Church School site which clearly lay outside it (Fig. 3.2).[9] An internal area of between 1.3 and 1.6 ha seems likely, which is exceptionally small for a fort of this date. There is relatively little evidence for the date of its construction, but what there is suggests that it was not built immediately after the demolition of the fortress but perhaps ten years later in the mid-80s, some years after most of the Flavian forts of Wales.[10] The only internal details known are a pottery kiln and five bread ovens in the area immediately behind its western rampart,[11] and, while this paucity of information inevitably limits any discussion of its function, there is a strong possibility that it was not a fort of the normal type. As we have seen, it is very close to Caerleon, indeed so close that it may well have fallen within the *territorium* of the fortress. All legionary fortresses were surrounded by a large area of land which was controlled by the army and which was intended to provide the fortress with many of the natural resources, including food, necessary for it to function. It is by no means impossible that Caerleon itself had been sited within the *territorium* of the original fortress at Usk, the fortress having, in effect, been moved to a more suitable site within it when the military requirements changed in the mid-70s.[12] If so the fort at Usk may either have been a works depot or have controlled one. This suggestion is supported by the presence of the pottery kiln near the western rampart, a structure which would have been totally out of place in a normal fort,[13] as well as by the large number of furnaces, mainly for

smelting and treating iron, which existed in the area in the 2nd to 4th centuries.

The existence of a works depot 8 miles from Caerleon need cause no surprise, for the main tileworks of its sister fortress at Chester were at Holt on the River Dee, which is a similar distance from Chester.[14] Whatever the explanation, the fort had a short life for its southern ditch was refilled around the end of the 1st century, although the eastern ditch remained open for another 50 years.

The dismantling of the fort or works depot did not mark the end of the Roman occupation of Usk, nor probably of a military presence on the site, for tiles bearing the stamp of Legio II Augusta were still being used at Usk in the middle years of the 2nd century.[15] The presence of soldiers from the legion is indicated by two tombstones from the

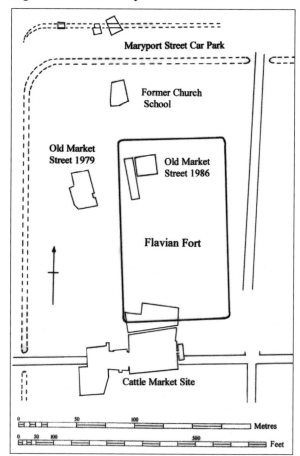

Fig. 3.2 The probable location of the Flavian fort. Only the east and south sides are known from excavation (after Marvell 1996)

site, one of the child of a soldier from the legion who was apparently still serving when the child died. The other is no more than a fragment which was found reused in later cobbling, but its quality indicates a military origin.[16]

Although the excavations in the north-western sector of the fortress produced some evidence of later occupation, it was too slight for its significance to be assessed.[17] Much the same applies to the excavations in the Priory Orchard, although areas of metalling, hearths and a metalworking furnace were found there suggesting that the area round the former *via decumana* was quite densely occupied in the later Roman period. The main area where the later history of *Burrium* could be examined in detail was to the east of the gaol and on the Cattle Market site. Unfortunately the latter area lay outside the later settlement, and while the former *via principalis* continued to be used, with new drainage ditches being cut on its north side and in places on the south as well, the rest of the area was largely devoid of occupation save for a series of inhumation burials dating from the 3rd and 4th centuries near the western end of the road. The acid soil had destroyed even the bones of the skeletons but careful excavation often revealed the shadow of the body and the outline of the wooden coffin. All lacked grave goods but a number had been buried with their boots, the hobnailed soles of which had survived (Fig. 3.3).

The large scale excavations to the east of the goal produced a far more complex story, although later ploughing had damaged many of the upper

Fig. 3.3 Hobnail soles found in a late Roman burial on the Cattle Market site

levels. The former *via principalis* had remained in use, as it had throughout the Middle Ages, with the drainage ditches alongside it being recut at regular intervals. In most cases these ditches continued across the line of the eastern defences of the fortress to turn and run south along the line of the fortress ditch. The minor road which ran east/west between the two sets of granaries also remained in use at least until the late 2nd century when its side ditches were recut, but it passed out of use in the 3rd century when it was cut by boundary ditches running diagonally across the site, ditches which in one form or another continued to divide the area until the end of the 4th century. The line of the east/west road appears to have marked the southern edge of the settlement which here ran alongside the main road, for save for a late 2nd-century enclosure there was little sign of occupation on its southern side. A handful of graves in the south-western corner of the enclosure confirmed that by then this area was outside the settlement.

The area immediately to the south of the former *via principalis*, however, was a different matter and here occupation extended to the western edge of the excavation, well beyond the defences of the former fortress — occupation which had continued from the mid-2nd century to late in the 4th century. It seems that in the period when the fortlet was in use, and for some years after, this area was not used, and when it was, in the mid to late 2nd century, it was in a desultory fashion which produced a few rubbish pits and little else. More systematic use began at about the time when the enclosure to the south of the minor east/west road was laid out at the end of the 2nd century. Near the eastern end of the excavated area a rectangular building, 13.5m long and 6m wide, had opened onto the road, its walls marked by a trench which had held the basal beams of the walls. Although there were no internal walls, light partitions could have existed. Building of this general type, built either of wood or stone, are common on Roman sites in Britain and probably served as workshops and dwellings. A large area around this building had been used for industrial purposes, and a number of furnaces, essentially trenches originally with stone linings, were found, together with one which was more complete and which had been protected by a small timber building. Whether the others had originally had lightly-built structures around them we cannot tell. Some of these furnaces were probably for smelting iron, for tap slag was found in a number of the pits; others were probably carburisation furnaces similar to those found at the eastern end of the excavated area. Several wells were probably related to this industrial activity, but there was no sign of larger buildings, although, as we will see, this need not mean that they had never existed. This industrial activity appears to have continued until late in the 4th century when large parts of the site

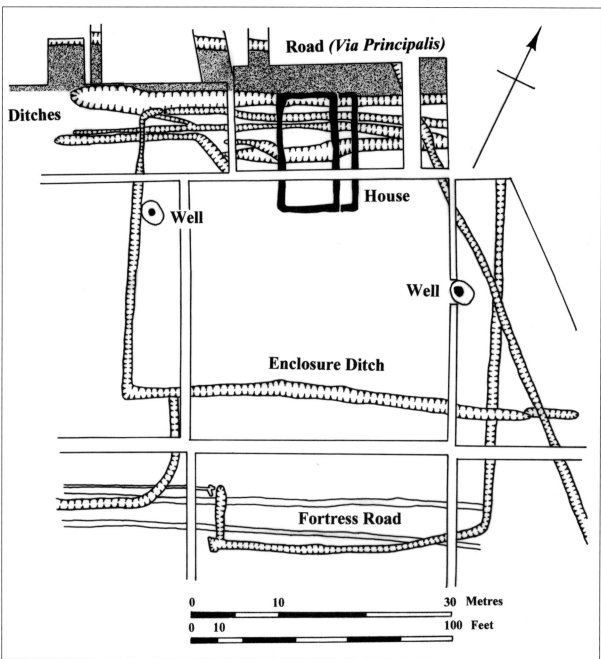

Fig. 3.4 The 3rd-century enclosure and buildings to the south of the former via principalis

were levelled up and covered by a layer of dark earth, possibly from middens, which in turn was cobbled over. Fortunately parts of this cobbling were sufficiently well preserved for fragmentary lines of stones which had clearly been packed against timber beams to have survived, marking the foundations of quite substantial rectangular buildings. The remains of such structures are easily destroyed, particularly by ploughing, and, apart from showing that one of them had been at least 13m long and 5.5m wide, few details of their plans survived. None the less they served to show that an apparent absence of buildings does not necessarily mean that they had never existed, and to suggest that if such buildings had been used earlier in the history of the site, the density of occupation may have been greater than the surviving structures suggested.

On the eastern side of this cobbling a large enclosure, 50m long and 33m wide, defined by a ditch and originally, no doubt, an internal bank, was constructed in the 3rd century (Fig. 3.4). On its northern side, overlying some of the ditches flanking the former *via principalis*, was a rectangular stone building 13.2m long and 7m wide to which a corridor or veranda 2.2m wide had been added on its eastern side at a slightly later date. The fact that the foundations of this addition were shallower than those of the original building suggests that they did not have to carry the same weight and it may have been no more than a lean-to structure, possibly giving access to rooms within the main building. It is clear that the surviving walls were no more than the foundations and that any doors must have been at a higher level. The foundations of the northern wall were slighter than those of the others, and this may indicate that it was not load-bearing, perhaps supporting a sill above which were removable shutters of the type probably used if that end of the building had been a workshop. Part of the enclosure close to the building had been cobbled over. The enclosure does not seem to have been used for industrial purposes; the fragments of furnaces found within it probably predated it and were the source of a mass of slag which had been used to fill one of the roadside ditches before

the construction of the building. Exactly when the building was demolished is uncertain but a well within the enclosure was refilled between the mid-3rd and mid-4th centuries, while another well, which had been built after the enclosure bank had been levelled was out of use by the mid-4th century.

The first sign of activity in the area to the east of this enclosure was the digging of a massive pit, probably for clay, in the 2nd century, but in the 3rd century the area began to be used more positively. The clay pit was refilled and the eastern end of the road, which still ran on the line of the *via principalis* of the fortress, was realigned to curve to the north-east, probably to run more directly to the mouth of the Olway valley. At much the same time the road which had run north/south along the outer edge of the fortress ditch was re-metalled and widened, and much of the area to the north of it cobbled over. A number of narrow trenches cut into the surface of this cobbling suggest the existence of timber-framed buildings, although they were too fragmentary for the details of the buildings to be ascertained. As with so many other parts of the site a large number of furnaces had been built in the 3rd and 4th centuries, all taking the same form, a narrow stone-lined trench with a central channel with the clay around it reddened and the stones cracked by great heat. The absence of slag from these furnaces and from the areas around them suggest that they were use to carburise iron, a process which produced a steel coating around bars of wrought iron.

To the south of the road which ran to the east was a large enclosure demarcated by a ditch, no doubt originally with a bank on its inner side (Fig. 3.5). A stone causeway crossed the ditch on its western side with a timber-framed gate at its inner end, its plan suggesting that it had resembled the lych-gate of a church. The interior of the enclosure had been dominated by a large, rectangular timber building, measuring 14m x 6m, outlined by stone-packed post-holes with a drainage gully running along its northern side. A well within the enclosure had been refilled in the late 3rd century. The absence of furnaces, and the degree of privacy given by its being set within the

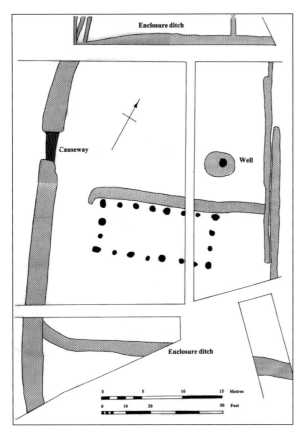

Enclosure ditch

Causeway

Well

Enclosure ditch

| 0 | 5 | 10 | 15 | Metres |
| 0 | 10 | 20 | | 50 | Feet |

Fig. 3.5 The late Roman enclosure and building at the eastern end of the 1968-71 excavations

enclosure, suggest that the building was a farm rather than another industrial area. The building was demolished late in the Roman period and the area covered with cobbling.

The Roman settlement which had developed at Usk in the years after the closure of the fortlet at the end of the 1st century was probably originally associated with the fortress at Caerleon, serving as a works depot principally, but probably not exclusively, for the production of iron. Whether Caerleon continued as a legionary fortress after the end of the 3rd century when many of the major buildings were demolished remains uncertain,[18] but even if it did, the military occupation was on a much smaller scale, and it is debatable if it would have required a works depot as distant as Usk. On the other hand, there is no reason to suppose that the demand for iron and steel was any less in the 4th century than it had been in earlier centuries and the craftsmen at Usk clearly continued to practise their metallurgical skills, no doubt alongside farming, until the end of the Roman period.

CHAPTER IV

Hospitals and Almshouses of Medieval Usk
by Geoffrey Mein

There were two medieval hospitals in or near Usk. The lesser known is that which stood upstream and across the river from the town where the Gwent Tertiary College now stands, the site known today as The Rhadyr (Fig. 4.1). The purpose of this hospital is not recorded but it was probably for travellers, including pilgrims.

For the second of the two we have a specific reference to the fact that it was originally a leper hospital. This stood outside the medieval town on the bank of the river where now stands the block of apartments alongside the bridge. What follows will draw together what is recorded of these two hospitals. The identity of their founders will be suggested as will a possible historical continuity from the town hospital to the Usk Almshouses.

Medieval Hospitals Generally
Medieval hospitals fell into three categories — leper houses, non-leper houses and almshouses.[1]

Fig. 4.1 The Rhadyr

By 1250 there were about 300 of each of the first two and 225 almshouses in England. The non-leper houses differed in the relief they offered — temporary accommodation and food for passing travellers, perhaps on payment, or the housing of permanent dependants. Occasionally the residents included those who bought the right to lifetime food and accommodation, but most provided only for the poor and infirm. Whoever they were, it was their duty to repay the founder by prayers for his soul.

The provision for travellers could be for pilgrims, in the case of Usk either those visiting the town's shrine to St Radegund or those passing through Usk to St Davids.

The purpose of each hospital was set out in the grant by the founder; they could be founded by the local bishop, a monastery, a member of the nobility, the sovereign or in later times some wealthy individual. A local example of the latter is the Haberdashers Charity, which still has its almshouses and schools in Monmouth and its fine row of almshouses in Newlands, Gloucestershire, where the founder was born in relative poverty. Occasionally the founders would be a group of the wealthy people of a town seeking to provide for their less fortunate neighbours, as in the case of the 24-bed hospital in Cardiff, founded by the burgesses at some time before 1396 but by then 'ruinous'.[2] Less frequently the object of the foundation was deliberately to deprive the donor's relatives of his estate on his death, as was the case with Roger Edwards, Usk's Elizabethan benefactor, who founded an Usk school and the still flourishing almshouses at Llanthowell, near Usk, after realising that his possible heirs had tried to murder him.

All hospitals were dedicated to a particular saint, many of the leper houses to St Mary Magdalene, as was that at Dixton, near Monmouth. Kissack suggests that this hospital may have changed its use after leprosy 'ceased to be a serious threat in the fifteenth century', a change suggested by its later dedication to St Michael.[3] All hospitals had a chapel and therefore a priest. Lepers were specifically prohibited by the Third Lateran Council of 1179 from living with the healthy or attending the same church; they were to have their own churches and cemeteries.

All had a master or warden, and a priest, the right of appointment usually being reserved to the founder and his heirs. Indeed the existence of such a right in favour of a particular family, as in the case of the Usk leper hospital, can be taken to indicate the identity of the founder where there is no other direct evidence.

All leper houses had a 'proctor' who acted as rent collector and business manager and as their licensed beggar, an important privilege in view of the severity of the laws against begging. English houses were permitted to maintain two proctors to beg for alms until the right was abolished as late as 1597, around the time of the Elizabethan reorganisation and regulation of charities. Such begging was usually limited to the immediate neighbourhood of the hospital which, with forethought, would be where travellers passed in numbers, as here in Usk alongside the river bridge.

The church favoured the selling of indulgences by their 'pardoner' to raise funds for leper houses, as at Dixton, where the possible early leper house was sited by the ferry across the Wye to Hadnock on the old road from Staunton to Monmouth.

The longevity of the medieval hospitals depended on factors such as their wealth from the original benefaction and its proper management, their local popularity and ability to attract alms, the continued need for their particular function in the community and their ability to change roles to cater for different local needs.

Some hospitals fell foul of international politics for, if they were dependant upon a hospital in a foreign country, they were classed as 'alien' when war broke out. As a result some had their assets seized by the Crown and were effectively extinguished, while others continued to operate and had their funds returned to them after the war. This was the case with the Rhadyr hospital.

The hospitals associated with monastic houses were closed at the time of the Reformation as part of the monastic property recorded in 1534/5 by Henry VIII's officials in the *Valor Ecclesiasticus*. The absence of Usk's hospital from the *Valor* shows that it was never an adjunct of the Benedictine Nunnery of St Mary's at Usk, although the existence of the nuns' own infirmary is recorded.[4] The priest in charge, its *firmari' IB'M* was the incumbent of *Eccl Sti David Ep'l*, which was until 2003/4 St David's Church, Llandewi Fach, just west of Llandegfedd village, now a private dwelling.

The Rhadyr

Known originally as the hospital of Aberthin from its position at the confluence of the Berthin Brook and the River Usk, it would perhaps better be called Aberberthin. It was a foundation dependent upon the Hospital of 'Santyngfeld', now known as Sant-Inglevert, a village 12km south of Calais, the remains of the medieval hospital lying below the fields of l'Abbaye Farm. It was here that one Oilard de Wimille, 'a knight of noble extraction', set up a hermitage shortly before 1116. In that year his signature *Oilardus Eremita* — Oilard the Hermit — appears on a document which may have been a charter grant.

The foundation charter of 1130 converting the hermitage to a hospital was by 'Etienne of Blois, count of Boulogne', the future King of England, Stephen (1135-1154). The hospital was specifically set up as 'a charitable shelter for travellers in distress', the poor being the 'preferred guests'. It lay just to the north of the old way from the port of Wissant to St Omer, a road which in the 12th century carried 'almost all the trade' and travellers between England and St Omer. A windblown area of very poor soil and sparse, leaning trees, the place had an air of the land of van Gogh's potato eaters and as such seems to have been an admirable place for such a haven, for it soon attracted sufficient donations from grateful benefactors for the brothers to built a fine church to be served by the canons of the local abbey.

The next recorded charter in favour of the hospital, this time granting land in England, was by Henry II in the year of his accession, 1154. The grant was signed by Thomas Becket, the witnesses including Henry's brother, William of Anjou. This resulted in the setting up of the two dependant hospitals of Farley, Luton, and Ludgershall near Andover together with a grant of land at Wiperley, presumably for their support.

The hospital and its church, having been left outside the English-held territory of Calais when the town was seized by Edward III in 1347, lay on the border between English and French territory and as such provided a semi-neutral area which became a favourite site for tournaments between the knights of the two countries, that of 1390 being particularly well recorded.[5] Horatia Durant tells us that one of the English knights who took part was the 17-year-old John Beaufort, ancestor of the Worcester/Beauforts of Raglan Castle and now of Badminton. Created Earl of Somerset at 24 he was later granted the forfeited estates of Owain Glyndŵr.[6] An even more spectacular event held not far away in 1520 was the Field of the Cloth of Gold in which Henry VIII is said to have jousted.

No founding charter has been discovered for the Rhadyr, the third dependant hospital of Sant-Inglevert in Britain, but there are two contenders as founders, Henry II and Gilbert 'the Red' de Clare.

The hospital was up and running by 1291 for it was included in the survey of monastic or ecclesiastical property, the *Taxatio Ecclesiasticus,* published that year. As Sant-Ingelvert, its 'mother house', had become a hospital in 1130,

the Aberthin daughter house must therefore have been founded some time between 1130 and 1291. Throughout the whole of this period Usk had been in the hands of the de Clare family or of their relations by marriage, the Marshals, as part of the Lordship of Striguil and from 1245 and the partition of the Marshal inheritance as part of the Lordship of Usk, with just two exceptions.

The first of these exceptions followed the deaths in 1136 of Henry I and in 1138 of Walter de Clare, the founder of Tintern Abbey, when the Welsh under Morgan and Iorwerth ap Owain took the opportunity of the lack of English control in the Marches to seize both Caerleon and Usk castles and virtually all of south east Gwent except Striguil — Chepstow — itself, and Newport. How long this occupation of Usk Castle continued is not certain, for while its seizure is recorded by the virtually contemporary chronicler Orderic Vitalis he does not date its recapture by the next lord of Striguil, Gilbert Strongbow de Clare.

The second occasion was in 1174 when the whole area was overrun by the Welsh of Caerleon. Occupied by them with royal approval the area was retaken by the English crown in perhaps 1184. Following the ejection of the Welsh, Usk town and castle were then to remain in royal hands for five years[7] until 1189 when the lordship became the property of William Marshal on marrying Strongbow's heiress Isabella.

Although the de Clares and Marshals had many more years of opportunity to found the hospital, it is more likely that it was Henry II who was the founder. As has been noted, Henry had granted the French mother house land in England in 1154, and it is suggested that, while holding the lordship of Usk during the minority of Isabella, he granted the Rhadyr lands to one of his favourite French hospitals.

It is possible that the idea was given to him by the Benedictine nuns of Usk who had probably been obliged to entertain visiting Welsh travellers who 'frequently descended on an Anglo-Norman house along the border or in South Wales with all the high-spiritedness of American cattle men reaching a small town'.[8] So onerous did this dispensing of hospitality become for Margam Abbey, for example, that their patron Gilbert III de Clare (d.1230) directed them to cease entertaining 'those coming to an assembly or the army', while nevertheless continuing to entertain 'neighbouring Welshmen whose frequent arrival burdens the house to excess'. There may also have been pressure on the nuns to provide hospitality to pilgrims visiting the chapel of St Radegund, which lay within the bounds of their nunnery and which seems likely to have been founded by Alicia de la Marche between 1271 and 1285, the year of her divorce from Gilbert 'the Red'.[9] The sisters could not house them within their nunnery and presumably had to accommodate them in one or more of their burgages in their Manor of Usk Priory.

Relief was granted to Brecon as early as 1155-1159 and later to Strata Florida and Whitland by the setting up of *ysbytai* or hospices at a distance from the monasteries to entertain guests. Cowley points out the extreme difficulty in establishing whether the numerous hospices in Wales, 'the forerunners of many a sixteenth-century inn ... were hostels or small hospitals'.[10] While the Rhadyr may have started as a hospice it had clearly become a hospital by the time of the *Taxatio* of 1291.

The name 'Rhadyr' derives from the Latin *oratorium* — a place of worship — but from about 1090 to 1533 'oratory' was a word regularly used to mean a 'bedehouse',[11] an endowed almshouse.[12] So did the Aberthin hospital eventually become an almshouse?

The only likely alternative to King Henry II as grantor is Gilbert IV, 'the Red' de Clare Earl of Gloucester (ob.1295) well over a hundred years later. However, there seems to be no evidence of any connection between any of the de Clare family and Calais to suggest a natural interest on their part in the hospital of Santyngfeld, although there is the possibility that such a gift could have arisen out of the negotiations with Edward I, leading to Gilbert's marriage, his second, on 30 April 1290 to Joan of Acre (ob.1307), the second daughter of Edward by his queen, Eleanor of Castile. The immediate problem here is whether there was sufficient time for such a grant between 1289, when Gilbert came into possession of the lordship of Usk, and the survey leading to the *Taxatio* in 1291 which records the hospital as a going concern.

Joan of Acre's mother, Queen Eleanor had inherited the county of Ponthieu, an area at the mouth of the Somme not far removed from Calais, its main town being the thriving port of Abbeville. Edward immediately took steps to confirm her succession with Philip III of France and undertook the administration of the area via a seneschal and exchequer based in Abbeville, paying Philip a substantial sum for his approval of Eleanor's rights in the county. It is possible that Joan of Acre, her mother or Edward himself had developed some connection with Santyngfeld, perhaps as benefactors, and that Joan through her father the king took the opportunity of the de Clare marriage negotiations to achieve a benefaction by her future husband. For this suggestion I am indebted to Dr Jennifer C. Ward.

Aberthin appears in the records again in 1382[13] and in 1386,[14] at which time it was still listed as a hospital. It may still have been offering shelter for pilgrims for some years after 1404, the year when Adam Usk prevailed upon the Pope to authorise for five years the sale of indulgences by the nuns of Usk to pilgrims to the shrine of St Radegund.[15] This produced the 'copious multitude' attending the shrine who Hartwell Jones suggests were accommodated in a 'hospice for pilgrims' — without identifying either its whereabouts or who was running it other than 'there was in Usk a hospice for pilgrims'.[16]

I will further suggest that what had been the leper hospital in Usk had become this hospice as early as 1316. Certainly by 1521 Aberthin had ceased to operate as a religious house and was being run, presumably by lay brothers, as a farm or grange. As such it was leased by its mother house to the Earl of Pembroke for 40 years. The Earl failed to pay the rent to Santyngfeld and was sued by its Master in the Star Chamber for the arrears. Pembroke acquired the property on the Dissolution only a few years later.

The Usk Hospital

While it is not possible positively to identify the founder of Usk's hospital for lepers, he was certainly a de Clare, as the right of advowson of both Usk hospital and Usk nunnery is recorded as vested in Gilbert V de Clare on his death at Bannockburn in 1314, and again in the survey of 1317 prepared for the division of his estates.[17] It is not impossible that he was the actual founder as leprosy was then still endemic.[18]

In the town reeve's account for the year starting 29 September 1316 there is an entry for the delivery to David Gregory, receiver of Usk, of food for the hospital inmates: 'salmon for the common hospice £9 11s 3d',[19] while his contemporary administering the Lord of Usk's financial affairs specifically records the place as a leper hospital. Thus in the minister's account for 1314-16[20] he records the receipt of one shilling burgage rent from William Hcved and Hawise Balli his wife for a plot 'which they hold of the hospital of the lepers in Elewith Street'. I have identified this street in chapter VIII as what is now Black Barn Lane. I cannot agree with Courtney's suggestion that the leper hospital itself was there, as this would have been contrary to the requirement of the Lateran Council for the isolation of lepers. It must be that the hospital owned a plot in Elewith Street which they had let to the Heveds.

Subsequent references to the hospital in 1322, 1327 and 1333 again mention the advowson[21] but after that there is no mention of the place. It is suggested that this was due to its destruction in the attack on the town in 1402 by Owain Glyndŵr and that the lord of Usk rebuilt it not as a leper hospital but perhaps for accommodation as suggested by Clark who records the Bridge Street hospital as 'a house of entertainment for guests'.[22] The 'guests' were possibly guests of the lord of Usk or an overflow from The Rhadyr of pilgrims to St Radegund's shrine.

Clark's house of entertainment had become 'the capital messuage' — or mansion — 'of the earl of Worcester' in the roll of 11 September 1569. It was then the property adjoining that on the river bank occupied by Thomas David Morgan, who held it rent-free. This suggests that his burgage had previously been part of the neighbouring holding of the earl or that Morgan had some personal connection with the 'hospice' or mansion next door, perhaps as its warden and perhaps living in the mansion, for as we shall see he did not build a house on his burgage plot. When the hospital had been rebuilt in this new form is not known, but by implication the mansion had been there by 1551, the year of Usk's first surviving rental.[23]

The fact that these rental rolls included these properties shows that by 1551 the bounds of the town had spread beyond the town ditch to the edge of the river. The lepers and their hospital had clearly ceased to exist by then, unless moved elsewhere away from the general population and to a place of which we now have no trace.

The earl's holdings in Bridge Street had included a further 3½ burgages further towards the town than his 'mansion', all held by John Thomas in 1569. By 1630 they had become Usk's House of Correction or prison, all mention of the lord's mansion having disappeared. In 1641 William Morris was recorded as the 'Master of the House of Correction for the county'.[24] It seems clear that this was land originally associated with the leper hospital, for upon it stood a chapel, or so we have been told by John Howard, the penal reformer, in his 1779 report on Usk's County Bridewell.[25] Perhaps originally the lepers' chapel, there is now no physical trace of this building. The property is now owned by Arthur Griffiths and within his set-back former warehouse is a pointed arched doorway (Figs. 4.2 and 4.3) which may have been mistakenly taken for part of this 'chapel' by Howard.

In 1801, Howard's suggestion was repeated by William Coxe: 'Part of the common prison, which is situated near the bridge, was formerly an ancient Roman catholic chapel; the gothic doorway, which formed the southern entrance, still remains; another gothic doorway to the north is filled up; the principal vaultings of the roof, with the cornice ornamented with dentels are visible'.[26] Coxe's southern gothic doorway must be the righthand one of the two major door-

Fig. 4.2 Mr Griffiths' former warehouse. The dotted lines mark the line on which stands the pointed arch shown in figures 3 and 3a

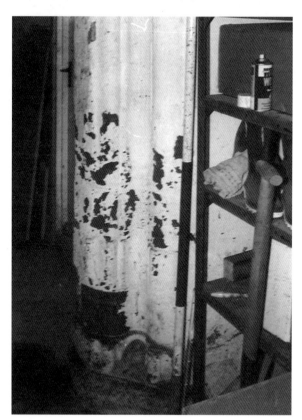

Fig. 4.3a Base mouldings of the pointed arch shown in Fig. 3; the north side from outside the doorway

ways in the front or southern elevation of the warehouse shown on Figure 4.2. Coxe seems not to have gone into the building and so missed the pointed arch shown in Figure 4.3 which penetrates the wall, the line of which is marked by the dotted line on Figure 4.2. Of his blocked gothic doorway to the north no trace remains; perhaps

Fig. 4.3 The pointed arched doorway within the former warehouse. Note the position of the hinges to the left of the archway

it was destroyed in the 'small improvement' in 1779 referred to by John Howard.

Howard started his report: 'This prison was formerly a chapel', but his purpose was to report on the health of the inmates, not to comment on historical architecture, and if he was referring to the doorway shown here, he clearly missed noting that its hinges were on the west side and that one therefore entered the building, whatever it was, from the east. It is perhaps unfair to suggest that he might have noticed the very convoluted mouldings of the doorway arch, but the fact that Coxe did not refer to them or suggest their date supports the suggestion that he did not go into the building, for surely he would have recorded the existence of this fine doorway. The dentels referred to by Coxe are possibly of the 15th century; this was confirmed to me by Mr A.J. Parkinson of RCHAMW,[27] who carried out a survey of the building in 1987, when the archway and another doorway were both hidden behind Mr Griffiths' floor-to-ceiling shelving.

An examination of the mouldings of the archway suggests that it too was of the 15th century, and it would seem to me that this was the doorway into the lord's mansion, although I reserve the question of whether this doorway had led directly into the mansion or into a separate gatehouse — this latter suggestion supported by the excavations made by my late wife and myself in the building after the 1979 floods. In addition to recording the arched doorway, we found the outer face of a heavily moulded, four-centred doorway through what appears to have been the outer, eastern, end wall of the mansion (Figs. 4.4 and 4.5). The then County Council Conservation Officer, Robert Wall, suggested a date for the doorway of 'about 1450', which would fit well with the construction of the mansion among the ruins of the leper hospital or hospice.

Figure 4.6 shows the blocking of the short passage on the inner side of this doorway, an opening in the western end wall of the former warehouse, viewed from the courtyard of Bridge Street Mews. This end wall exhibits numerous blocked windows and doors of various ages, one

Fig. 4.5 Detail of the moulding of the doorway shown below

Fig. 4.4 The doorway into the lord's mansion through what appears to have been its outer, eastern wall

of which includes among its random filling a brick from the Gwehelog brickworks.

By 1759 the site of the lord's mansion had become The Angel Inn, then still owned by the Earl of Worcester's descendant, the Duke of Beaufort, and sold that year by his divisee the Earl of Lichfield.[28] It later became The Beaufort Inn, which in turn became The Bridge Inn, The Angel seemingly being reborn to stand on the same side but further down Bridge Street.[28] Demolished in the early 20th century for a bus garage next door to Mr Griffiths' warehouse, the riverside land of the Angel/Beaufort/Bridge Inns was left open and eventually became the District Council's works yard (Fig. 4.7). Since July 1989 all have been part of Usk Bridge Mews.

The position of the hospital 'at the bottom of Bridge Street, adjoining the old Bridewell' had been a matter of folk memory for many years when recorded by J.H. Clark in 1891.[30] Mr Griffiths' warehouse was the westernmost part of the Bridewell or 'House of Correction' and Clark placed the hospital beyond this. As we have seen, the present western gable end of the warehouse may well have been the eastern gable end wall of the 'mansion of the Lord', but it was no part of the original leper hospital which must have stood somewhat nearer the river and set back well from the street, as was its successor, the 'mansion'.

That they were set back from the street is known from the layout of the now demolished bus garage. The front half of the garage floor was flat concrete but there was a cross wall with a gap for an apparently low doorway to its rear and in line with the front wall of the warehouse next door. In 1988 Councillor Dave Rennels told me that he was sure that the opening was an arched doorway but could not remember whether it had a round or a pointed arch. The

Fig. 4.6 The blocked doorway seen from its original inner side

Fig. 4.7 The council yard with the bus garage partly demolished adjoining Mr Griffiths' former warehouse

lack of height of the doorway had required the lowering of the floor to allow the single-decker buses to be driven through the arch to the back of the garage. Beyond had been the stables of the earlier inn, as dividing stall walls showed on the floor beyond the arch and hay racks were still on the walls.

When work started on Usk Bridge Mews I examined the foundation trenches for both the new flood defences and the apartment block nearest to the river. This part of the site had been

the riverside land adjacent to the old Beaufort Inn which in 1569 had been the rent-free property of Thomas David Morgan. No earlier buildings had stood there so wherever Morgan had lived it was not here and equally this area had not been the site of the leper hospital.

The easternmost block of the Mews, the part which fronts on to Bridge Street, is separated from the riverside block by an entrance to the courtyard and parking area to the rear of both of them (Fig. 4.8). Its eastern end stands on the

Fig. 4.8 The eastern block of Usk Bridge Mews. The gable end of Mr Griffiths' former warehouse is on the left

Fig. 4.9 The courtyard of Usk Bridge Mews, the probable site of Usk's leper hospital

site of the former bus garage and on the removal of the concrete floor of the front of the garage for the new foundations, the cellar walls of the Beaufort Inn, formerly The Angel, were exposed. I noted that these walls had been dug into previously undisturbed subsoil, no sign appearing of the walls of the leper hospital or of the later mansion. Both must have stood to the rear, but unfortunately the position of neither of them could be established in the construction work as no trenches were required in what was to become the courtyard.

While therefore we can be fairly certain that the hospital lay under what is now the western part of the Mews courtyard (Fig. 4.9), its chapel and graveyard still awaiting discovery. The latter may have lain under what is now Mr Griffiths' garden, shown as it was in 1988 in Figure 4.10, but to date he has not encountered any of the remains of late inmates when digging his garden.

The Usk Almshouses

As we have seen, the 'Lord's mansion', the successor to the leper hospital, disappears from the records of Usk between 1569 and 1630. It had probably been allowed to fall into ruin due to a succession of absentee lords of Usk, including the Mortimers and later the Crown, and to the shift of local power from Usk to Raglan. This started with the creation of the lordship of Raglan out of that of Usk in March 1465,[31] Usk finally becoming merely a part of the Raglan lordship in the 1550s by a grant of Edward VI. Even before that Usk had been included in an Act of Parliament of 1543 relating to the repairing of decayed houses in the towns of south Wales[32] while by 1587 the castle itself was ruinous.[33]

Despite the undoubted decay and decline of the town, the care of its poor and needy must have continued to be a matter of concern. This was met occasionally by gifts of money by local

Fig. 4.10 Mr Griffiths' property in May 1988. The warehouse and the bus garage are to the right of the main block, formerly Usk's House of Correction. The garden may be the site of the burial ground of the leper hospital

benefactors such as Roger Edwards of Llangwm, the founder of the Usk Grammar School and of the almshouses at Llangeview, who died in 1624 leaving money for his executors to give £20 to poor tradesmen and shopkeepers on Usk's fair days and another £10 to the poor of Usk.[34] The generality of the wording of these gifts makes it clear that by Roger Edwards' death there was no accommodation provided for the town's poor, so we must look elsewhere for the benefactor who eventually provided the land and the money to build the twelve small tenements 'together with the garden attached' in Bridge Street.[35]

Built after 1670, there being no mention of them in that year's rental,[36] by 1825 they were ruinous and thought totally unfit for the residence of the poor. The suggestion by the present writer that it was one of the Beauforts who built the Bridge Street almshouses, while admittedly intuitive, is based not only on the fact that it was a later duke who provided for their replacement on land he owned alongside the gatehouse to the Priory in Church Street,[37] but that their original site in Bridge Street appears to have been land which had very probably been in his ancestors' hands for centuries. Their site, identified by Bradney as that of four shops on the south side of Bridge Street,[38] is that of the tall building, now three shops and an office, shown in Figure 4.11.

Small though Clark reports them to have been, they cannot have been smaller than the 12ft-long frontages of the tiny cottages in Mill Street, Tewkesbury, and measurement suggests that these twelve Usk almshouses cannot have fronted onto the street, as does their tall replacement. They probably formed a 'U'-shaped block with the garden in the centre and reaching back towards what is now Usk's central car park. Standing as they do where there is a slight kink in the line of the street, I would suggest that their site was land still vacant, having been a space left in the original planning of the town for one of the 'streets planned but never developed' on my suggested original layout plan of the town. As such this land would have remained in the hands of the successive lords of Usk and would have come into those of the Beauforts. Perhaps the original benefactor was Henry Herbert, 1st Duke of Beaufort, the occasion of his becoming aware of the plight of the poor of Usk being his visit on 19 August 1684 towards the end of his official progress through Wales as Lord President of the Welsh Council.[39]

The funds for the Bridge Street almshouses was met by the rent of various pieces of land known as 'the lands of the poor of the town'. Given for that purpose by various people largely unknown but almost certainly including William

Fig. 4.11 The site of Usk's original almshouses in Bridge Street

Addams-Williams of Llangybi or his ancestors,[40] some of the lands had originally belonged to Usk Priory. Addams-Williams was chairman of the committee appointed to sell the old Bridge Street almshouses in 1825 and build their replacement on the land given by Henry, 7th Duke of Beaufort. These Church Street almshouses were run by the vicar, churchwardens and overseers of the poor of Usk, funded with the rents of the remaining pieces of the lands of the poor of the town which had not been sold to defray the cost of their erection.[41]

By 1883 our historian James Henry Clark, as chairman of the Local Board, reported that the new almshouses were 'getting into dilapidation'.[42] This continued to be their unhappy state until they had to be abandoned in the 1960s, were demolished in about 1970 and were replaced by the Usk UDC before its own demise in 1973.

Today known as Priory Court and still housing elderly people, their function as almshouses, as successors to the hospice for the entertainment of pilgrims, and in turn as successors to Usk's leper hospital and even to the hospital at The Rhadyr, has ended, but with an appropriate and worthwhile continuing use.

CHAPTER V

The Medieval Priory and its Community
by Madeleine Gray and Sian Rees

Foundation

Medieval Wales was poorly endowed with nunneries. While Ireland and Scotland had around 40 and 15 houses respectively, only four houses for women were established in Wales throughout the whole of the middle ages; all were small and one probably barely survived its year of foundation. Of the three more long-lived establishments, two were rural Cistercian houses in mid Wales founded by Welsh princes. Several, sometimes contradictory, explanations have been suggested for this — the higher status of women in Welsh society so that they had less need to retreat to religious communities, the apparently lower regard for female chastity in Welsh culture, the fact that under Welsh law women could not hold land and could not therefore endow religious houses — but it remains a puzzle for medieval historians. Why, therefore, is it at Usk that we have the only Benedictine nunnery in Wales, founded apparently by Norman benefactors, and the only women's religious house in an urban setting?

It would be useful to be able to begin to answer this question by looking at the date of the foundation and the name and thus perhaps the motives of the founder. Unfortunately, that is easier said than done. Glanmor Williams and Fred Cowley, following Knowles and Hadcock, say only that it was there by 1236, when a charter confirming the original founding was issued.[1] In his account of the history of the community in the *Monmouthshire Antiquary*, David Williams[2] suggests a date

before 1135, the year of the death of Richard de Clare, earl of Hertford and lord of Usk, to whom he attributes the settlement and whose son Gilbert continued to act as benefactor to the nunnery. The one extant charter we do have dates from 1330 and in it Elizabeth de Burgh confirms the grants of lands to the community made by her predecessors Richard and his son Gilbert. This Richard, however, is probably Richard Strongbow, earl of Pembroke (d.1176); Mein[3] tries to narrow down the date of his charter by analysing the list of witnesses cited as being present, and thereby suggests a date between 1154 and 1170. By the Dissolution the nuns regarded Richard de Clare and Gilbert his son as their founders, but there is evidently much opportunity for confusion amidst the series of Richards and Gilberts who succeeded one another during the 12th and 13th centuries and the lack of specific dates in the early charters provides little help.

This very uncertainty, however, may hint, albeit obliquely, at the nature of the earliest community of religious women and its relationship with the castle. Recent research by Sharon Elkins, Sally Thompson and others has demonstrated that many post-Conquest women's houses in England originated in informal groupings of women which eventually became part of one of the established orders.[4] There is also evidence for a tradition of reclusive, eremitical religious women in pre-Norman Wales, usually attached, however loosely, to a church, a tradition which continued throughout the medieval period. This certainly does not answer the question as to why, if such a community existed at Usk, it led to the foundation of a nunnery there and not in similar towns with Norman castles elsewhere. However, it seems probable that the community at Usk originated with such a woman or group of women, who would almost invariably be widowed or unmarried and of gentle birth, possibly including women from the castle household. Such communities usually settled in close proximity to a church or monastery, sometimes in cells adjoining the church building. They might take vows of enclosure as anchoresses or undertake charitable or educational work in the local community. Eventually, though, most came under pressure to regularize their status: the church at the beginning of the second millennium was becoming increasingly uneasy about the role of women, and independent and informal female communities were seen as a particular threat. There were advantages, too, in becoming part of one of the established religious orders. The formal structures of a religious order offered support and spiritual guidance, as well as protection for young members who might be under pressure from their families to leave the community and marry. The adoption of a recognised rule also enabled the community to look more effectively for endowments in order to ensure its continued existence.

Architecture

The fabric of the priory church may give us a hint of when this process of formalization took place.[5] The oldest part of the church, the tower and crossing, is 12th century, and probably early 12th century at that. The south wall of the nave with its blocked door is also 12th century. The arcade separating the present nave from the north aisle, however, is 13th century. As was usual in Benedictine communities, the nuns shared the church with the local community. Unusually, though, instead of occupying the western part of the church, the parishioners of Usk occupied the north aisle, which they eventually extended until it was as wide as the nave. We might conjecture, therefore, that the north aisle was built when the community of religious women took on the Benedictine rule of strict enclosure and needed a separate part of the church in which to worship.

While the fact that an existing church and its community stood here would explain the position of the formalised Benedictine nunnery of, perhaps, the late 12th or the early 13th century, it is perhaps worth examining the choice of this site at the point we can first detect the building in the early 12th century. We have suggested that a community of religious women, probably of good birth, might well have been situated at a reasonable proximity to the castle as this would provide some protection and ease of communication. We know little of the appearance and character of any pre-Norman settlement at Usk and we have no evidence for any community or church on the site before the Norman foundation of the castle. There is a hint of a pre-Norman cult in that we know that in the outer enclosure of the nunnery was a chapel devoted to the 6th-century Merovingian saint Radegund (see below) but Mein[6] has suggested that the association is later, and probably derives from Alicia, first wife of Gilbert de Clare, who came from the Poitiers area where Radegund's relics lay in the church dedicated to her. The dedication of the church to Mary is a standard Norman practice, as at other Benedictine foundations in the area at Monmouth, Abergavenny and Chepstow. The position of the priory, close to the castle but utilising an existing pre-monastic church on the site, may be paralleled by Monmouth, where, we know, a pre-foundation church had to be adapted for the new Benedictine religious community.[7]

The site of the priory lay to the south-east of the castle, on low ground between the river Olway to the east, always prone to flooding, and the Usk, the course of which may then have been some way east of its present bed. Whether or not the site was undeveloped before the Norman incursion, one may assume at least that all traces of the defences of the Roman fort at Usk had been erased, as knowingly to build a church over the silted ditch of a Roman fort, with all the potential difficulties of construction over soft fill, would have been ill advised indeed. The structural problems which do seem to have bedevilled (and to some extent still bedevil) the building complex were, however, largely the result of building on what we know to have been the north-east corner of the defences of the earliest legionary fortress in south Wales.[8] Excavations subsequent to the main fort excavations in the 1970s have shown that the ditch did indeed turn under what is now the Garden of Rest, east of the existing church's chancel.[9]

What may we discover about the form of the original Norman church from the remaining 12th-century architecture and from the several small-scale pre-development excavations that have periodically been undertaken around the church? The present church is used for parish worship and comprises nave, north aisle, the tower now used as the chancel, two porches and a modern vestry on the site of the north transept. Of these, only the tower and nave are Norman, while the original chancel and transepts have been demolished. The nave has itself been lengthened westwards. However, excavations in 1987 prior to the extension of the burial ground to the east of the

church revealed a robbed out wall of substantial size, running north/south, 9.5m long which the excavators interpreted as the east wall of the presbytery.[10] This underlay the more recent boundary wall between the Garden of Rest and the Duke's Yard to the east. If the interpretation is correct, which seems likely, it shows that the presbytery would have measured some 22.6m, the same length as the nave, thus giving a symmetrical plan to the church. This confirmed the results of investigations in the same area carried out in 1964 when Isca Bowen and Rudge Humphreys excavated a north/south running trench 11.75m east of the tower which uncovered footings of the ashlar built north and south walls of the presbytery.[11] The trench revealed no traces of floor tile but pieces of stone slabs and mortar suggesting that the presbytery floor was slabbed. The excavations therefore served to disprove Stephen Williams' theory that the presbytery was shorter, with the east wall about 28 foot east of the tower.[12] Further excavations in 1998 in advance of the building of the new vestry uncovered footings of the east wall of the north transept, while a watching brief in

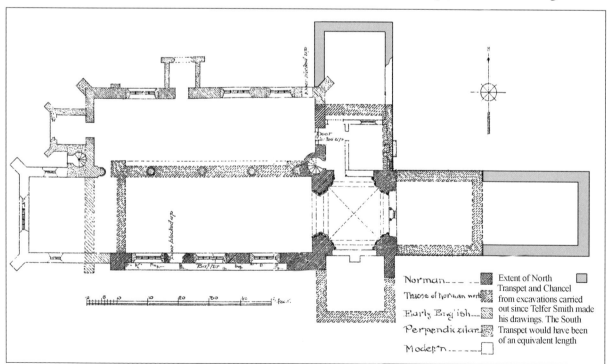

*Fig. 5.1 Plan of Usk Priory in 1886 by Telfer Smith (*Arch Camb *1886, 90), showing the original extent
of the north transept and chancel/presbytery since located by excavation*

41

1994 found the position of the north-east corner; together these showed the internal length of the transept as being 13.7m. Interestingly, the north wall was found to have had deeper foundations than the east, perhaps reflecting its position over the Roman ditch that had led to structural failure requiring subsequent strengthening.[13]

We may assume, therefore, that the monastic church would have had a conventional cruciform shape, some 52m in length, the four arms each having a width of around 7.3m, the transepts 13.7m long with the tower forming the crossing, rather than the chancel as it now does. The outline of the east crossing arch with traces of the simple vault for the presbytery and the crease line for the roof above can clearly be seen from the exterior of the church. Similar evidence for the transepts survives in the tower masonry to the north, partly obscured by the existing modern vestry, and the south, visible only from the gardens of the Priory House. This shows that the roof was of one height with the transepts, with a steep roof crease somewhat higher than the existing built into the masonry.

The tower is of two stages with simple chamfered 12th-century windows and unadorned belfry and ringing chamber, and a circular stair turret built into the north-west angle. The newel stair retains its internal dimensions from ground to roof, and is clearly of one build with the tower,

Fig. 5.2 South-east view of Usk Priory in 1886 by Telfer Smith (Arch Camb *1886, 90*)

only the battlemented upper courses of which are recent. The stair has the normal series of simple rectangular lights, the lowest of which, originally external, is now within the north aisle. The topmost rectangular opening, a crawl through to what is now the valley between nave and aisle roof, may be an original opening to give access to the space within the slightly loftier Norman nave roof. The lack of other openings confirms the simple form of the church, with no doors giving access to triforium or clerestory as was found at Monmouth. The south wall of the 12th-century nave survives, albeit with inserted windows. The blocked doorway at the east end would have led to the cloister and would have been the main entry point to the church for the nuns — this too can only be seen from the Priory garden, the interior of the church having recently been rendered.

From the interior, the church gives several clues about the nature of the original Norman church. The early 12th-century crossing is completely preserved, though the tower has been vaulted internally as a convenience for its use as the chancel. The impression is one of solid simplicity, with only scant concessions to decoration. The piers have plain scallop caps and their bases are now below ground level which tends to emphasise their heaviness. The crossing arches are in simple, unadorned two square-angled orders. There is a late 12th-century font comprising a square bowl with chamfered angles and a circular stem surrounded with four attached shafts with scallop caps. The rendered south wall of the nave gives nothing away, as the remnants of the blocked door to the cloister and the joint between the original west wall and the 19th-century extension are only visible from outside.

We may safely assume that the main conventual buildings stood to the south in the normal way, designed to lie so that the tall church walls did not block the sunlight from the cloister. The south nave door is in the conventional position to give access to a cloister which presumably was surrounded by the sleeping, dining and storage quarters of the nuns. So few nunneries survive that we cannot be sure that the conventional pattern of monasteries appertained to womens' houses, but it is reasonable to suppose that the nunnery buildings extended into what is now the Priory House garden and probably into the house as well. Whether any monastic medieval masonry survives within the existing Victorian house is not possible to say, though the east wing of the house is aligned directly with the south transept with the main house at right angles to it. The main house lies about 23m south of the church, the same distance as the length as the nave. It is entirely possible, therefore, that the house stands on the footprint of the refectory and south end of the dormitory range, which would result in a cloister of around 23m square. It is tantalising to imagine the wealth of information that may be hidden beneath the garden and house.

Fig. 5.3 North-east view of Usk Priory in 1886 by Telfer Smith (Arch Camb 1886, 90)

Modest in scale and decoration though the monastic church appears to have been, there presumably would have been decoration on the lime plastered walls, the roof timbers and possibly the flooring. Tiles probably deriving from the nunnery have been excavated in various parts of the town, but all date from well into the later medieval period and cannot inform us as to the form of the Norman church flooring, which, as we have seen above, may have been stone slabs.

The extent of the monastic precinct is unknown. The monastery appeared to have been reasonably well endowed and planned in a relatively spacious fashion within the south-eastern side of the Norman town. The open area known as The Priory Lands and bounded by Pook Lane and Market Street may give us an idea of the precinct layout. The precinct was certainly large enough, we know, to house at least one chapel, presumably near to the church, though we have no specific evidence for its date of construction, appearance or position. Mein suggests that the chapel to Radegund, an important focus for pilgrims to the priory and thus an important source of income for the nuns, may have been the building drawn by Colt Hoare as standing outside the west end of the north nave, but demolished when the nave was extended in the 19th century.[13] Whether the existing gatehouse on Sanctuary Street, to the north of the priory, apparently a late medieval, possibly even post-Dissolution structure, stands on the position of the original Norman entrance is also unknown, though it is certainly convenient for the town.

The cemeteries of townsfolk and nuns would have lain respectively around the church and probably adjacent to the claustral buildings. The 1987 excavations mentioned above found substantial numbers of male and female inhumations of adults and children just outside the presbytery wall, clustering around the mid part, at the nearest point to the high altar. This would have been a prestigious position for burial, and Maylan suggests that it may have been a private graveyard set aside for minor benefactors. No pre-cemetery features were found, suggesting that this area immediately east of the church was unoccupied before its use for burial, and its separate identity is suggested by the lack of burials found during excavation to north, east and south. The main graveyard to the north of the church was probably part of the priory's precinct but was not sold at the Dissolution, being retained for parish use. Burial of the nuns would probably have been within a separate graveyard to the south, nearer the claustral buildings.

It was entirely normal for Benedictine houses to share their church with parochial lay use, but the general rule was that the nave was used by the town, the crossing, transepts and chancel by the religious community. Why this was not adopted at Usk, where the chancel was of a reasonable size, is not clear, though several English nunneries have the same pattern. The church, we know, held a chapel and three chantries as well as St Radegund's chapel. Did the position of these, or perhaps the requirements of some community service provided by the nuns, make access through the nave a convenience or necessity? For whatever reason, it was decided to extend to the north by the building of a new aisle in the 13th century. It comprises four bays with strong circular piers with boldly projecting moulded caps, their moulded bases largely hidden below ground level.[14] The easternmost free-standing pier has four slender attached shafts and now stands at the junction between chancel and nave, but Newman suggests that it originally marked the division between the nuns' east bay and the townspeoples' three west bays of the aisle. If that is the case it is curious that all the piers show signs of the attachment holes for the screen that separated nun from parishioner. As time passed, the aisle proved insufficient again and it was extended northwards in the 15th century to achieve the same width as the nave, giving a harmonious symmetry to the interior. The windows in the extended north aisle exterior wall appear to be the original 13th-century fenestration rehoused in this new position.

The nuns' part of the church would have been screened off, and the two sections of the church could have been decorated quite differently. But however solid the screen was, it would never have been a complete barrier. The presence of the nuns would have been clearly felt in the parish church; their regular services would have been audible, and the scent of their incense would have drifted through the arches. Roberta Gilchrist has suggested that communities of religious women were always expected to be more closely linked with the local community than male communities. Women's houses tended to be smaller and to have less in the way of landed endowments; as a result they were more dependent on regular charitable donations in return for prayer and their spiritual presence.[15] This was certainly true of Usk. The prioress in 1374 was godmother to Roger, son and heir of the lord of Usk, Edmund Mortimer. Evidence of tiles found at the priory suggests that the Mortimers contributed substantially to the repair and rebuilding of the priory church at the end of the 14th century. In the 1460s, the Herbert family of Raglan Castle added a north porch and may have contributed to other work on the church.[16]

By the late medieval period, therefore, the church had been considerably extended from its original Norman build. The north aisle had

Fig. 5.4 The 15th-century north porch

doubled the area of the west end of the church, while the two porches added in the 15th century are the most conspicuous and flamboyant additions, both giving access to the lay part of the church (Fig. 5.4). The monastic church appears to have been accessed only from the cloister on the south nave wall, though there may have been an entry point from the dormitory, probably within the south transept. The two 15th-century porches, added perhaps by Sir William Herbert (d.1469) appear to have been built at the same time as the extension to the north aisle as they share the same plinth moulding, though the aisle is of Old Red Sandstone and the porches are of coursed limestone ashlar. The porches are almost identical with two storeys and two beautifully vaulted bays, though that on the north has angle buttresses while on the west porch they are diagonal. Each has a richly decorated entrance arch flanked by slender shafts. The Herbert badge is set in the parapet of the north porch, with a bearded king's head above. Each porch has an image niche over the doorway while in the west porch is a fine stoup on a head corbel. These are flamboyant additions departing significantly from the Norman original, and it is suggested by Newman that by this time the town's aisle was much more splendid and prominent than the nave of the nunnery.

Nonetheless, it may have been at this late period of the monastery's history that the splendid gatehouse was built, rather like the apparently late flowering of activity in the late 15th or early 16th century at Monmouth (Fig. 5.5). The two-storeyed gatehouse has square-headed windows with a west stack for a hearth to heat the room above the passage. The uncusped lights suggest to Newman that the build is 16th century and possibly post-monastic, built to lead, as it does now, into the house of the post-Dissolution owner of the property,[17] though Mein is more inclined to consider it late monastic with perhaps a gatekeeper's lodge attached to regulate entry to the precinct.[18] The blocked doorway on the east wall, he suggests, may have led to such a lodge from which the gatekeeper would have been able to inspect potential callers and regulate entry.

The life of the community[19]

We know very little about the daily life of the nuns at Usk. The community was probably never large, though Archbishop Peckham's instruction that the two treasuresses should make their accounts before the prioress and five or six senior nuns suggests that in 1284 they had at least the conventual number of 13.[20] In 1534, the prioress and five nuns acknowledged the Royal Supremacy. In his petition to the pope on the nuns' behalf in 1404, Adam Usk was at pains to point out that 'only virgins born of noble ancestry' were admitted to the community. There may have been some exaggeration here, but this was clearly a community with an aristocratic ethos. The nuns would not have been expected to work with their hands: they probably undertook the work which was regarded as acceptable for their secular sisters — fine sewing, embroidery, perhaps a little gentle gardening. The account rolls of similar communities elsewhere (such as the convent of St Radegund in Cambridge) suggest that they employed servants for manual work.

There is evidence from other communities of nuns undertaking embroidery for money, but it was more usually done as a social and spiritual activity, for gifts or for their own use in church and as an acceptable way of using their time. There is also some anecdotal evidence of nuns spinning. John Aubrey spoke to an old man who remembered the nuns of Kington St Michael sitting in their garden and spinning with wheels and distaffs — though again this was probably as a social occupation rather than an economic one. Nuns might also do occasional work in the fields at harvest; they seem to have treated this as a holiday (and the authorities criticised it as an occasion for misbehaviour).[21] Some nunneries

*Fig. 5.5 The gatehouse of Usk Priory as seen from inside the Priory House garden, in 1801.
Note the surviving medieval roof finials (Coxe Historical Tour I, 132)*

had a limited educational function. They could not teach to a high level, of course, but the novices had to be taught, and Power quotes evidence for young boys as well as girls living as boarders in nunneries, learning their early lessons. In smaller houses girls might sleep in the nuns' dormitory (or in later years in their private chambers). Girls would learn reading and possibly writing, music, embroidery, basic medicine, household management, deportment — all the things they could also have learned in a big aristocratic house, but possibly in a safer environment. As well as the regular distribution of alms at the convent gate, some communities also did a certain amount of nursing and other charitable work. There is a possible connection between Usk Priory and a hospice or leprosarium in 'Elwithstreet'. Much of this was an extension of what any large aristocratic household would have done. A nunnery was a large household like any other, and household management was usually a woman's job.

The daily routine of the convent would have been based around the requirement for regular prayer, the sevenfold monastic office. This shaped the monastic day as the sequence of saints' days and other church festivals shaped the year. This was the *opus dei*, the work of God. *Laborare est orare*, their founder St Benedict had said, to work is to pray: but to pray was also to work, and that was what they did. They got up for the night office of Matins and Lauds at 2am, then went back to bed until Prime, which was at 6 or 7am depending on the time of year. There was another mid-morning service, Tierce. Sext, originally at mid-day, gradually moved to late morning. Nones, originally mid-afternoon, by the late medieval period had become the noon office. This left from mid-day to about 5pm in winter, 6 or 7pm in summer, for work or study. The evening office of Vespers and Compline finished at about 7pm in winter, 8pm in summer, and the nuns were supposed to go to bed immediately after.

In addition there was the daily Mass. As women the nuns could not celebrate Mass themselves so they would have needed a chaplain. Rhys Hays found references to a prior (possibly connected to Archbishop Peckham's direction

in 1284 that they should appoint a 'senior priest to be master of all your goods') and to monks serving the church in 1330. There is no hint of which community these monks came from: Usk is roughly equidistant from Abergavenny, Monmouth, Chepstow and Goldcliff, the main male Benedictine houses in the county, with Llangiwa a little further away. This may have been a short-lived expedient; it would be more usual for the nuns to have had a secular chaplain.

The reorganization of the daily routine gave the nuns most of the afternoon for work, meditation, private prayer and study. This would have been spiritual reading rather than learned study; nuns were not encouraged to learn Latin, or to study theology or philosophy. Even the formidably spiritual Bridgettine nuns of Syon in Middlesex appear not to have been able to read Latin. Other aspects of the daily routine of the priory would have included meeting in the chapter-house to read a chapter of the Rule, to make their regular confession of faults and to transact daily business. In the early years they would have shared communal meals, but this practice was breaking down by the late medieval period. The austere diet of the refectory was increasingly replaced by the more relaxed diet of the *misericordia*, and in many houses the nuns ate in virtually independent households. (This was not necessarily a reprehensible development; we could compare it, for example, to the *foyers* of the brothers at the modern community of Taizé.)

In theory, the Benedictine life for women was one of complete enclosure and separation from the world. Gilchrist even describes enclosure as 'a fourth cardinal vow'.[22] Nuns were expected to take fresh air and exercise in the cloister, where they might also be able to talk to each other, but contact with the outside world was in theory restricted to senior nuns in the convent's parlour. There are some clear inconsistencies here. On the one hand, the community of nuns was supposed to be closely linked with the local community; on the other hand the nuns were supposed to be kept away from the world. On the one hand they were supposed to use the cloister for fresh air and exercise; on the other hand, as Gilchrist points out, many women's houses did not have a full claustral range.[23] They were of course fully enclosed: but within the enclosure their buildings were often similar to secular manor houses, with only a small courtyard. Usk was in fact built on more spacious lines, but it seems to have been acknowledged that some flexibility in the rule was needed. In his visitation report of 1284, Archbishop Peckham only felt it necessary to instruct the nuns that they should not go outside the cloister without suitable companions, nor should they stay in lay people's houses for more than three or four days.[24]

Spirituality

We can glean a surprising amount of information about the distinctive spirituality of the little community at Usk from a consideration of the saints commemorated there. We can look first at the priory seal. Medieval seals were more than mere authenticating devices: they were a crucial part of what we would now call the visual identity of the institution or individual using them. We could even go so far as to describe them as brandmarks. The common seal of Usk Priory survives in the National Archives and in the National Museum in Cardiff. It shows the Virgin Mary, crowned and seated on a rather Byzantine throne, with the Christ-child on her lap. The priory was dedicated to the Virgin Mary and this depiction of the Virgin and Child seems on the face of it a straightforward and appropriate image for a community of religious women vowed to chastity and humility. However, when we look at the seal in detail, it becomes much more complex.

Medieval iconography had two rather different ways of depicting the Virgin and Child. One appears in poetic descriptions of the statue of Mary at the shrine to her at Penrhys. Here she was shown standing, with the child in her arms, 'nursing Jesus for a kiss': an image of tender and affective motherhood. The other was the version chosen for the priory seal of Usk, the 'Throne of Wisdom', which by contrast emphasised Mary's unique power and status as queen of Heaven. This image seems to have appealed particularly to women. Gilchrist notes that a few women's religious houses had the standing Virgin and Child on their seals, but far more had the Throne of Wisdom.

The child in Mary's arms is also iconographically significant. Images of the Virgin and Child almost always depict Jesus not as a baby but as a well-grown toddler or even a miniature adult. The medieval church was not really interested in the human pathos of the infant Jesus: there are very few depictions of the Nativity in medieval Welsh art. However, although the child in Mary's arms on the Usk seal is clearly well grown, it is equally clear that Mary is breast-feeding him. This is a strange and even disturbing image to modern eyes, accustomed as we are to modern ideas about breast-feeding and women's bodies, but it was quite a common medieval picture, and it had many meanings.

First, and perhaps most basic, breast-feeding (then as now) was a sign of good mothering. The medieval theory was that breast milk was a kind of modified blood, and that it could transmit moral and intellectual qualities. A really devoted mother would insist on breast-feeding her own children, or at the least would ensure that they had a wet-nurse of good moral calibre. Lives of medieval saints are full of stories of holy royal women who fed their children themselves in spite of the inconvenience and the fact that it was usually something which women of low status did. There are also some strange stories of particularly saintly babies who refused to take milk from wet-nurses of bad character.

The Virgin Mary's milk was even more important. At its simplest, the image of a humble virgin who was also queen of Heaven feeding a helpless baby who was also the all-powerful God encapsulated in all its paradoxicality the doctrine of the Incarnation. But the Virgin Mary was also seen as a type or figure of the church. Both were spoken of as the bride of Christ: and in her willing co-operation with God's plan of salvation Mary provided a model for the ideal relation of the church to God. Her milk therefore came to symbolise the nourishment which the Church offered to the faithful. Medieval understanding interpreted breast milk as modified blood, so Mary's milk paralleled both Christ's blood shed for human sin and the conse-

48

crated wine of the Eucharist. Caroline Walker Bynum points to the links between the image of the breast-feeding Virgin and the imagery of Christ's wounds, also displayed in the Last Judgement but frequently described in mystical writings as feeding the soul.[25]

Mary's actual suckling of her child was presented as evidence of her humility, and relics of her milk were venerated all over the Christian world. The Usk Priory seal places its emphasis on Mary's uniquely powerful status, but at the same time the fact that she is nursing the child makes her more human and approachable. Images of the breast-feeding Virgin may also point to some of the mystical practices found in medieval convents, nuns who shared visions in which they fed and cradled the infant Jesus.[26] However, the child on the Usk seal is no infant but a well-grown child, sitting upright on his mother's knee. She offers her breast to him, and he receives it, almost as a sacrament.

Usk also had a statue of the Virgin Mary before which William Baker, rector of Tredynog, asked to be buried in 1514.[27] Unfortunately, we have no idea what form this carving took, or where it was in the church. As the patronal image it should have been sited to the north of the high altar (or possibly of the people's altar): but many churches had more than one image of the Virgin Mary.[28]

The nuns also celebrated devotion to some rather more unusual saints. Somewhere in their outer enclosure was a chapel to the obscure Merovingian saint Radegund, as discussed above.[29] Born in about 525, a princess of the Thuringian royal house, Radegund was unhappily married to Clothar, king of the Franks. She eventually ran away from him when he killed her brother, and sought refuge in Poitiers. Clothar eventually accepted her decision and helped her to found a religious community there.[30]

Although she was the founder, she never took the office of abbess. Instead, she chose deliberately to humble herself. At first she chose an active religious life, devotedly performing the most menial tasks, cleaning out privies, ministering to the sick, washing sores, even caring for lepers. Her biographer, the great hymn-writer Venantius Fortunatus, described her as 'busy as a new Martha' in her care of sick paupers.[31] Eventually though, she moved on to a life of complete enclosure as an anchoress, walled up in a cell but still able to dispense spiritual advice. She was also renowned for her practice of extreme self-denial and even self-punishment, chaining her body with iron bands and scarring herself with hot coals. However, reading between the lines of another biography written by one of her fellow nuns, Baudonivia, we can see that, in spite of her vow of complete enclosure, she remained a powerful political figure. Without giving any details of specific conflicts, Baudonivia praises Radegund's skill as a mediator and peacemaker:

> She was always solicitous for peace and worked diligently for the welfare of the fatherland ... Whenever she heard of bitterness arising among [the different kingdoms], trembling, she sent such letters to one and then to the other pleading that they should not make war among themselves nor take up arms lest the land perish. And likewise, she sent to their noble followers to give the kings salutary counsel, so that their power might work to the welfare of the people and the land ... So, through her intercession, there was peace among the kings ... Aware of her mediation, everyone rejoiced, blessing the name of the Lord![32]

An illuminated manuscript of Fortunatus's biography of her dating from the later part of the 11th century depicts her as enclosed in her cell but reaching out to perform miracles of healing and reconciliation.

How, then, did the cult of this holy woman from Merovingian France reach Wales? Geoff Mein makes the illuminating suggestion that it may have been an aspect of the close connection between Usk Castle and the priory. The most likely link is through Alicia de la Marche, first wife of Gilbert de Clare, 'Gilbert the Red'. Her family estates were in Poitou, their *caput* near to Poitiers where Radegund's relics lay in the church dedicated to her near her convent of Holy Cross. The marriage between Alicia and Gilbert was not a happy one; she bore him no sons, and he eventually divorced her to marry Edward I's daughter, Joan of Acre. Geoff Mein suggests that Gilbert's powerful mother, Matilda, and the nuns of Usk may have offered Alicia sympathy and that she gave a relic of the saint to the priory church.

The cult of a royal saint who became an enclosed nun was appropriate for an aristocratic community of Benedictine nuns. More surprising, perhaps, is the fact that the nuns also had a chapel with a cult image of Mary Magdalene. Mary of Magdala or Mary Magdalene is named in the Bible as the woman from whom Christ cast out seven devils (Luke 8.2). It was she who accompanied the Virgin Mary and Mary Cleophas at the Crucifixion and first saw Christ after the Resurrection. In medieval tradition, she was identified with Mary of Bethany, Mary the sister of Martha, who sat at Christ's feet and heard his words and later anointed him with spikenard and wiped his feet with her hair (Luke 10.39; Mark 14.3, John 11.2, 12.3). She in turn was conflated with the anonymous penitent woman who, in an alternative version of the anointing story in an earlier chapter of Luke's Gospel, anointed Christ at the house of Simon the Pharisee and washed his feet with her tears (7.37-50). She was forgiven 'because she loved much', and from this stemmed the assumption that her sins were of a sexual nature.[33] The medieval legend, based on apocryphal gospel texts, continued her story after the Resurrection with a tradition that she was present at Pentecost and received the gifts of the Spirit, travelled to southern Gaul as a missionary and eventually became an ascetic hermit.[34]

This legend of a reformed prostitute who became the 'apostle to the apostles' was one of the most powerful and ambiguous of medieval stories. On the surface, it is a story of abjection and forgiveness. It is subversive in that Christ welcomes a polluted woman in the home of one of the leaders of his own society, but conventional in that it sees purity as the most important thing for a woman. However, as the story develops, it is clear that it makes claims for the status of women which would be resisted by the institutional church. Mary's anointing of Christ's feet and her readiness to anoint his dead body with sweet spices linked her with the anointing in the sacraments of baptism, confirmation and Extreme Unction. Her presence at the tomb and the fact that she was the first person to see the risen Christ qualified her as the *apostola apostolorum*. This was embroidered on in the apocryphal gospels and later traditions which presented Mary Magdalen as a prophetic church leader.[35] Some church leaders countered this by pointing to Christ's commandment to her, 'Touch me not', arguing that this explicitly forbade women from touching the sacraments.[36] Just over the border in Shropshire, the prior of Lilleshall, John Mirk, wrote a book of sample sermons for clergy in the mid-15th century who were unable to preach. His sermon for Mary Magdalene's Day describes her announcement of the Resurrection and her retirement into ascetic contemplation in the wilderness, but her time as a preacher forms the bulk of the sermon.[37] Mirk even challenged the use which his fellow-churchmen made of Christ's commandment, claiming that Christ 'suffyrd her to towch hym and kys hys fete'.[38]

The chapel and statue of Mary Magdalene were a focal point of pilgrimage for the region around Usk in the later middle ages. An anonymous early 16th-century poem, *Mair fadlen mawr yw dwrthie*, was written to the saint at her shrine there. Cast in the form of a dialogue between the pilgrim and the statue, it addresses Mary as 'Mary Magdalene, bride of John ... merciful Mary Magdalene ... Mary Magdalene of Bethany ... Mary Magdalene, fair maid'. The poet asks for advice on relieving poverty of the body and spiritual need. The saint advises him to be just and charitable, to offer regular masses and to pray regularly. Unfortunately, the poem gives no hint as to the appearance of the statue or the location of the chapel.[39] It must have been at some distance from the priory enclosure, possibly on the marshes. In 1543 the priest Henry Morgan (younger son of Sir William Morgan of Pencoed) left money to repair the causeway 'between the town of Usk and Mary Magdalene's Chapel'.[40] (The implications of this bequest are twofold: the chapel was outside the town bounds, and it survived the Dissolution.) The chapel may have had some connection with the leprosarium in 'Elwithstrete'.[41] Leper hospitals were often dedicated to Mary Magdalene because her brother Lazarus (who Jesus raised from the dead) was conflated with the poor leper in the story of Dives and Lazarus. It is possible that the chapel survived when the hospice went out of use as leprosy became less common (see also chapter XII).

These two saints were perhaps unusual patrons for a community of celibate women, but the nuns of Usk had more conventional cults as well. As well as one or more statues of the Virgin Mary, they had a relic of St Elvetha (also known as Eluned or Eiliwedd), one of the Welsh virgin martyr saints. The story of Eluned/Elvetha in Baring-Gould and Fisher's *Lives of the British Saints* is a typical folk tale of a determined young woman, the daughter of the local king Brychan, who vows herself to celibacy but is pursued by a young man who eventually kills her. A chapel and well dedicated to her about a mile east of Brecon were the focus of a very strange medieval cult. Gerald of Wales describes how young men and women gathered there on the saint's day and danced around the graveyard in a trance, miming the work they had done on the Sabbath contrary to the commandments. They were then led into the church where they made penitential offerings and woke from their trance knowing they had been absolved and pardoned.[42]

While the nuns venerated a married saint and a saint who was identified as a reformed prostitute, their shrines were outside the nuns' enclosure. In the holiest part of the church, near the altar, were statues and relics of virgin saints, Elvetha and the Virgin Mary. The nuns accepted the validity of married sanctity and the possibility of holiness for even the worst sinner, but it was the virgin saints who were nearest to their hearts.

Endowments and economic life

The priory's estates were well focussed, consisting of land and rents in the Usk and Olway valleys, the rectories of Usk, Llanbadoc and Llangyfiw and tithes and pensions in Raglan, Llandenni, Cilgogean and Trostrey. The only significant holdings outside this area were in Badgeworth, Uphatherley and Downhatherley in Gloucestershire, where the nuns held the rectories and a small amount of land.[43] Their holdings in this area were so substantial that it has even been suggested that they had a dependent cell there, but there is no firm evidence for this.[44] This was an easily-managed estate producing a little over £60 a year net in 1536, comparable with Monmouth and considerably better off than Chepstow or the Cistercian abbey of Grace Dieu.[45]

There is a suggestion of slack financial administration in Archbishop Peckham's report. His visitation of the priory in 1284 was part of a whistle-stop tour of Wales following the collapse of Welsh independence in 1282-3. He made a flying visit to Usk and actually wrote to the nuns from Llanthony. While he saw no major spiritual problems, he described the priory as 'desolate' and clearly diagnosed financial mismanagement. The remedy he prescribed was that two 'provident and discreet' nuns be elected as treasuresses. All the priory's income was to be paid to them and they would distribute it to the prioress and other nuns as necessary. The treasuresses were to render accounts three times in the year, at Lent, Whitsun and Michaelmas, to the prioress and five or six senior nuns. As has been noted, Peckham also instructed that the nuns should have 'a senior priest, circumspect in temporal and spiritual affairs, to be master of all their goods'.

Clearly Peckham felt that the financial problems of the priory were the fault of silly women who could not manage money. This was a common medieval assumption. Recent archaeological investigation, however, has suggested another explanation. The nuns could hardly have been expected to realise that their church had been built over the rampart and ditch of the Roman fortress. This caused repeated problems with subsidence: the north transept had to be rebuilt and the floor of the church was relaid and retiled at least twice. It is possible that other parts of the claustral range were affected as well.[46] The drain this caused on the priory's financial reserves must have been considerable. Problems with the building may also explain the amount of time which some of the nuns were spending staying with families and friends.

The problems which the priory faced a century later were of an entirely different order. Usk was caught up in nearby fighting during the Glyndŵr uprising. Adam Usk's petition to the Pope described the 'burnings, spoilings and other misfortunes' caused by the war and claimed that the priory had come to such want that, unless some remedy be quickly provided, the nuns would be forced to beg for food and clothing by wandering about the country, or to stay in the private houses of their friends; 'whereby it is feared that scandals are likely to arise'.

Geoff Mein suggests that there is more than a little special pleading in Adam Usk's petition. If the nuns were really from aristocratic families, it is unlikely that they would have been left to starve. There is an element of moral blackmail in Adam's warning that they would be forced to rely on lay hospitality and scandal might ensue. Finally, given the involvement of the Cistercian abbot of Llantarnam in Glyndŵr's army, it might seem unlikely that they would have attacked a religious house, even one of a different order and with different allegiance. It would clearly have been politic to blame rebel troops for the devastation rather than general decay caused by problems with the site.[47] The problems of the early 15th century may also be connected with a rather odd episode in 1398, when two nuns from Minchinbarrow in Somerset (another aristocratic house) left their own priory and came to Usk, but subsequently went back to Minchinbarrow.[48]

By the early 16th century the priory's estates were being managed with exemplary firmness. At a time of rising rents and food prices, keeping land 'in hand' and farming it with hired labour made good sense. Usk had a higher proportion of its land in demesne than any of the other religious houses of Gwent. And the land which they had let out to tenants was on comparatively short-term leases so that rents could more readily be put up in line with inflation. This, as much as the continuing ability of the nuns to attract local patrons, may explain the amount of building work done in the late 15th and early 16th centuries. It was also the county's largest Benedictine community, with six religious to Abergavenny's five and the two each at Monmouth and Chepstow.

The Usk Frieze

A few years ago, we would probably have concluded this chapter with a discussion of the carved wooden frieze which is now in Cefntila but is traditionally assumed to have come from Usk Priory. The frieze has coats of arms of local families and of the Tudor dynasty, the Beaufort portcullis, the Tudor rose and Katherine of Aragon's pomegranate, portrait heads, symbolic carvings such as a wounded stag and a shield with three fishes, and shields with the *Arma Christi*, the Five Wounds of Christ and the implements of the Crucifixion. There is also a shield with the initials E.W., traditionally supposed to be the initials of Eleanor Williams, the last prioress of

Fig. 5.6 The Usk Frieze, now at Cefntila

Usk. However, in a lecture to the Gwent County History Association subsequently incorporated into the CD-ROM which accompanies Peter Lord's book *Medieval Vision*,[49] John Morgan-Guy has argued that it was originally commissioned not for Usk but for Raglan Castle, by Charles Somerset, first Earl of Worcester.

The frieze was certainly at Raglan in 1832 when the antiquarian and clergyman John Skinner drew it on a tour of south Wales.[50] John Morgan-Guy also makes a good case for an earlier date for the frieze than 1529, the earliest known date of Eleanor Williams's term of office as prioress. The royal coat of arms has as its supporters the dragon of Cadwaladr and the greyhound of Richmond. By 1520 the greyhound had been replaced by a lion in official heraldry. The pomegranate was a common emblem but as Katherine of Aragon's device it was unlikely to have appeared on public display after 1528 when Henry announced that he believed his marriage to be invalid. John Morgan-Guy concludes that the frieze with its blend of religious and secular imagery has remarkable parallels with the Worcester chantry at Windsor and may have

been installed in memory of Elizabeth Herbert, Charles Somerset's wife. The EW monogram would then refer to her by her title of Elizabeth Worcester.

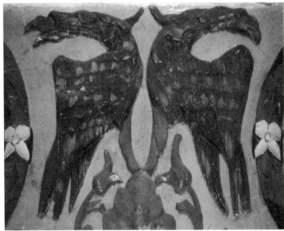

Figs. 5.7 to 5.11 Details of the Usk Frieze. The initials E.W. could relate to Eleanor Williams, the last prioress, but may refer to Elizabeth Worcester

However, this argument does not indicate where the frieze was between the slighting of Raglan Castle in 1646 and the restoration of the great hall in the late 1820s, nor does it explain why the frieze subsequently went to the Priory House in Usk rather than going to Badminton with the rest of the panelling from the great hall. John Morgan-Guy suggests that the frieze might have been sent to Troy House with the panelling from the great hall and some of the other treasures of Raglan as the Parliamentary army approached, but no evidence for this has yet been found. It is also extremely unlikely that Elizabeth Herbert would ever have used the EW monogram: peeresses do not use their titles as surnames.[51] The royal coat of arms and the pomegranate suggest a date between 1509 and 1520. Eleanor Williams does not appear as prioress until 1529 but the last datable reference to her predecessor Joan Haryman is in 1518. It is just possible that Eleanor Williams was in post by 1520 and ordered the frieze to commemorate her appointment. Joan Haryman was still receiving her pension in 1535 but the early retirement of heads of religious houses was common at this period.

We also need to bear in mind that there may have been a time-lag in changing the design of royal coats of arms in remote religious communities. As for the pomegranate, although we now know that Henry and Katherine's marriage was in difficulties by the mid 1520s and that he was actually seeking an annulment in 1527, in his Bridewell speech to the dignitaries of London in the autumn of 1528 he claimed that 'if I were to marry again, if the marriage might be good, I would surely choose her above all other women'. Did Eleanor Williams take him at his word, naively or with deliberate irony? The jury, as they say, is still out.

Dissolution and aftermath

Whether or not Eleanor Williams was defying Henry VIII in the redecoration of the priory buildings, she was certainly managing the priory estates with considerable efficiency. She may also have been one of the very few heads of religious houses who saw the way the wind was blowing in the early 1530s. While the monks of Tintern were trying to reduce the net income recorded for their house in *Valor Ecclesiasticus* by claiming for servants' wages and the wine, wax and oil used in the abbey church, a strategy which resulted in Tintern being dissolved in 1536 when it could have survived for a few years longer, Eleanor Williams was quietly leasing her priory's lands to local relatives.[52] She may simply have been providing for her own old age, but it is also possible that she was making provision for the whole community.

Eleanor Williams and her five nuns acknowledged the Royal Supremacy in 1534. The convent was finally suppressed on 29 August 1536. The prioress received a pension of £9 a year, but no provision was made for her sisters. Nuns suffered more hardship than male religious at the Dissolution. Monks and friars could choose to become secular priests or could transfer to larger houses. For nuns the first option was not available, and the nearest large house could well be some distance away. And when the larger houses were closed as well and the ex-religious were pensioned off, nuns received lower pensions than the men, in spite of the fact that they were still expected to keep their vows of chastity.

Little wonder, then, that much of the evidence we have for the survival of religious communities relates to groups of women. Elizabeth Throckmorton, last abbess of Denney (Cambs) took some of her nuns back to her family home at Coughton (Warwks); the last Abbess of Wherwell died in 1569 and left bequests to seven of the nuns who were apparently living with her.[53] Was this what Eleanor Williams had in mind when she leased part of the demesne to her cousin Philip Williams of Mathern? We will never know. By this time the connection with the castle was presumably long broken — but it may cause us to reassess our ideas on local attitudes to the little priory and its dissolution.

CHAPTER VI

Welsh Space and Norman Invaders: Usk Castle 1136-1245
by Jeremy Knight

The Timber Castle

Since the last full length account of Usk Castle in 1977[1] much has happened — Malcolm Thurlby's recognition that the 12th-century keep was a gatehouse like that at Ludlow; the new chronology of the Marshal castle at Chepstow, in whose lordship Usk stood; and the publication by Turner and Priestley of Minister's Accounts detailing building work on the castle in the 14th century. Between them, these have altered our understanding of the three main periods of the castle's history. A fresh account, relating this new evidence to the standing remains, may help to put these discoveries into perspective.

Usk Castle is first mentioned in 1136 in a context which shows that it already existed, and probably had done for some time. Can the historical background help us to date its foundation any closer than between 1067 and 1136?

The inscription on the Trellech sundial of 1689 claims the late Neolithic standing stones there as a war memorial erected by Harold Godwinson after his invasion of Gwent and his building of a base at Portskewett, on the site of the llys (court) of the pre-Norman king of Gwent. In the next century, the incursions of his army were still remembered at St Gwynllyw's church at Newport, but any intended conquest was sidelined by the events of 1066.[2] After Hastings, William fitz Osbern, lord of Breteuil in Calvados, inherited Harold's role and founded castles at Chepstow and Monmouth, but how far his control extended is debatable.[3] In the years immediately after the conquest he was involved in consolidating Norman rule in places as far apart as Yorkshire and the Isle of Wight and would have had little time to devote to south Wales. In his grants to the Abbeys of Lyre and Cormeilles in Calvados, known only from a later confirmation and from their claims to tithes from individual settlements, all the places named are on the eastern fringes of the modern county. Apart from Chepstow, they are all in the Monmouth-Trellech area: Llangua with its church; Grosmont; Mitchetroy; Cwmcarfan; Nova Villa (Newcastle) and the forests between Usk and Wye ('*inter Waiam et Oscham*'). A later charter of Walter Bloet, confirming the tithes of Raglan to Lyre and Cormeilles, and mentioning fitz Osbern, suggests that Raglan, commanding the road from Monmouth to Usk, may also have been in fitz Osbern's hands.[4] As David Crouch has said, 'apart from the references to specific settlements in the shadow of his castles, Earl William's authority in Gwent seems more apparent than real'. His tenure was in any case brief. He left for Normandy in January 1071 and the following month was killed in battle at Cassel in Flanders.[5]

His son, Roger fitz William, is a more substantial figure in relation to Gwent. At the Norman

Fig. 6.1 Map of Anglo-Norman Gwent, showing the lordships of Ewias, Monmouth, Abergavenny, Chepstow, Edelicion (Edlogan) and Glamorgan

conquest, Rhydderch ap Caradog ruled in Gwent Iscoed and Ewias, his cousin Caradog ap Gruffydd in Gwent Uwch Coed and Gwynllwg. Caradog's territory included Edelicion and Lebenydd (broadly the later lordship of Usk west of the Usk, with Caerleon). He was a descendant of Morgan the Old, who in the previous century had given his name to the kingdom of Morgannwg or Glamorgan ('Morgan's Land'). Caradog had become king on the death in battle of his father Gruffydd ap Rhydderch in 1055. He now allied himself with Roger fitz William. The two defeated Caradog's rival, Maredudd ap Owain of Deheubarth, on the banks of the river Rhymney in 1072.[6] Thereafter Caradog was 'king of the Glamorgan people' (*regis Glatmorganensium*). When another Welsh ruler, Caradoc ap Rhiwallon, granted land at Llangwm, east of the river Usk, to the Church in 1071-5, it was with the consent of Roger fitz William 'Count of Hereford and lord of Gwent', but a similar grant of *Tref Rita in Edelicion* west of the Usk by Caradoc ap

Gruffydd about 1072 had no mention of an over-lord.[7] This suggests that Roger claimed overlord-ship as far as the Usk. His alliance with Caradog continued. Monmouth Castle was garrisoned by three of Roger's knights, Humphrey, Osbern and William the Scribe (William Scriptor). In 1075 Roger was involved in a rebellion against William the Conqueror. He was imprisoned and his lands taken into royal custody. On his fall, three knights, presumably the same, fled to the *subregulus* (underking) Caradog, provoking a royal attack on Gwynlliog.[8] Nevertheless, Caradog's alliance with the Normans continued. He attended the consecration of the castle chapel of St Cadoc at Monmouth, but was killed at Mynydd Carn in Dyfed in 1081 in a battle between two alliances of Welsh princes, one supported by an army of Danes from Waterford and Dublin. Caradog's kingdom went into eclipse. He may be the subject of an elegy on a ruler killed in the battle, possibly written by the bard of a later lord of Caerleon, Hywel ap Iorwerth.[9]

By 1086 Caerleon was in Norman hands, held by Thurstin fitz Rolf. David Crouch has suggested that the motte on the corner of its Roman walls may have been built by William the Conqueror on his 'pilgrimage' to St Davids in 1081 when he made a settlement with Rhys ap Tewdwr and possibly built the similar motte inside the Roman walls of Cardiff. Mynydd Carn had caused a power vacuum in south Wales which William needed to fill. Thurstin also held six carucates of land beyond the Usk, in Caradog's former terri-tory. The king retained land for one plough and fisheries on the Usk, strengthening the possibility that Caerleon Castle was a royal foundation.[10]

Usk thus lay at the boundary between Norman Gwent and the Welsh lordship of Caerleon in Edelicion and Lebenydd, temporarily in eclipse at the time of Domesday. Its strategic position, at the point where the Roman road from Monmouth met that along the Usk Valley, so controlling stra-tegic river and valley routes, would have made its fortification essential. Though there is no direct evidence, Roger fitz William may have been the founder of Usk Castle. Its situation on the inter-face between Welsh and Normans is reflected in its history until William Marshal built his new castle at Usk and simultaneously eliminated the Welsh lords of Caerleon.

The first castle of Usk bears a marked resemblance to the first phase of White Castle, also held by Roger fitz William. Both show under their later stone defences the earthworks of an early timber castle.[11] Both have a sub-circular scarped and ditched Inner Ward, entered through a crescentric hornwork, with a large Outer Ward or enclosure opposite. Both were later turned through 180 degrees, so that the hornwork is now to the rear and entry to the Inner Ward is via the original outer enclosure. Llantilio Crossenny (where White Castle stands) was granted to Payn fitz John, a trusted lieutenant of Henry I, in 1100-35. Though not specifically mentioned until 1162-3, White Castle thus probably existed by the early years of the 12th century, and by implication in the time of Roger fitz William.[12]

After Earl Roger's forfeiture, fitz Osbern's holdings were split up by the crown. Thurstin fitz Rolf died without issue, and about 1115 King Henry I granted his land to Walter de Clare. Caerleon was in the hands of Robert de Chandos, founder in about 1113 of Goldcliff Priory, where he was buried in 1120.[13] The Welsh lords of Caerleon were generous patrons of this house. Caradog had been succeeded by his son Owain Wan ('the weak'), but after his death the kingdom of Gwent was revived by Owain's sons Morgan and Iorwerth. When Henry I died in 1135, the Welsh rose against the Normans and recovered much of their lost lands. It is in this context that we first hear of Usk Castle. In 1136 Morgan ap Owain seized 'Ucham' after he had killed Richard de Clare, lord of Ceredigion. David Crouch has recently suggested that an unidentified site called *Wetuna*, granted to the church of Llanlywel by William de Tancarville (d.1129), chamberlain of King Henry I, may have been an earlier predecessor of Usk, the centre of a lordship in the Usk valley, perhaps founded following the death of Robert de Chandos in 1120, and lost to the Welsh in 1136. Crouch concludes that this 'cannot at the moment be said to be estab-lished', but if correct it would put the foundation of Usk, and presumably the castle, back by around a decade.[14] Despite these military activities, the local Welsh alliance with Norman rulers continued. Morgan and Iorwerth did homage to Earl Robert of Gloucester, whom they called in a charter *dominus noster*, 'our lord', whilst Orderic Vitalis called Morgan '*Morgan Gualas Ucham'*, Morgan the Welshman of Usk'. They issued charters giving land to Bristol Abbey and Goldcliff Priory and after the anarchy of Stephen's reign (in which they supported Earl Robert) received a confirmation of the 'Honour of Caerleon' from the new king Henry II.[15] On the death of Robert of Gloucester in 1147 they found a new patron in Earl Roger of Hereford, witnessing his charter to Llanthony Secunda, with Morgan in first place as king of Glamorgan, '*Morganno rege'*. Morgan died in 1158 in battle against Ifor Bach, lord of Senghennyd, fellow Welsh rulers proving as usual more lethal opponents than Norman invaders. After Morgan's death, Richard de Clare recovered Usk and Caerleon, probably between 1165 and 1170.[16]

In 1174 Henry II spent money on 'the castle of Usk, which the men of Earl Richard [de Clare] captured from the Welsh'. In the same year Morgan's nephew Hywel ap Iorwerth rose against the king, ravaged Gwent Is Coed, 'won all except the castles' and even took hostages from some of the Norman lords. Shortly afterwards, he recovered Usk from Strongbow and held the castle for the next decade as a client of Henry II.[17] Just as Caradog was allied with the Norman Roger fitz William, now Hywel was an ally and vassal of the English king. In 1175 or 79 he founded the Cistercian Abbey of Llantarnam or Caerleon, a daughter house of Strata Florida. In 1183 he was holding both Usk and Newport for the king.[18] Shortly after this, however, Hywel was mortally wounded in a surprise Norman attack on Usk Castle.[19]

The First Stone Castle

By 1185, after the death of Hywel, Usk was in royal hands. £10 3s was spent on repairs to the castle and the houses in it. Its garrison comprised ten sergeants, ten archers, four watchmen, and a flying squad of fifteen 'mobile' sergeants. Ralph Bloet of Raglan served as keeper of the castle.[20] Conditions on the March required urgent action. In 1182 the Welsh had attacked Abergavenny castle in revenge for de Braose's massacre of 1175 and killed the sheriff of Hereford at Dingestow, where he was building a new castle. Between 1183 and 1187 Grosmont, Skenfrith and White Castle were being strengthened against Welsh attack by Ralph of Grosmont, a royal official.[21] This was the context for the building of the stone curtain wall and tower at White Castle and possibly of a now vanished hall or tower at Skenfrith. It may also have been the context for the building of the gatehouse at Usk. Logically, this should have been accompanied by a stone curtain wall, as at White Castle. If so, the two castles would have been very similar in the late 12th century. Only foundations remain of the White Castle tower. It overlooked the crescentric hornwork giving access to

the castle, but its angle to the former shows that it cannot have been a tower-gatehouse, like that recently recognized at Usk.

Recent stripping of creepers from the exterior east face of the keep at Usk revealed the ashlar springing of a large entrance arch, showing it to have been a tower-gate like those at Ludlow and Sherborne (Figs. 6.2 and 6.3).[22] This entrance occupied the two lower of the present three floors. The upper floor was a hall, of which three original round-headed openings, all now blocked, survive. One was placed centrally over the entrance arch. The other pair, set in the south wall and visible externally, are double-splayed windows with rubble external arches and pale freestone window surrounds set back from the wallface (Figs. 6.4 and 6.5). Geological analysis identifies the latter as Middle Jurassic Box Ground stone from the quarries at Box outside Corsham in Wiltshire.

Fig. 6.2 The recently revealed springing of the original entrance arch in the tower-gatehouse (keep) at Usk

Fig. 6.3 The entrance tower (keep) at Ludlow Castle, showing the blocked arch (Malcolm Thurlby)

Fig. 6.4 The tower-gatehouse at Usk showing the two original window openings in the south wall

Usk Castle and William Marshal

In the summer of 1189, Isabella de Clare, the young daughter of Earl Richard Strongbow, was married to a distinguished soldier, William Marshal, then in his early 40s. Isabella was heiress to large estates in southern England, south Wales and Ireland, a rich prize for a man whose landed wealth, despite years in royal service, was modest. William Marshal had been born about 1147, the younger son of a Berkshire knight.[23] He made his own way in the world as a soldier and in the tournament field, and in 1168 entered the household of Eleanor of Aquitaine, the estranged wife of Henry II. He was subsequently part of the household of King Henry's son, Henry 'the young king', until the latter's death in 1183. Marshal fulfilled the dying wish of the prince, who had taken the vows of a crusader, by taking his cloak, with its crusader's cross, to the Holy Sepulchre in Jerusalem. Marshal was in Palestine from 1184 to 1186. On his return, he was among the few who remained loyal to Henry II during the revolt of his sons Richard and John, who were aided and abetted by the French king, Philip Augustus. Henry II promised Marshal the hand of Isabella de Clare and after his death at Chinon in July 1189 the new king, Richard, kept his father's promise, even though Marshal had unhorsed him shortly before, during a skirmish near Le Mans, when Richard had been pursuing his fugitive father.

Marshal acted swiftly to take possession of the de Clare lordship of Striguil. New evidence shows that he started work on Chepstow Castle and its twin towered gatehouse, previously dated to the 1220s or later, soon after his marriage. In

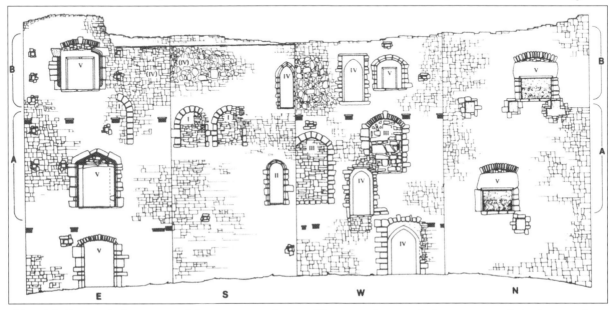

Fig. 6.5 Internal elevations of the tower-gatehouse. The recently revealed entrance arch in the east face is not shown (Knight Usk Castle and its affinities)

1991, Kevin Booth, excavating within the gate-house, found a cut silver halfpenny of Henry II of c.1180-9, 'not greatly worn when lost'; sealed within its construction levels.[24] This early date was confirmed in 1998 when tree ring dating of timbers of the original gatehouse doors gave an estimated felling date range of 1159-89.[25] Marshal was at Chepstow in March 1194 when he received news of King Richard's release from captivity, and no doubt took the opportunity to inspect his new fortifications.[26.] For the rest of Richard's reign he was in France, fighting against the king of France, Philip Augustus.

The earldom of Pembroke had been created for Gilbert de Clare in 1138 by King Stephen, but Henry II confiscated it in 1153-4 as a royal estate wrongly alienated. Gilbert styled himself Earl of Striguil (Chepstow). Pembroke, commanding the direct sea route to Ireland, was politically sensitive, since the king was suspicious of his over-mighty subjects there. Henry II and Richard both retained Pembroke in their own hands. Only when the new king, John, invested Marshal as Earl of Pembroke in 1199 and allowed him to take possession the following year was he able to exercise control. Late in 1200 the new Earl of Pembroke visited his new possessions in Pembroke and in Ireland.[27]

John's loss of Normandy in 1203-4 created problems for Marshal, as for many English nobles who held estates of both John and Philip Augustus. Initially, he was able to expand his territory. John granted him Goodrich in April 1204 and at the end of the year he recovered Cilgerran from the Welsh. However, John's suspicions over his divided loyalties grew. By 1207, with Marshal in Ireland, John was rescinding his earlier grants of Gloucester, St Briavels and Cardigan and demanding Marshal's sons as hostages.[28] Marshal did not return permanently from Ireland until 1213 and would in any case hardly have courted suspicion by work on a major new castle. Usk must therefore date from after his return.

By 1213, the political wheel had turned full circle. King John was faced with rebellious barons, who had offered the throne to Philip Augustus's son Louis (who invaded southern England) and allied themselves with King Alexander of Scotland and Llywelyn ap Iorwerth (Llywelyn the Great) of Gwynedd. Marshal was one of the king's few loyal supporters. That October John granted him Cardigan, Carmarthen and Gower, restoring his pre-eminence in south Wales (though within a few years he had lost them to Llywelyn). With this new status went the need to defend his territory. In the uncertain political climate, prudent men looked to the defences of their castles and in David Crouch's words England at this time 'was a disturbed anthill of military activity'.[29]

This was the background to William Marshal's decision to re-fortify Usk. At the time of John's death in October 1216 and the crowning of the child king Henry III, Marshal was in Gloucester, where he could watch events both in England and in south Wales. Morgan ap Hywel of Caerleon was allied with Llywelyn and the coronation banquet at Gloucester was interrupted by news that Goodrich was under siege, presumably by the Welsh. The turning point of the crisis was Marshal's last and victorious battle at Lincoln the following May. Morgan continued hostilities even after peace had been made. In 1217 there was fighting in Gwent in which several of Marshal's knights, including Roland and Walter Bloet of Raglan, fell. Late in September 1217, Marshal's bailiff, probably John of Earley, seized Caerleon from Morgan, who did not finally make peace until 1218.[30]

The capture of Caerleon is relevant to the date of Usk, since the arrow loops on the surviving tower of Caerleon Castle, next to the Hanbury Arms, are of the same distinctive type as those on the Garrison Tower at Usk and work at Caerleon, in the characteristic style of William Marshal, cannot have begun before the spring of 1218 (frost would have made winter working in masonry impossible).[31] A date bracket of 1213-9 would suit the parallels with the Middle Ward at Chepstow and (bearing in mind that construction would take a number of seasons), a central date of two years on either side of 1216 would fit. The construction of a new castle was often seen by neighbours as a hostile act, even a *causus belli.*

It is possible that Morgan's belligerence before the seizure of Caerleon was provoked by the new fortifications at Usk.

William Marshal transformed Usk from an earthwork with a stone gatehouse and (probably) curtain wall into a major castle in the state of the art defensive mode of the early 13th century (Fig. 6.6). The Inner Ward was enclosed with a curtain wall of sandstone rubble enclosing a rectangular area, its four sides angled outwards in shallow echelons. Its corners, oriented to the cardinal points, were protected by circular towers, save on the east, where the earlier tower-gatehouse was retained as the entrance. A second entrance comprising, so far as can be seen at present, a simple pointed arch and portcullis was added a little north of this, at the top of a steep slope. A larger circular tower, the 'Garrison Tower', faced

the rear of this entrance across the Inner Ward, at close archery range. Of the three original circular corner towers, only a small fragment of the South Tower remains.[32] That on the west was removed when the 14th-century domestic range was built, and the North Tower was rebuilt by Gilbert de Clare in about 1289.

The Garrison Tower
The large circular tower facing the entrance arch across the width of the Inner Ward is traditionally known as the Garrison Tower (Fig. 6.8). It is contemporary with the adjacent curtain wall, the angled ashlar quoining linking them surviving in part. Of four storeys, with an added corbelled out and battlemented top, the raised ground level within the ward makes it appear one storey shorter. As was normal in these round Great Towers,

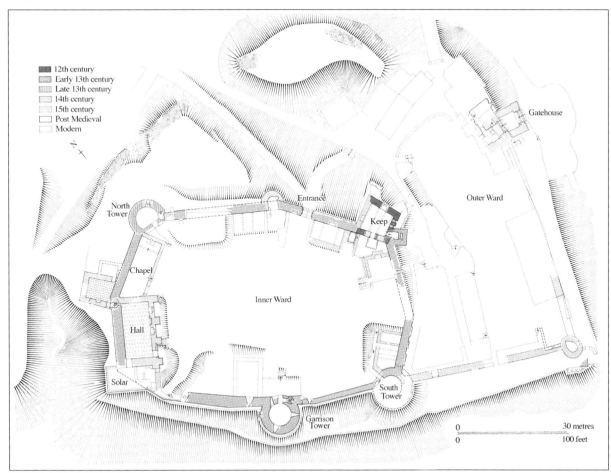

Fig. 6.6 Plan of Usk Castle showing periods of construction (© National Monuments Record for Wales, Royal Commission on the Ancient and Historical Monuments of Wales)

61

Fig. 6.7 Tomb of William Marshal, Temple Church, London

access was at first floor level, via a vertical two storey wooden porch (a lateral stair would have blocked one of the openings on either side). A spiral stair from the first-floor landing gave access up and down. Often the ground floors of such towers could only be reached by a trap door from above, but here the spiral stair led down to an original ground-floor doorway which survives inside a secondary late 13th century door. A later opening cut through the external walling now gives ground floor access.

The original entrance, its sill 8 feet above original ground level, is a tall opening with two rings of small squarish voussoirs.Comparison with the surrounding ground level suggests that in late stages of the castle's history, the ground floor of the tower had been filled in and this now served as a ground-floor entry. Both lower floors are lit by sets of three splayed loops with round-headed rear arches, which emerge externally as

Fig. 6.8 The exterior of the Garrison Tower

Fig. 6.9 The Hanbury Arms Tower at Caerleon

long firing slits with serifed bases, similar to loops at Chepstow and The Hanbury Arms Tower at Caerleon, the only surviving part of the castle (Fig. 6.10). The ashlar dressings of rear arches and loops are from the Dundry quarries outside Bristol, a stone particularly favoured by William Marshal.

The spiral stair continues to the second-floor landing, lit by a shorter loop, now ruined, directly over the entrance door. Two wall passages lead to the wall walk and to a latrine. In order to accom-

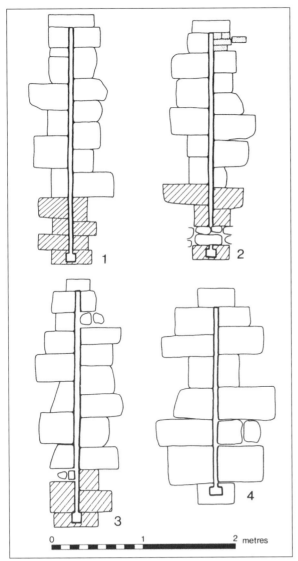

*Fig. 6.10 Comparison of Caerleon (1, 2 & 3) and the Garrison Tower (4) arrowslits. The shaded stones are Dundry limestone (*Knight *Road to Harlech)*

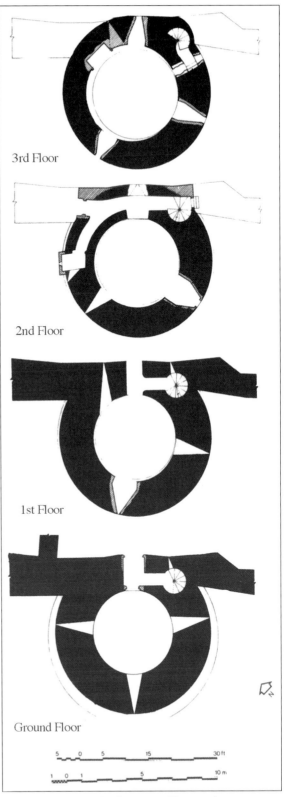

3rd Floor

2nd Floor

1st Floor

Ground Floor

*Fig. 6.11 Garrison Tower plan (*Knight *Usk Castle and its Affinities)*

modate the latter, there are only two loops at this level. A curving wall stair rises to the top floor and roof. A line of beam holes on the exterior face of the Garrison Tower marks the position of an external timber gallery allowing access between the adjacent wall walks without entering the tower. Before the addition of the later corbelled and battlemented top, the tower might have been crowned by a timber hourd or fighting top, like those known to have existed on other round keeps, notably at William Marshal's Pembroke.

In the late 13th century, a number of doors and windows were altered, a fireplace inserted on the upper floor, blocking one of the loops, and the latrine remodelled, with an added projecting ashlar chute. These alterations, designed to make the accommodation in the tower less spartan, may be part of the documented work of John Mayel in 1289 and are considered in the following chapter.

The Entrance

One major puzzle of William Marshal's castle is its gateway (Fig. 6.12a). The simple entrance arch is surprisingly weak for an up to date major castle. O'Neil saw it as typologically early, but the new early dating of Chepstow outer gatehouse shows that this is not the answer. However, the Usk entrance is very like William Marshal's middle ward gateway at Chepstow (Fig. 6.12b). If the Usk tower-gatehouse remained in use as part of Marshal's castle, both would have been secondary entrances, accounting for their simple forms. It is uncertain however when the tower-gatehouse was converted to its present form and its archway blocked. There are also indications that the entrance was more complex than

*Fig. 6.12a The gateway
to the Inner Ward at Usk*

*Fig. 6.12b The gateway
to the Middle Ward at Chepstow*

it appears at present. The portcullis slot shows the one-time presence of a first-floor chamber of some kind above the gate and it was seemingly provided with a drawbridge in 1320-21.[33] There also may have been an earthwork barbican to the east, covering its approach. In 1302-4, a new brattice (a timber fence or palisade, often in prefabricated sections) was erected 'outside the gate of the castle, towards the garden'.[34] Early 13th-century castles often had earthwork barbicans, defended with timber brattices, blocking the direct approach to the main gate. For example at Montgomery in 1228-32 Hubert de Burgh added a barbican defended by brattices, blocking the direct approach to the Outer Gate along the neck of the ridge on which the castle stands.[35]

Date and Affinities

The castle was first attributed to William Marshal by Bryan O'Neil in 1936. He compared the simple gateway with Hubert de Burgh's work at Skenfrith and Grosmont, begun after 1219, the year in which Marshal died.[36] In 1977 I expanded this, comparing Usk with the French castles built by Philip Augustus, and with work at British castles, including Chepstow. On the basis of these parallels and William Marshal's varied fortunes I suggested a date of 1212-19 for Usk. This can now be fine tuned to 1213-1217 (see above).[37]

Richard Avent identified three phases of work at Chepstow under William Marshal.[38] The first was the Outer Gatehouse and its curtain wall of c.1189-95, previously thought to be no earlier than the 1220s. The second comprised the curtain wall, towers and entrance arch of the Middle Ward, the third the Upper Bailey. In contrast to earlier interpretations, this left only the Barbican beyond the latter as the work of his sons.

Architectural parallels between Usk and Chepstow have long been noted. It can now be seen that these are concentrated in the second phase of Marshal's work at Chepstow, i.e. the Middle Ward. Its simple entrance arch resembles that to the Inner Ward at Usk, and both can be seen as secondary entrances, rather than as simply typologically early. To the rear of the Chepstow arch is a short arrow loop with square

basal stop, paralleled on the upper floor of the Garrison Tower. The Garrison Tower has courses of squared stone marking the first floor levels externally. On the Buck print of 1732 (Fig. 7.7) these appear as chamfered offsets, which can be matched on the towers of Chepstow's Middle Ward (and in the castles of Philip Augustus). Both at Usk and Chepstow, the towers were originally entered at wall walk level, or by an external stair, with a spiral stair giving access to other levels. We cannot say whether the now vanished corner towers at Usk had similar arrangements.

In broader terms, Usk belongs to a distinctive family of geometrically planned castles of the early 13th century, associated in France with Philip Augustus (1179-1223).[39] From about 1170 there had been experiments in England and France with various forms of polygonal great towers ('keeps') leading to cylindrical towers like Henry II's Tour du Moulin at Chinon (Indre-et-Loire) before 1189 and Thibaud, Count of Blois's great tower at Châteaudun (Eure et Loire) of 1170-90.[40] Philip Augustus developed a distinctive, almost standardized, version, which he combined with the parallel development of castles with a square or rectangular 'geometric' form (Fig. 6.13c). Round towers at each angle, often set to the cardinal points, gave covering fire to each face of the curtain.[41] Sometimes, as at Usk or at King John's Dublin (Fig. 6.14), the four sides are echeloned out in a shallow V to give a more efficient angle of fire along each sector of wall face. The circular Great Tower (*Tour Maitresse*) can be either placed centrally, as at the Louvre in Paris (1190-1202) or Skenfrith (Fig. 6.13d)[42] or can form an enlarged corner tower as at Dourdan (1220-2) or, later, Edward I's Flint;[43] or can be integrated with the line of the curtain, as at Usk. These were all castles built *de novo*. Circular Great Towers could also be added to pre-existing castles, sometimes on top of a motte (Longtown, Bronllys) or within an earlier shell keep (Tretower). Four of Philip Augustus's Great Towers can be dated by their *devis* (building instructions) to 1204-12. Sadly, the only survivor is Villeneuve-sur-Yonne (Yonne) (Fig. 6.13b).[44] All the necessary elements — a geometric trace,

Fig. 6.13b

Fig. 6.13c

Fig. 6.13a

66

Fig. 6.13d

The geometric planning of Usk and its circular Great Tower (the Garrison Tower)
link it to other contemporary major castles:

Fig. 6.13a) Kilkenny Castle, caput of the extensive Irish lands of the Marshals. The existing structure is
mostly post-medieval, but recent research and excavation have found much of the Marshal castle, with
close parallels to Usk

Fig 6.13b) Villeneuve-sur-Yonne (Yonne, France). A circular Great Tower built by the French king
Philip Augustus in 1204-12

Fig 6.13c) Lillebonne (Seine Maritime, France), another circular tower of Philip Augustus. The great
towers (tours maitresses) of Philip Augustus probably served as models for Welsh round towers like Usk
and Skenfrith but show significant differences

Fig 6.13d) Skenfrith Castle, built by Hubert de Burgh in 1219-1232, shares with Usk its 'geometric' plan
and circular great tower (Print by Samuel and Nathaniel Buck, 1739)

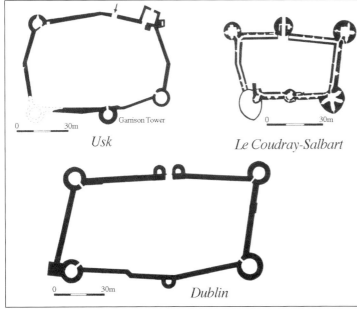

Fig. 6.14 (left)
Comparative plans of geometrically designed castles. The 'geometric' planning of Usk was an international style, as plans of these contemporary castles show. The early 13th-century Le Coudray-Salbert is near Niort (Deux Sèvres, France), where Hubert de Burgh was seneschal before King John's loss of Normandy in 1204-5. Dublin, built under a 1204 mandate of John, is, save for one tower, buried under the post-medieval castle, but is known from early plans and recent excavations. All three show a rectangular outline, with corner towers and a fifth tower opposite the gateway

Great Tower and architectural details were thus in place before Marshal began work on Usk around 1215.

The careers of men like William Marshal or Hubert de Burgh, builder of Skenfrith, were passed as much in France as in Britain. It is therefore hardly surprising that their work and contemporary French castles show such close affinities, extending to details such as the use of chamfered ashlar offsets to mark each floor level externally. There are however differences. The French Great Towers are floored with stone vaults and often surrounded by a circular stone lined moat, crossed by a bridge. British examples are normally floored in timber, Pembroke being a rare exception, and the first-floor entry was reached by an external wooden porch or stair, of which traces sometimes remain. Both in Britain and France, the towers were crowned by timber hourds or fighting platforms, set on radial timbers. An impressive example survives at Laval (Mayenne).[45]

William Marshal's widow Isabella de Clare held the lordship of Striguil in her own right after his death in 1219 until her own death the following year. Her five sons then successively inherited, though all had died without issue by 1245. During this time, Usk underwent two of its few sieges. In August 1233 Richard Marshal, in dispute with Henry III over the imprisonment of Hubert de Burgh, fled to Wales. The king assembled an army at Hereford, invaded Marshal's lands and laid siege to one of his castles. Roger of Wendover could not remember its name ('*cujus nomen neo teneo*'), but Usk is the obvious candidate on geographical grounds, and the Tewkesbury Chronicle confirms this. When the king failed to take '*castrum Huske*' after a siege and his food supplies were running out, a deputation of bishops negotiated a face-saving compromise whereby the castle was to be delivered to Henry for 15 days and then returned. When he failed to return it within the agreed time, Richard brought up his siege engines and retook the castle by force, killing several of the king's knights and officials in the process.[46]

CHAPTER VII

De Clares to Herberts:
Usk Castle after the Marshals
by Jeremy Knight

Gilbert II de Clare, 1262-95

Anselm Marshal, the last of William Marshal's sons, died childless in 1245 and Usk became a separate lordship under his nephew Richard de Clare. Richard's son, Gilbert II de Clare, succeeded his father in 1262. Some items in a Minister's Account of 1289 can be related to the surviving fabric. Locks were bought for the door of the castle chapel and for the door of 'the new tower where the Lord Earl's treasure is placed for safe keeping' (the North Tower), whilst a stone-mason, John Mayel, was paid 7 shillings under contract for altering the windows of the Round Tower of the castle (the Garrison Tower).[1] Taylor identified these with the altered windows on the two upper floors of the Garrison Tower. The offerings in the castle chapel on Easter day amounted to 2s 6d and another entry 'for the purchase of a cocker dog' was, as Taylor pointed out, the earliest known reference to a cocker spaniel.[2]

The North Tower

The D-shaped North Tower replaced an angle tower of the Marshal castle (Figs. 7.1 and 7.2). A doorway with renewed stop chamfered jambs and a recent arched head leads from the Inner Ward. On its right, a latrine is contrived in the angle between tower and curtain wall. Externally, cross-oiletts (cruciform firing slits) cover the area outside the tower, though those on

its western half have been lost in later refacing, leaving a series of prominent putlog holes. The first-floor chamber, reached from the ward by a stair, has a central fireplace in its flat inner wall, resting on three corbels, with a lintel of joggled blocks. The central corbel is an impost with dog-tooth decoration, reused from Marshal's castle. The fireplace is flanked by the entrance door, with quarter round ('bull-nosed') jambs and by a window opening. Attached shafts on the inner side of the door and window emphasise the tripartite division of the wall space. Of the upper (second) floor, little survives, though the Buck print of 1732 shows the tower standing to full height with a corbelled out top and cross-oiletts. The 'bull-nosed' jambs, cross-oiletts and squinch arch above the slit lighting the latrine match contemporary work by Gilbert de Clare at Caerphilly and Llanblethian. At the same time, the spartan accommodation in the Garrison Tower was remodelled. New ground-floor doors with bull-nosed jambs now gave access to the ground floor. Such secondary inserted doors are common in round towers of this type, as at Skenfrith.

In Gilbert de Clare's large building programme of those years, emphasis shifted from lesser castles like Usk and Caerleon to major fortresses like Caerphilly, Llanblethian and Llangybi. The alterations to the Garrison Tower were domestic,

Fig. 7.1 'The new tower where the Lord earl's treasure is placed for safe keeping' (1289). Exterior of the North Tower. The doorway to the right is modern, cut through the original walling

not military, and the well-appointed North Tower was probably the lodging of a steward or treasurer. With such a building programme on hand, the collection of revenue would have loomed large in Usk, but Gilbert's revenues were hard hit when much of central Monmouthshire was laid waste in the war between Edward I and Llywelyn ap Gruffydd.[3] When Gilbert died in Monmouth Castle in 1295, 180 houses in Usk were 'void and burnt in the war' and another 104 'void and ruinous' due to the poverty of their owners.[4]

Gilbert III de Clare, 1307-14

Usk remained in the hands of Gilbert's widow, Joan of Acre, until 1307. There were minor repairs and alterations, including the building of a timber brattice 'outside the gate of the castle towards the garden', but no major building works.[5]

It is tempting to interpret this gate as the tower-gatehouse and claim that the present garden already existed, but this area is usually called the Outer Ward, and the small William Marshal gate is probably meant. Joan's son Gilbert III de Clare stayed frequently at Usk, both in his youth and as Earl.[6] In 1308-9 an isolated

Fig. 7.2 Interior face of the North Tower

building account records work carried out on the 'tower over the prison', probably the Garrison Tower. It was roofed with lead, and the wall adjoining it repaired. This seems to have been part of a prolonged building campaign, still in progress in 1312-3, followed by the construction of a new domestic range. The work may have included the removal of the timber hourd which we can assume originally crowned the Garrison Tower, the construction of the present heightened corbelled and battlemented top and its reroofing. 'The round tower over the prison' is mentioned again in 1315-6.[7]

The Domestic Range (Fig. 6.6)

The domestic hall range is aligned along the inner face of the early 13th-century curtain wall between the North Tower and the vanished West Tower. It comprises three elements: a buttressed hall on the south, a square two storey chamber block at the upper angle of the hall, projecting outside the curtain, and a chapel range to the north. It is not a structural or architectural unity and date-able original features are scarce. On documentary evidence, Priestley and Turner have suggested dates of 1308-9 for the chamber block, 1315-6 for the chapel and 1314-9 for the hall. However, they seem to represent piecemeal replacement of a pre-existing hall range and it is possible that some references could relate to now demol-ished features, particularly since the sequence of surviving Ministers Accounts is incomplete.[8] There are however early 14th-century details in the chamber block and the excavation of the chapel produced a sculptured capital representing a long-haired noble youth wearing a fillet, with long bobbed hair and curvilinear curls (Fig. 7.3). My colleague, the late Stuart Rigold, suggested a date of c.1325 for this, plus or minus 20 years (i.e. 1305-45), agreeing with the date suggested by the documents, though the head could also belong to later work under Elizabeth de Burgh.

The First-floor Hall

The Receiver's account for 1318-9 records 'a hall newly built in the castle' by William Keys, Receiver of Usk in 1314-5. By 1318 it was being

Fig. 7.3 Carved head from the chapel

roofed. A plasterer, 'Master Hugh', was making a louvre for the roof and tenants at Llangovan were making stone roofing slates for it and carrying them to the castle.[9]

The buttressed hall is of three bays, the curtain forming its north wall. Entry at ground-floor level is by a door at the lower end, with renewed stop-chamfered jambs. The first-floor door to the screens passage is immediately above. The other two bays have ruined window openings between the buttresses. A now blocked doorway with pointed head and ashlar jambs led from the lower angle of the hall to a now largely destroyed solar block. The doorway was later blocked, the solar demolished and the wall refaced with a series of putlog holes like those on the secondary external patching of the North Tower. There was no conventional service range with pantry and buttery. The first-floor hall has a large 15th-century fireplace with renewed head in the north (inner) wall and a large rectangular window in the gable end. This now lacks its head, but the 1732 Buck print shows it as mullioned and transomed. This 15th-century remodelling was probably contemporary with that of the keep. The renewed entrance door and fireplace are part of the work

Fig. 7.4 *The first-floor hall at Brinsop Court, Herefordshire,
the same size and probable appearance as that at Usk*

carried out by Albert Addams-Williams in 1899-1920, 'repairing arches and fireplaces that were on the point of going to ruin'.[10]

The hall is similar to other first-floor halls of the early 14th century. Markenfield Hall, near Ripon in Yorkshire, licensed in 1310, has the same modest-sized hall, buttressed on one side, with entry at one of its lower angles and no apparent service block. A door in one of its upper angles (i.e. from the High Table) leads to a long first-floor range at right angles, incorporating a chapel.[11] At Brinsop Court, Herefordshire, the buttressed first-floor hall of *c*.1340, almost exactly the same size as that at Usk, has two superimposed doorways at its lower end and a large central first-floor fireplace in its opposite wall, as at Usk (Fig. 7.4). The surviving original roof trusses and panelling give an idea of the possible original appearance of the Usk hall.[12]

The Chamber Block

The chamber block in its projecting tower is of two stories, with a spiral stair in the south-east angle. Priestley and Turner suggest that it may be the 'New Chamber' roofed with tiles in 1308-9, though this could refer to an earlier now demolished chamber block.[13] However, the architectural evidence agrees broadly with such a date.

The Chapel

The chapel was identified and excavated in the 1930s. Only the west wall, forming part of the curtain, survives to full height, with the foundations of the east and north (liturgical east) walls. The remains have been conserved as a family chapel and burial place, with an altar and niche in the north wall. A chapel is mentioned in 1289, but the existing remains probably belong to the documented rebuilding of 1314-6, begun by Gilbert de Clare III before his death in June 1314 and finished by his widow, Countess Matilda. Work was still in progress in 1315-6. A ruined wall 'facing the chapel' was rebuilt and a door and window inserted, possibly in the now vanished east wall.[14] Medieval domestic chapels were usually on an upper floor when there was more than one storey, to prevent unsuitable activities

taking place above the altar. In this case, references to an oriel, a landing or porch lit by a large window, suggest that the chapel was reached from the Inner Ward via a (probably wooden) stair leading to an oriel before the door of the chapel. The ground floor probably served as an ante-chapel. One chamfered door jamb through the north wall of the chapel survives at first-floor level, as does a second door leading from the upper floor of the north Tower.

It is sometimes thought that Llangybi was intended by Gilbert as a major new fortress like his father's Caerphilly, which, had Gilbert lived, would have replaced Usk and Caerleon. However, Priestley and Turner suggest that it was a grand hunting lodge and rural retreat, where he could escape from the busy administrative centre and large household at Usk. Perhaps unfinished at Gilbert's death at Bannockburn in 1314, it was soon completed with all necessary apartments and conveniences. Elizabeth de Burgh visited for short periods with part of her household, leaving the rest at Usk.

Elizabeth de Burgh and the Despensers

On Gilbert's death, Usk passed to his sister and co-heir, widow of John de Burgh, Earl of Ulster, though Gilbert's widow, Matilda retained Usk in her own hands in dower until 1320. Elizabeth and her second husband, Roger Damory, then began a major programme of building works, initially rounding off the amenities of the hall complex. In 1320 a 'dresser house', where food was dressed for the table, was built between the kitchen and hall. The kitchen is likely to have been a squarish detached structure lying inside the south-west curtain between the hall and the Garrison Tower. An oriel window was added for the goldsmith, next to the door of the countess's chamber, presumably on the first floor of the small block whose foundations remain in the angle between the chamber block and the north-east curtain.[15]

In 1320-1, in a worsening political climate, attention shifted to the defences of the castle. Almost £22 was spent on a new gate at the entrance from the castle to the town — the present, still inhabited gatehouse. A mason,

David Godeway, was paid for an arch of free-stone and a reference to carpentry suggests that the upper floor may have been half timbered. The existing gatehouse is of two periods. References to an added drawbridge and bridge show that the outer half is the work of 1320-1. The earlier inner half, on a slightly different alignment, may have been the work of Gilbert de Clare. A second drawbridge was provided for the Inner Ward gate and the castle was furnished with armour, arrows, crossbow bolts and catapults.[16]

Roger Damory was a leader of the baronial revolt of 1321 against Edward II and the Despensers. After the collapse of the rising (in which Roger was mortally wounded) Elizabeth was arrested in her castle of Usk (*le Chastel Duske*) in January 1322 and sent to Barking Abbey near London with her children. Her account of her tribulations is preserved in a collection of Mortimer charters.[17] In June, the king forced her to exchange Usk (her own property, not that of her husband) with Hugh Despenser the Younger for Gower, which was of much lesser value. Later, she was summoned to York and pressure was put on her not to remarry or alienate her land without the king's consent. Finally, in 1324, Despenser used the hard up William de Braose, lord of Gower, to lay claim to Gower, which he then passed to Despenser.[18]

Despenser was not alone however in making use of the disturbed conditions following the baronial revolt. Damory and his steward had a long-running dispute with the Prior of Goldcliff over some monastic lands, including a mill and its leat. Writs and counter-writs in chancery had flown back and forth. In 1322 a group of Damory's Welsh servants seized Prior William of St Albin, stole the priory's seal and cattle, looted grain from its granaries and held the prior prisoner for a week in the '*Morbu*' near the donjon in the castle of Usk (*prés le donjon en la chastel de Usk*), only freeing him on a ransom of 100 marks.[19] Oddly, the whole episode was to be repeated in 1442 with a subsequent prior. Despenser held Usk for the next five years. Small amounts were spent on repairs, but Despenser's main efforts went to the building of the magnificent hall and kitchens at

Caerphilly. On his fall in October 1326, Elizabeth rapidly regained her possessions, and was in residence in Usk Castle by mid November.[20]

She evidently intended to take up residence in her newly regained castle with a household suitable to her rank and status. Repairs were made, including to the 'Lady's chamber' and, significantly, a large masonry stable was added in 1329-31, presumably in the Outer Ward. However, since Despenser had seized her papers ('remembrances and evidences') it took her until 1334 to sort out some of her personal finances and debts.[21] In 1341-2, new chambers and chimneys were being built 'at the Lady's order' and carpenters, plasterers and roofers were at work. Later records are incomplete, but in 1348-50 Lady Elizabeth was again in residence and alterations included a new bell tower ('*campanila*'), presumably of wood, at a cost of 25s 4d, perhaps for the chapel. New chambers and latrines were being built 'next to the new tower towards the park', which Priestley and Turner suggest may be the small semi-circular tower next to the entrance gate of the Inner Ward.[22]

These minor new works, presumably by the resident 'works squad', can be put into context by two factors, the itinerant nature of the medieval noble household, travelling between its castles or great houses, and its very size. Medieval household accounts sometimes list repairs and alterations 'against the coming of the lord thither'. This phrase occurs at Newport Castle in 1457 when Ralph Plomer was mending holes in the roof, windows were being repaired and new furniture bought before the arrival of the Duke of Buckingham. Similarly at Usk in 1329 buildings were being repaired '*contra adventum comitisse*'. The process was even made the subject of a poem by George Herbert.[23] A noble household would contain many servants and officials of various grades, all requiring accommodation appropriate to their rank. The list of provisions for Elizabeth de Burgh's Christmas feast at Usk in 1326 shows the number of mouths that required feeding, again each in a manner appropriate to their status.[24] Many castles have traces of foundations and fireplaces from lodgings for this medieval Great Household. The chimneys and latrines mentioned in the documents may even have been perquisites of a certain rank, much as carpets once were in the civil service. Elizabeth's household accounts include impressive quantities of bread, wine and ale, a variety of livestock, poultry and fish and oysters from her Suffolk estates. Even after she left Usk for the last time in April 1350, it continued to provide her London household with provisions — beef and pork, salmon and lampreys, herons and sparrowhawks, and even a porpoise 'caught in the water of Usk'.[25]

The Outer Ward

The Outer Ward, in the area of the present house and gardens, originally at the rear of the castle, was turned through 180 degrees when the keep-gatehouse was built and the early hornwork abandoned. The date of the curtain wall and the south corner tower are uncertain, but the outer half of the Outer Gatehouse is known to date from 1320-1 (Fig. 7.5). The earlier inner half and the curtain (with which it is aligned) may date from the time of Gilbert de Clare. Little now remains of the curtain.

The South Tower, looking out over the town, is of two storeys, with a corbelled and once battlemented top. It was later converted to a columbarium and the conical roof shown in the Buck engraving suggests that this had already happened by 1732. Documentary sources refer to a large medieval barn and stables in the outer ward.

Usk Castle in the Fifteenth Century

Elizabeth de Burgh's daughter Philippa married Edmund Mortimer, Earl of March. Their son, Roger Mortimer, born in Usk in 1374, was killed fighting in Ireland in 1398. Her grandson, Edmund, 5th Earl of March, who had a good claim to the throne, was kept in prison during the reign of Henry IV. Whilst he was in prison, Usk castle 'in some measure repaired for defence' and with a garrison of 20 lancemen and 60 archers was attacked (12 March 1405) by the forces of Owain Glyndŵr, resulting in the Battle of Pwll Melin (see chapter IX). The year after the battle,

Fig. 7.5 The Outer Gatehouse at Usk Castle

one of the victors, Sir John Greyndour, Sheriff of Gloucestershire, was appointed steward of the lordships of Usk and Caerleon.[26] The revolt had severley affected Usk. 'All the tenants had fled' it was reported, 'certain of them had been killed; and their lands are in the lord's hands because of the lack of tenants'. The The castle however had been kept in repair and in 1411-2 a new camera (or private chamber) was built.[27] Mortimer's estates were restored to him by Henry V on his accession, but he died childless in 1425. The Mortimer heir, Richard, Duke of York was killed at the Battle of Wakefield in 1460. When his son became king as Edward IV the following year, Usk became a royal castle.

Edward IV's daughter, Elizabeth of York, married Henry VII in 1486. Henry VIII purchased the other shares in the lordship in 1511 and Usk formed part of the dowry of both Anne Boleyn in 1532 and his last Queen, Katherine Parr, in 1543. Neither visited Usk, the main result for the tenantry being an entry fine of 500 marks on each occasion.[28] After Katherine's death, the castle was to become a quarry for building stone.

Usk Castle and the Herberts
In 1431, Richard Duke of York appointed William ap Thomas, progenitor of the Herberts, steward of the lordship of Usk. Ap Thomas was a new man, who had married the heiress of Raglan. He exploited his new position with vigour. In 1442, one of two rival priors of Goldcliff, Lawrence de Bonneville, complained to the Pope that Sir William ap Thomas's men, during a dispute over the priory's properties, had broken into the priory, led de Bonneville 'by the bridle, like a thief' to Usk Castle and kept him there for four days chained by one foot, before taking him to Abergavenny. Sir William (or Sir Thomas Herbert as he was becoming known) had sworn to 'make him resign ... even if it were on the high altar of the priory'.[29] His son, William Herbert, succeeded in 1455. Ten years later, Raglan became a separate lordship. Herbert became Earl of Pembroke, of the second creation, in 1468, but the following year was beheaded after the battle of Edgecote. In the 17th century Sir Thomas Herbert of Tintern recorded that as soon as Sir William Herbert was made a Baron (in 1462) 'he was at great charge in repairing several castles within his jurisdiction', as well as 'hereditary seignories of his own'.[30] Usk came into the first category and comparison with work at Raglan suggests that this included the remodelling of the interior of the Great Tower and the Hall.

After the death of Katherine Parr in 1548 Edward VI granted Usk to Sir William Herbert, who in 1551 allowed his steward, Roger Williams,

Fig. 7.6 The tomb of Sir William ap Thomas, Abergavenny Priory

Fig. 7.7 The Buck brothers' print of Usk Castle in 1732

to strip the castle of stone for the Great House, the new residence he was building in Old Market Street. References to the 'Exchequer' (probably the North Tower), the Hall and Chapel and the Chamber block suggest that much of the stone came from the domestic range in the Inner Ward, though he also demolished the Great Barn (measuring 70ft x 35ft) in the Outer Ward and stripped 'tablestones' and 'battlements' from the curtain wall. The gap in the curtain near the North Tower may have been made by Williams to take away his cartloads of stone. These would have been difficult to get through the arch of the Gateway, and he demolished 'a house jutting to the exchequer' which probably lay along the inner face of the curtain next to the gap. The Great Hall was 'dismantled', probably for its timberwork. The dressed stonework of the doors and windows of the chapel and the chamber block and the spiral stair[31] (35ft high and 70ft in compass) leading to the 'Prince's Chamber' in the latter were also removed. Williams's handiwork can be seen today in the many ruined openings, robbed of their dressed stonework, in the castle. Thomas Churchyard in 1587 lamented the ruinous state of the county's castles. Usk Castle, 'a seate where kings and princes have been borne', (though 'full neare great woods and many a mightie oak') was 'all to torne' and Churchyard feared that it was 'readie down to fall'.[32]

The gatehouse however remained in use as the residence of the steward of the lordship. In the 17th century this was Thomas Herbert, (sheriff 1673), half-brother of the Civil War parliamentary Colonel Henry Herbert of Coldbrook. Thomas Herbert died in 1693, his widow six years later. By the time Coxe visited a hundred

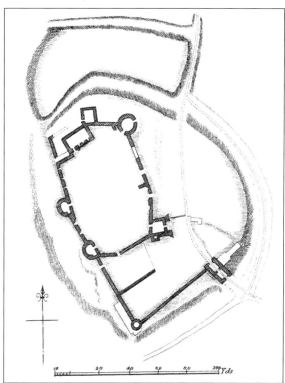

Fig. 7.8 William Coxe's plan of Usk Castle, 1801

years later it had become a farmhouse.[33] In the meantime, the castle itself had passed out of the hands of the Herberts and was eventually sold to Valentine Morris of Piercefield, whose mounting debts forced him to sell it on to Lord Clive of India. Towards the end of the 18th century it was bought by the 5th Duke of Beaufort. In 1899 the castle was sold for £16,250 to Albert Addams-Williams of Llangybi.[34] In 1908 John Humphreys and his family came to live in the gatehouse (the only habitable part of the castle), and in 1933 the Humphreys family purchased the castle ruins, and created a garden around them — see chapter XIV.

Plate 1 The 12th-century tower of St. Mary's Priory Church, showing the entrance arches and roof lines of the original chancel and north transept, the latter partly obscured by the modern vestry

Plate 2 The Garrison Tower of Usk Castle, built at the same time as the curtain wall by William Marshal c.1213-1219

Plate 3 The Keep, initially a tower-gatehouse, at Usk Castle, showing the south and east walls

Plate 4 The herbaceous border in the gardens at Usk Castle,
with the Keep to the left and Castle House to the right

Midsummer
1934

The Vinery Jersey.

*Plates 5-14 (this page and opposite) Watercolours of and from the castle garden
by Kitty Humphreys, c.1924*

Plate 15
An elegant coffee pot, an
example of Usk japanned tin plate,
circa *late 18th century*
(Pontypool Museum)

Plate 16 The screen at St. Mary's Priory Church. In 1455 Sir William Herbert succeeded to the steward-
ship of the lordship of Usk. He was a fairly new man. His father, William ap Thomas, had risen from rela-
tive obscurity as a Yorkist supporter and Herbert may have felt the need to consolidate his position.
This wooden screen, together with the two 15th-century ashlar porches, may therefore represent an
embellishment of the church of the seat of his lordship. The screen is unlike other Monmouthshire screens
and the workshop responsible may have been based in Somerset or Gloucestershire. The screen has been
heavily restored and possibly moved from its original position, but now stands on a low stone plinth
which destroys its proportions and resulted in the removal of its wainscot and middle rail

Plate 17 Usk Bridge in autumn. The first stone bridge was built in 1750, but 100 years later the bridge had become too narrow and steep for the ever increasing volume of traffic. A man fell off a hay wagon into the river and was killed. The magistrates took over its management and the people of Usk and Llanbadoc had to find £200 for repair and widening

Plate 18 Inside Usk Rural Life Museum: part of the museum showing the farming year. The museum has over 3,000 rural artefacts dating from 1850-1950

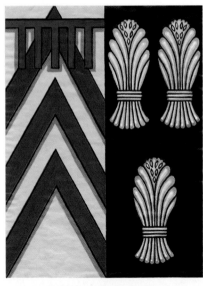

Richard de Clare
and Eva MacMurrough.
Or, three chevrons gules, a label
(suggesting that he bore the arms in
his father's lifetime) of three points
azure. Sable, three garbs or.

William Marshal
and Isabella de Clare.
Per pale or and vert, a lion
rampant gules, langued and
armed azure.
Or, three chevrons Vert

Gilbert de Clare
and Isabella Marshal.
Or, three chevrons gules.
Gules, a bend fusilly or
(the Marshal family coat)

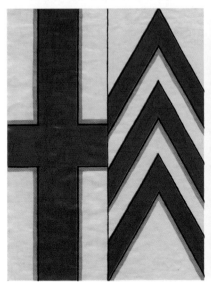

John de Burgh
and Elizabeth de Clare.
Or, a Cross gules (Ulster).
Or, three chevrons gules

Henry Tudor
and Elizabeth of York.
Quarterly, France Modern
(azure, three fleur-de-lys or)
and England (gules, three lions
passant guardant or, langued
and armed azure).
Quarterly (1) The Royal Arms,
as daughter of a king; (2) and
(3) Ulster; (4) Mortimer (azure,
three bars or, on a chief of the
first, two pallets between two
base esquires of the second.
Overall an inescutcheon argent)

Plates 19-23 The banners on this page each bear the coat-of-arms
of lords of Usk, with that of their wives on the right. A shield or
banner is described, or blasoned, in the archaic language still in use
today, from the standpoint of the bearer (behind the shield). The staff
of the banner is always to the left. In heraldry there are five essential
colours or hues: gules (red), azure (blue), vert (green), purpure
(purple) and sable (black), along with two metals: or (gold or
yellow) and argent (silver or white).

CHAPTER VIII

The Development of the Norman Town
by Geoffrey Mein

The town was founded by Richard Strongbow de Clare sometime between December 1154 and May 1170, with a view to his own financial profit. It was populated initially largely by those who were tenants on his own widespread English estates, settlers who had 'gone west young man' in a time of good weather, good crops and therefore burgeoning population, to what they saw as a new land of opportunity. Offered building plots laid out for them by the lord's surveyor and town planner, possibly the Osbert *Cementarius,* Osbert the mason, mentioned in the town's first charter, they paid the annual one shilling 'burgage' rent wherever their plot lay in the town. Each undertook to build a house and perhaps a shop within the year, which they could either occupy themselves or sub-let if they continued to live elsewhere. The town was planned so as to attract trade to the town centre from neighbouring settlements by routing all the main roads through its market place, now Twyn Square but perhaps originally known as *Twyn y daley du* (the hillock of the black leaves). With each burgage rent set at a shilling, the narrowest plots were in the square, and became ever wider the further the plot lay from the centre. Thus plots in what is now Maryport Street are double the width of those in Twyn Square, but all had long back gardens and were separated from their neighbour by open passages giving access to the rear of the property. Business was promoted by prohibiting the marketing of goods by the native Welsh country people elsewhere than in the town, coupled with a ban on their customary practice of barter.

Apart from the layout of the streets, the lord provided a defensive ditch round the town, the town and market hall fronting the main street, one or more mills with their feeder leats from the Olway (Fig. 8.1), the Benedictine nunnery,

Fig. 8.1 The Dairy Farm, Four Ash Street in 1986, the site of Usk's Upper Mill

with perhaps an integral parish church in place of the small chapel in the castle, a communal bread oven which certainly by 1591 was on the west side of what is now Maryport Street, and a smithy, the earliest being out beyond the town ditch towards the river until the leper hospital was built. The finding of iron slag may suggest that its second site was in Church Street, west of the priory gatehouse.

Local government was run by the burgesses, initially the rent-paying occupiers of the houses and shops. With the passage of time the position

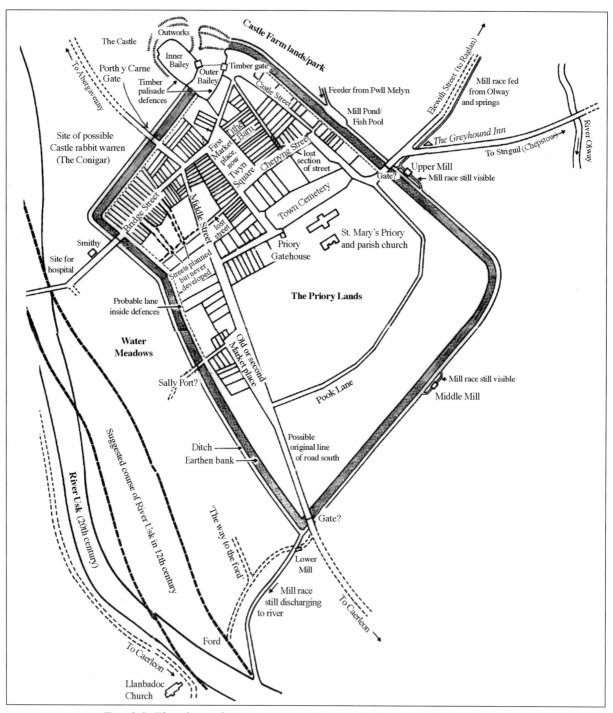

Fig. 8.2 The planned Norman town showing the layout of burgage plots

became more complex as properties were sold, leased out or inherited, as can be seen in later surveys.

The lord of Usk profited by charging a rent for just about every activity in the town, including entering the town to go to market. The market used the shelter provided by the street-level parts of the market hall, which stood where Mulberry House stands in Twyn Square. There was also a charge for using the town oven and mills, and the still unidentified 'kiln' in Sanctuary Street. The brewing of beer, which was much healthier to drink than the water from the town's many wells — these were usually sunk very close to the primitive latrine arrangements of each burgage — also provided the lord of Usk with a regular income, the 'prize [tax] of ales'. Presumably less was charged for brewing for home consumption than for brewing for sale. Interestingly, this imposition became a source of income for the Inland Revenue by Victorian times and an example of a license for home consumption brewing can be seen in the brewing section of Usk's Rural Life Museum.

The buying and selling, or sub-division, of the burgage plots was closely controlled and had to be enrolled 'at the gate of the castle', as was their passing, with the approval of the lord and on payment of a levy, to the next of kin on the death of the burgage holder.

The only thing provided free was the shelter of the castle in times of attack for those fleet enough to reach it in time. They would then be expected to assist in its defence, along with the major and minor tenants of the lord, who held their lands by military service, including 'castle guard'.

The changes in the layout of Usk from that of the planned town of the 1100s (Fig. 8.2) to that seen today were sporadic rather than gradual, accelerating in the early 1600s so that by 1642 and the outbreak of the Civil War the centre of the town would have been much as it is now. During the town's early centuries a number of events occurred which must have had a demoralising effect on the townspeople and on possible incomers, whilst others cost many of them their lives or wrecked their homes and businesses.

The earliest arose from the tension between the Norman lords of Usk and the Welsh lords of Caerleon (see chapter VI).[1] We have no idea of the degree of damage caused by the Welsh assault of the 1170s, for instance, any more than we do the number of houses originally planned for the town. However, I have suggested something like 100 for the latter.[2] We do however have some tentative figures for the size of the town in the next century.

An account of the income of the lordship for the period June 1262 to February 1263 suggests the figure of 130 full burgages or house plots. This number increased substantially in the following 20 years or so. By the time an Extent was prepared on the death in 1289 of the Lady of Usk, Matilda, widow of Richard IV de Clare, the number had increased by something like 280. But then disaster struck. By the winter of 1295 and the death of their son and heir Gilbert IV 'the Red' in Monmouth Castle, 180 houses in the town had been burnt and a further 104 were not paying rent because they were ruinous and their tenants impoverished as a result of the recent Welsh wars.[3]

The effects of the successive Welsh wars of independence, not all of which seem to have involved the town, were added to by major outbreaks of livestock disease, be it murrain or scab, the latter wiping out virtually the whole sheep population in Glamorgan in 1281.[4]

Then came the series of epidemics known collectively as the Black Death. This will have killed many of the population of urban south Wales, but fewer in the rural areas. The first outbreak, the 'Great Pestilence', reached Usk in the spring of 1349. Llantrisant, Trellech and Monmouth were also affected, whilst Caldicot and Abergavenny were hardest hit, the son of the Lord of Abergavenny being among the victims.[5] We have no details of the effects of this outbreak on the townspeople, but it is thought that on average 10% of the population perished. There is however some information from the accounts of Elizabeth de Burgh, who was resident with her household in Usk Castle in this period. One of the three sisters of Gilbert III de Clare, killed at Bannockburn in 1314, she came into her inheritance of Usk, Caerleon and Tregrug (later known as Llangybi) in July 1320 on the death of Gilbert's widow, Matilda, though her troubles with the Despensers and with Edward II meant that she did not come into full possession of Usk until October 1326. Thereafter she visited Usk frequently, often for considerable periods, until some ten years before her death in 1360.[6] The plague reached England in the summer of 1348, entering via Elizabeth's port of Weymouth. It spread to London and Bristol by the late summer. By that winter, the death rate in Gloucester as high. The risk of catching this disease does not seem to have deterred Elizabeth from following her normal social round, or entertaining guests, both friends and relations, at Usk, Llangybi, Tintern or Trellech.

Among the guests she entertained at Usk during the time of plague were, according to recent work by Frances Underhill, John Paschal, bishop of Llandaff, along with the abbot of Evesham, whose household had recently suffered many deaths. Only weeks later Usk saw her entertaining Lady Berkeley, of Berkeley Castle across the Severn, Lady Elizabeth Bloet, wife of John Bloet of the well established Raglan family, and Lady Margaret Monthermer, her sister-in law. At Tregrug/Llangybi Elizabeth entertained the Ladies Berkeley and Zouche, perhaps the wife of William la Zouche, lord of Glamorgan in 1329,[7] a name still remembered in the Midlands town of Ashby de la Zouch. Also present were two still acceptable members of the Despenser family, Hugh III and Gilbert.

Whilst Elizabeth was fortunate in escaping the plague, many of her guests in that dreadful year of 1348 were less so. Three of them were dead by the next spring. One was her friend Elizabeth Bloet, another her sister-in law, Lady Monthermer. The third was Elizabeth's nephew Hugh Despenser III. She also lost her own daughter Isabella Ferrers who, we are told by Frances Underhill, died that year in East Anglia, where mortality was particularly high.[8]

Another major event which seriously affected the growth of the town was the destructive attack by Owain Glyndŵr's supporters in 1402.

According to Adam Usk, then in Rome, Owain took the castles of Usk, Caerleon and Newport, and fired the towns. Doubts have been raised as to the accuracy of this report in Adam's *Chronicon* because of his absence from the scene, and a record of emergency defence works at Newport Castle at this very time make it clear that Owain's forces never got there. However, the doubters have overlooked the fact that Adam was back in the country soon afterwards and could have seen the state of the town for himself and talked with survivors, adding details learnt in this way to his narrative.[9]

The renewed attack of March 1405 ended in the Welsh defeat of the Battle of Pwll Melin. This 'Yellow Pool' can still be seen about a third of a mile up the lane north of the castle, and not where I placed it when giving details of the battle in my *Norman Usk*.[10] The 'abandoned railway reservoir' I mentioned is now the ornamental pool in the modern Castle Oak development and was the site of the burial of a number of the casualties, Welsh and perhaps English, whose bones were excavated by the solicitor Isca Bowen and his friend, the historian J.E. Lloyd, in 1933.[11] Details of this battle are given in the following chapter.

While no doubt causing renewed panic in the town, the attack of 1405 seems to have caused no damage or casualties, save perhaps among those locals who 'came out' for Glyndŵr, several of whom were later pardoned. Recent 'watching briefs' on planning developments in Church Street and Priory Street have shown evidence of intensive burning in the former and the rebuilding of an original street-front house at 14 Priory Street. Both could be evidence of damage inflicted on the town in the early 1400s which could also have been the cause of the demolition of several houses on the east side of Priory Street, and opposite number 14. These had all stood in what is now the garden and drive south of one of the parts of Ty Brith, 'The Speckled House', which for some reason, least of all a sense of history, has been re-named 'Priory House'.

As I have suggested in my *Norman Usk*, the town ditch was too long to be defensible and was probably designed to impress, or overawe, the Welsh of the surrounding countryside as well as acting as a defining limit to the administrative area of the town. It was probably the first element of the Norman town to disappear. By 4 April 1460 it had been so completely forgotten along part of its length that in a lease of land east of the priory that straddled the ditch where it ran between 'the street called Pokelane' and the Olway, the ditch was not even mentioned (Fig. 8.3).[12] In the centre of the town, on one side or another of Bridge Street, the ditch had become by 1569 a lane or *venella* known as *Clawdd du,* the Black Ditch, described as the boundary between two burgages. This is probably the lane to the car park alongside the present Spar stores.

The lease of 1460 shows that housing had now developed along Pook, or Puck, Lane, now reduced to a footpath around the south of the priory. The lane's name is derived from the Welsh *pwca*, a hobgoblin, and associated with spooks or ghosts. Roman ghosts perhaps, for it stood within the confines of the Roman legionary fortress of *Burrium*. The feeling that people had been there long ago may have arisen from finding pottery, and perhaps coins, when digging gardens in the 15th century. Eventually abandoned, perhaps

because of the cyclic economic depressions of the 17th and 18th centuries, and the still regular winter flooding of the Olway, there were probably 18 houses along the lane just prior to the 1569 Burgess Roll, which lists 16 houses. Later Rolls give 15 in 1630, 14 in 1670 whilst by 1800 and Coxe's map of Usk, they had all gone.[13]

The same early roll shows that by then the town had spread beyond its former limits and houses had been built along the present Chepstow Road beyond the town gate, which must have stood where the road crossed the line of the town ditch. These houses seemingly went as far as the Olway, the parish boundary, at which point the property description of the roll would cease. Study of the 1630 and 1670 rolls printed by Bradney[14] is difficult since one cannot usually tell which way, and on which side of the road, particular burgage plots lay. In what are now Black Barn Lane (formerly Elewith Street, see Fig. 8.2), Four Ash Street (formerly Chepyng Street, see Fig. 8.2, and extending to Upper Mill) and Chepstow Road it is particularly difficult, since street names have changed and two bridges are mentioned — the Olway Bridge and Pont y Clifion (*Cleifion*), 'the bridge of the sick people'. Bradney suggests that this refers to the supposedly curative well in the

Fig. 8.3 The land leased in 1460, shown flooded in 1987 when part of the then Usk Dairy Farm

fields south-east of and behind the Olway Inn. Bradney also mentions Croes Lloyd,[15] a corruption of Croes Lwyd — 'the holy crossing' — at the junction where now stands the Greyhound Inn. This crossing may have gained its now forgotten name as the possible site of the lost chapel of St Mary Magdalen lay in the field across the Chepstow Road from the inn (Fig. 8.4). Alternatively the name could be derived from the curative well known locally as the 'Holy Well' and so marked on the old 6 inch Ordnance Survey map of Usk.

The two later rolls again show a marked decrease in the numbers of houses, or house plots, in both Black Barn Lane and the Chepstow Road. In 1630 there were 20 burgage plots in Black Barn Lane, by 1670 reduced to 4, whilst in the Chepstow Road the number had fallen from 16 to 6, an even more marked decrease than in Pook Lane.

Strangely, the opposite can be seen in Baron Street, known by the Welsh as 'the way to the ford', the ford across the river Usk to Llanbadoc church. There, the number of burgages increased from 25 in 1569 to 28½ in 1670, one former property owner being one of Usk's few known Royalist army officers, Captain Sandiford, whose holding was almost certainly that now belonging to Mr and Mrs Dick Lewis, whose garden centre and house must lie partly over many of the early building sites.

A change in layout which appears in many medieval planned towns results from what may be termed 'trespass building'. This is the gradual encroachment onto the highway in front of the original building line, of which there are four examples in Usk. The first, on the west side of Twyn Square, is the block that now ends with the HSBC Bank, an encroachment that clearly took place at an early date. Opposite the bank the encroachment on the site of what was the nonconformist chapel took place fairly recently, with dire results for the stability of the front part of the building, since made good. The third example, again probably very early, is the projecting southern portion of the eastern half of Four Ash Street (Fig. 8.5). The fourth is the block of build-

Fig. 8.4 The Greyhound Inn at Croes Lwyd, with the possible site of the Chapel of St Mary Magdalen in the field beyond

Fig. 8.5 Four Ash Street cottages and the trespass building adjoining Black Friars

ings which virtually block off the northern end of New Market Street, reducing its width by more than half.

This forward encroachment is usually due to the property concerned first having been used as a shop. The shopkeeper would have exhibited his goods on benches or on the pavement in front of his shop, as still sometimes takes place in Twyn Square and Bridge Street, and to protect his goods he would erect a temporary canvas or other light

Fig. 8.6 The massive Ty Brith in Twyn Square with beyond it the late 16th or very early 17th century The Laurels blocking a lost street heading towards the river

roofing which, when it became worn and tattered, he would replace with a timber roof supported on posts. Wind and wet weather then required sides to be erected and, when no one objected, the whole forward display area became permanent. No doubt the occupier would then begin to repeat the process if space allowed. The extent of this accretion or trespass building in the case of the west side of Twyn Square is astonishing and can be seen from an examination of a modern Ordnance Survey map of the town. From this it is clear that the rear boundary line of the HSBC property is an extension of the building line of the front of the properties in Priory Street, the swing forward commencing with 8 Priory Street, which marks one side of one of the town's lost streets.

Of these there are certainly four. The first, leading westwards out of Twyn Square is the longest and would have been a continuation of the present western portion of Four Ash Street, once known as Old Chepyng Street,[16] meaning 'Old Market Street' (not to be confused with the current Old Market Street), thus identifying it as one of the first sites of the very moveable market of Usk. One could have walked towards the river along the front of shops, now the site of Ty Brith, out across the north end of Maryport Street between the Museum and the house known as The Old Maltsters (Figs. 8.6 and 8.7)

Fig. 8.7 The western end of the lost street from Twyn Square to New Market Street

A second lost street, of which the central half still exists as the rear entrance to the Castle Inn from Castle Parade, would have continued southwards. Up until a few years ago it was still to be seen as the entrance to the last of Usk's slaughterhouses from Four Ash Street, but is now the garage entrance of the new no. 3 Four Ash Street (Fig. 8.8). This lost street divided into two equal blocks the group of properties between the east side of Twyn Square and Castle Street. Presumably its northern end led up to the castle.

A third lost street is the extension of Castle Street to the front of the castle gatehouse. This can still be walked, with the permission of the Humphreys family, as a garden path via the gate on the north side of Castle Parade across from Ty Basket, one of the town's two remaining toll houses.

A fourth lost street joined the one described at the castle gatehouse and led down to Twyn Square via what is now the gate between Castle Cottage and Mulberry House, the site of the original market hall (see chapter XII). This street has been divided lengthwise, the other half being the drive to Castle Parade House. There may have

been a fifth lost street leading south out of Bridge Street into what is now the car park from the point where Bridge Street develops a slight kink on its way to the river bridge.

Also lost is the former north-eastern length of Black Barn Lane. This was part of the Elewith Street (see Fig. 8.2) which led via Factory Lane towards the lost village of Elewith, which I suggest lay downslope from Pentwyn Farm towards Llanolway Farm and close to the southern boundary of Cefntilla. According to Professor William Rees, Elewith was a demesne manor of Usk and the vill was probably the home of some of the Welsh workers of the lord of Usk or their successors as his tenants, as happened at nearby Raglan.[17] It presumably got its name from the old name for the Olway Brook — the Eleui. Usk's leper hospital seems to have owned property in the town end of Elewith Street.

One of the minor changes in the layout of the town has been the infilling or covering and turning into tunnels by trespass or agreement of the back access lanes between individual burgages. These access lanes are a regular feature of medieval towns. Some remain in Bridge Street and a group can be seen in Priory Street. Another, between the present flower shop and the Castle Inn, was obliterated by a sideways expansion of the inn, the evidence for its former existence remaining in the blocked stair window in the southern wall of the flower shop. Another lane between two of the adjoining cottages to the north now comprises a shared rear garden exit. Something akin to the blocked stair window can also be seen in the museum, blocked in this instance by the later erection of the house to the south in New Market Street (see chapter XII).

Usk's major post-medieval development was its spread towards the river. Excavation and documentary research suggest that Old Market Street developed piecemeal in the late 16th and early 17th centuries, and followed the growth of properties in 1591 and 1602 in Maryport Street. The nearby Mill Street, formerly known as Walker Street after the occupation of some of its residents at the fulling mill at its southern end (a fuller walking backwards and forwards along a long bath or trough to tread the cloth), had developed by 1630 to contain 27 burgage plots.

New Market Street, or at least the western side of its northern end, had been the site of houses since at least 1469,[18] whilst it is suggested in chapter XII that further down the street at least one major house, now the Rural Life Museum, had existed before 1402 and was badly damaged that year by Glyndŵr's supporters. When the two houses that virtually closed the end of New Market Street were erected is unknown, but it was clearly after the building, or possible post-Glyndŵr rebuilding, of the property now divided between The Nook and The Maltsters.

Allied to this dating problem is the date of the extension of Bridge Street beyond the medieval town ditch, which underlies part of the present Spar shop and, across the road, under the western half of H and R's store. There is no evidence that any of the properties on the south side of the road pre-dated 1402 because no archaeological examination has yet been possible, but it nevertheless seems likely that development would have taken place before the Glyndŵr era towards the bridge and opposite the hospital — unless the proximity of the lepers inhibited development. All that can be said is that in 1826 there was at least one house on the site of what is still known as 'Bunnings' and that it was occupied by Evan Jones, one of the proprietors of the Usk japanware factory around the corner in New Market Street. At least two of the small properties east of 'Bunnings', the present Alcove Antiques and the Café en Fleur, seem to be buildings of some age, but perhaps no earlier than the 18th century, when they would have been opposite Usk's House of Correction. The front wall of the antique shop is of late brickwork, but the rear may suggest an early date.

On the other side of the road, again beyond the town ditch, is the fine Cross Keys Inn, which shows several classic features of a Monmouthshire building of the end of the 1500s or early 1600s, whilst beyond the inn there is no evidence of any early building until one reaches the hospital by the bridge. Recent excavations have clarified something of the history of this area (see chapter IV).

Fig. 8.8 The lost street up to the castle from Twyn Square

The greatest changes in the appearance of the town were made first by the cutting through of the direct road towards Chepstow and Monmouth under the powers of the county Turnpike Acts, and second, the building of Usk prison a few years earlier. The major road building took place immediately before the publication of the Tithe Map of 1846 and involved the demolition of the tithe barn, presumably originally the property of the priory, together with one or two other properties, to form the present Castle Parade. This meant cutting off from the castle both Castle Street and the street left forming the back entrance to the Castle Inn. It saw the building of Ty Basket as one of the town's turnpike cottages and cut off the end of Elewith Street, as did the railway some years later and even later the building of the first Junior School and its grounds.

The building of the new prison contributed to these changes, involving a realignment of Maryport Street[19] and an increase in the population by way of prison officers and the houses for them in Mill Street, Baron Street and Maryport Street. Changes in the legal system led to the construction of the new Courthouse and brought to town the attendant lawyers, witnesses and litigants, all of whom needed to be fed and sometimes accommodated, along with those attending Usk's markets. This encouraged the growing number of inns.

These two major events saw the passing of Twyn Square as the centre of commerce in the town and its replacement by Bridge Street. These were the precursors of the housing developments of the 20th century.

CHAPTER IX

Adam Usk and Owain Glyndŵr
by Chris Given-Wilson

Adam Usk, renowned for his Chronicle recording events in which he was to an extent caught up, is one of Usk's best known sons and was a contemporary of Owain Glyndŵr, the Welsh patriot who, for a brief time, created an all but independent Wales. This chapter considers the life of Adam and what it tells us of Usk, the Glyndŵr Rising and its effects on Usk and what Adam thought of Glyndŵr.

Adam Usk was born around the middle of the 14th century — according to local tradition, in a room of Usk Castle gatehouse.[1] As a boy, he witnessed the abortion of a two-headed calf in the house of Llugu, the daughter of Watkyn, in Llancayo, two miles north of Usk.[2] Nothing else is known of his youth.

A little more is known, or may be inferred, about his kindred. His claim to blood-relationship with several of the 'virgins of noble stock' to whom membership of Usk Priory was restricted implies that he regarded himself as, in some sense, noble-born.[3] In his will of January 1430 he bequeathed 40s each to a sister, Joan, and an unnamed brother, and a copy of Ranulf Higden's *Polychronicon* to his kinsman (*consanguineo meo*) Edward ap Adam.[4] At the height of his influence, in the months following the Lancastrian revolution of 1399, he secured livings near Usk for two further kinsmen, Thomas ap Adam ap William de Weloc, and Matthew ap Hoel.[5] His affecting account of the last hours of John of Usk, abbot of Chertsey, who was born and baptised in

Usk, is also suggestive of kinship — although it would probably be rash to make too much of the fact that, with almost his dying breath, the abbot bestowed upon Adam 'that same blessing which the Blessed Virgin bestowed upon her son the Lord Jesus, and which Isaac bestowed upon his son Jacob'.[6]

The *Polychronicon* which he bequeathed to Edward ap Adam was his personal copy, and included his continuation of Higden from 1377 to 1421. It is from his chronicle, in parts autobiographical, that we learn much of what we know about Usk's life. Fortunately — for he does not always tell us the whole truth about himself — he enjoyed sufficient prominence (not to say notoriety) to ensure that he also features steadily in the public records of the time.

From 1368, as a consequence of the marriage in that year of Edmund Mortimer, earl of March, to Philippa, daughter and sole heiress of Lionel duke of Clarence, until 1425, when his grandson, another Edmund, died childless, the lordship of Usk was held by three successive earls of March of the Mortimer family. It was from the Mortimers therefore that Adam initially sought patronage, nor was he disappointed, for Earl Edmund (d.1381) it was who sent him up to Oxford, presumably around 1370, to study civil and canon law, also providing for him while he was there.[7] No record of his studies at Oxford survives from the 1370s, but by 1381 he had made sufficient progress to be created a notary public (though ineffectually, apparently) by the papal legate Pileus de Prata, archbishop of Ravenna.[8] Two years later, in September 1383, he was instituted to the rectory of Mitchel Troy (Monmouthshire), then in the king's gift because of the minority of Roger, heir to the earldom of March, and in April 1384 he was ordained subdeacon by John Gilbert, bishop of Hereford, at Sugwas.[9] He exchanged benefices regularly over the next decade, indeed did so on many occasions throughout his life. Meanwhile he read and taught law. He described himself in December 1387 as an 'extraordinary in canon law living in Oxford',[10] and probably remained at Oxford for a further seven or eight years.

He was still described as a bachelor (and subdeacon) in November 1388, and the first surviving reference to him as a doctor of laws is from 1393.[11] He tells us that he subsequently held a chair of civil law (*cathedram ciuilem*), which, when he left Oxford, he resigned to Henry Chichele, and that after this he worked for seven years as an advocate in the Court of Arches for the archbishop of Canterbury.[12] It is unlikely that he entered the archbishop's service before April 1394. He was still described as an advocate of the archbishop's court in February 1400,[13] and there is no good reason to think that he ceased to act in that capacity before his departure for Rome in February 1402. This would mean that he acted as an advocate for three archbishops of Canterbury — William Courtenay, Thomas Arundel, and the intruder Roger Walden (who served whilst Arundel was exiled at the end of Richard II's reign).

Adam's employment in the Court of Arches was soon to bring him into contact with the man who would act as his principal patron for much of the next 20 years, Thomas Arundel, archbishop of Canterbury 1396-7 and 1399-1414. Since the death of Edmund Mortimer in December 1381, Adam had lacked a powerful adult patron, for Edmund's heir, Roger, was only seven at his father's death (he was born, at Usk, in April 1374), and did not receive livery of his inheritance until February 1394.[14] That Adam regarded the new earl of March as his patron, and maintained his connections with the Mortimer family, there can be no doubt. He speaks in fulsome terms of Roger as 'a young man of the highest character', and lamented his early death in July 1398.[15] His continued service to the earl is indicated by the fact that in August 1397 he and Thomas Overton, confidential clerk and executor of the young earl, received 500 marks each for the earl from the royal exchequer.[16] His association with the Mortimers also generated ties with other patrons: Philippa, the daughter of Adam's first benefactor Earl Edmund, and herself one of his patrons,[17] married (as her second husband, in August 1390) Richard earl of Arundel, brother of Thomas Arundel; while Eleanor, the widow of Earl Roger, married Edward Charlton of Powis in June 1399, just at the time when Charlton — later to prove a powerful supporter — began to patronise Adam.[18]

Adam's appointment to the Court of Arches precipitated his entry into the service of the Crown as a civil lawyer, initially as royal commissioner to hear appeals from the courts of admiralty and chivalry.[19] After Richard II's 'Revenge Parliament' in 1397, which saw Archbishop Arundel exiled, events at which Adam was appalled, he seems to have remained in office under Roger Walden. However, when he heard of Henry Bolingbroke's landing in 1399, he hastened to join him and Arundel at Bristol and accompanied their march to Chester. Having gained the confidence of the new regime, the next two and a half years saw him at the height of his influence. His counsel was sought by many.

The outbreak of the Glyndŵr Rising saw suspicion fall on Welshmen generally and the passing of racist legislation by parliament. This, and his desire for clerical preferment to a bishopric, led Adam to Rome in February 1402. Arriving in Rome on 5 April he had soon been appointed a papal chaplain and auditor of causes in the apostolic palace, and remained in the Curia until 1406.

This is not the place to explore the grievances that led to the outbreak of the Glyndŵr rising. Suffice to say that they were many and genuine and eventually led to rebellion. The spark was a dispute between Owain and Lord Grey of Ruthin in September 1400. Ruthin was sacked along with other towns in north Wales and Shropshire before the rebels were defeated by Hugh Burnell. But the rebellion continued. Henry IV led a chevauchée through north Wales and then attempted negotiation. On 1 April 1401 Conwy Castle was captured and only regained by Hotspur towards the end of June. Skirmishing continued with 'victories' for either side, until Owain won the battle of Hyddgen in the summer. This gave the rebellion the impetus it needed, with raids then taking place ever further south.

For the first two years of the war Owain Glyndŵr and his men experienced varying fortunes, but on 22 June 1402 they defeated an English army at the battle of Bryn Glas or Pilleth in Radnorshire, in the process capturing Edmund Mortimer, the then head of the Mortimer family until his nephew came of age, and several knights and esquires. Victory was to crown Owain's endeavours for another two years; the English under Henry IV's uncertain leadership failed to regain the initiative. Mortimer's subsequent defection to Glyndŵr left the central Marches, formerly under Mortimer control, wide open to Welsh raids. Owain became Prince of Wales, ruling with his own council and parliament; he made alliances with Scotland, France and the pope. His triumph at Pilleth does much to explain why the war dragged on for eight more years.

In the August following Pilleth, 'Owen', writes Gruffydd Hiraethog, 'came to Glamorgan and all Glamorgan rose with him; Cardiff and Abergavenny were burnt.'[20] The possibility has been mooted that this daring stroke was conceived by Owain Glyndŵr and his captains as their principal operation for that summer, and that it was postponed because of the unexpected outcome of the invasion of Radnorshire. Whatever the truth may be, Owain enforced the moral impact of his stunning victory over Edmund Mortimer, and kept the momentum going with this new offensive.

The English chronicles are strangely silent on these events, but Adam Usk, writing in Rome, comes to our aid with a highly emotional and rather garbled report:

My heart trembles when I think of this dire blow against English rule inflicted by Owen; backed by a force of thirty thousand men who would issue from their caves, he seized castles everywhere throughout Wales and the march — including Usk, Caerleon and Newport — and burned the towns. What more can I say? Like another Assyrian, the rod of God's anger, he vented his fury with fire and sword in unprecedented tyrannies.[21]

Adam's hatred of his famous contemporary helps to explain why, for the next three centuries, Owain was to be so unfavourably regarded by his own countrymen. In this war some of the Welsh themselves suffered as much from his men as from the English. Gwent does not seem to have shown any of the sympathy for Owain's cause evident in Glamorgan. Adam makes no mention of Cardiff or Abergavenny, probably because he was so distressed by the ruin brought to his homeland of Usk and Caerleon, both belonging to Mortimer. Newport was a lordship of the Earl of Stafford, and the damage done there was so great that in 1403 no revenue could be collected.

On 7 August commissions were sent to 18 sheriffs to array troops at Chester, Shrewsbury and Hereford, commanded by Prince Henry, the king and the Earls of Stafford and Warwick respectively, for a triple assault on Wales. The chancellor of the county palatine of Lancaster was ordered to send his men to Chester to join those from Derby and Shropshire. The shires of Hereford, Worcester and Gloucester sent men to the Earl of Stafford, who was lieutenant for the Marches from Wigmore to Chepstow and south Wales; his deputy was Richard, Lord Grey of Codnor. The lieutenant for the Marches from Wigmore to Holt was the Earl of Arundel. The offensive began at the end of August — and failed. Wales threw her very worst weather at the invader: rain, hail, even snow. King Henry himself had a narrow escape when a torrential downpour overthrew his tent when he was encamped in a meadow. A lance or perhaps the heavy central pole fell across him; he survived only because he was sleeping uncomfortably in full armour. He was lucky not to have been struck by lightning.[22]

Parliament's contribution to the Welsh problem was wholly negative, and can have done nothing to conciliate the Welsh. It presented a series of petitions to the king, asking for punitive measures which Henry was very willing to grant; 'le roi le voet' gave them the force of law. Unless they were of approved fidelity, Welshmen were severely restricted in their freedom in their own country: they were forbidden to try Englishmen, to carry arms in public, and to hold defensible houses or responsible offices. Arms and supplies might only be brought into towns or castles if they were English-held.

During the winter of 1403 Owain besieged castles which were still in English hands, including Harlech and Aberystwyth. In March the king appointed Prince Henry, then 15 years old, royal lieutenant in Wales and the Marches, with powers to order the sheriffs of the border counties to supply troops. Despite his youth, Henry was fast acquiring the grasp of detail and flair for administration with which he was to win the Welsh war, and which were finally to place him far above any other commander of his time. In May, as Owain gathered fresh forces and prepared to resume operations, Prince Henry moved to Shrewsbury.

Owain was planning to overrun south-west Wales and insurrection soon spread to the area. During June the people of Builth and Brecon rebelled, but this was quickly put down by John Bodenham, sheriff of Herefordshire. After his victory Bodenham withdrew to Hereford, apparently unaware of the menacing developments in Carmarthenshire, where Dinefwr Castle near Llandeilo and Llandovery Castle were besieged. Then came news of the arrival in the area of Owain Glyndŵr in person with his retinue. Both castle garrisons requested aid, but the king's attention was focused on events in the north of his kingdom.

Carmarthen fell to Glyndŵr on 6 July; Newcastle Emlyn, guarding the middle Teifi valley in Cardiganshire, had already been given up by Jenkin ap Llywelyn. Although the king was preoccupied with his intended expedition against the Scots, on 10 July he belatedly ordered £1,000 to be paid to his son. Some good news came when Lord Carew's forces met and killed the greater part of a detachment of 700 of Owain's men.

But the king's and Prince Henry's eyes were focussed on new events in the north. Hotspur, son of the earl of Northumberland, felt a number of grudges as regards his treatment by Henry IV. The refusal of the Percies now to obey the king illustrated only too clearly a political problem confronting any usurper: it was hard for Henry IV to command the respect and obedience of a powerful family whose support had helped him to the throne and who thought that they had been ungenerously treated.

Hotspur rose in revolt and the outcome was the best known event of the reign: Henry's hard-won victory at Shrewsbury. Hotspur's army was made up not of the northern Percy affinity, but of men from Cheshire and north Wales, loyal to the memory of Richard II, who had raised his retinue there. Hotspur and his uncle Thomas, Earl of Worcester, advanced on Shrewsbury. If they hoped to find Owain Glyndŵr there, they must have been badly out of touch with recent events in south Wales, where Owain and his army were too deeply committed to come to their aid. Faced by this dire threat to his throne, Henry acted vigorously and decisively. After a forced march he reached Shrewsbury before Hotspur, and defeated and killed him on 21 July 1403. The casualties on both sides were heavy. Worcester and other leaders of the rebellion were executed after the battle.

During the battle Prince Henry sustained a nasty wound in the face from an arrow, and needed surgery. Two days later the Earl of Arundel, Lord Berkeley, Edward Charlton, Hugh Burnell and Lord Audley were appointed 'to govern the marches of England towards Wales and resist the invasions of Owin de Gleyndourdy' in the prince's absence.[23]

Henry's victory at Shrewsbury did nothing to ease the situation in Wales, which became even worse. The Welsh were by then in the vicinity of the Black Mountains; soon they were in Herefordshire. In response King Henry moved to Worcester, from where, on 8 September, he issued orders for the re-equipping, repairing and restocking of 22 castles in the southern Marches. He then undertook another chevauchée into Wales, and at least succeeded in regaining Carmarthen, but little else.[24]

When Parliament met in January 1404, the king handed 'the custody of our country of Wales to our very dearly beloved son the Prince as our lieutenant in those parts'. Presumably he was now fully recovered from his wound. This may seem a very heavy burden to place upon so young a man, but the signs are that Henry was eager for responsibility; in the last four years he had already gained much experience. Decisive action was more desperately required than ever, for Shropshire and Herefordshire in particular were falling prey to marauding bands of Welshmen.

The situation in Herefordshire was indeed serious. 'The Welsh rebels in great numbers have entered Archenfield, which is part of the county of Hereford, where they have burned houses,

Fig. 9.1 Owain Glyndŵr as depicted on his own seal

killed people, taken prisoners and ravaged the land with great dishonour to the king', the sheriff and his colleagues reported to the king's council on 10 June.

Towards the end of June Prince Henry was in Worcester, from where, on the 26th, he described the situation in sombre terms. Rebels from south Wales, victualled for 15 days, were burning and destroying in Herefordshire. The prince had ordered enough men from the four border counties to help Richard of York, brother of Edward, duke of York, who had responsibility for protecting the borders of south Wales. He warmly commended the Earl of Warwick to the royal favour for the fine body of troops which he had provided at his own expense. Perhaps it was now that the nunnery of Aconbury, about six miles south of Hereford, suffered grievous damage from the Welsh. Another payment, of five marks, was ordered to assist Llanthony Priory which had also suffered badly.[25]

Further disasters followed. The fall of Aberystwyth and Harlech castles gave the signal for the overrunning of south Wales, not just a great raid like that of August 1402. The principal event was the capture of Cardiff, which is mentioned only in the *Eulogium*. It sounds as if the damage was probably very much worse this time:

> Owain took the town and burned it, except for the street in which the Friars Minor lived, which for his love of the friars, together with their convent, he allowed to stand. In addition he took the castle and destroyed it, and took away many valuables which had been deposited there. When the Friars Minor asked him for their books and silver which they had deposited in the castle he replied: 'Why did you put your goods in the castle? If you had left them at home, they would have been safe.'

The incident gives a rare glimpse of Owain's character and humour.[26]

By midsummer 1404 Owain's writ ran throughout most of Wales. The English still held eight castles round the edge of north Wales: Welshpool, Oswestry, Flint, Rhuddlan, Denbigh, Conwy, Beaumaris and Caernarfon, but the country outside them was controlled by Owain's troops. Owain's power was at its zenith. In August there was an air of despondency in a review of the situation by the council. The Cheshire revenues of the Prince of Wales were not enough to maintain the Mortimer castle of Denbigh, as well as the prince's own castles in north Wales, and the king was asked for a grant of £1,000. He would have been even less pleased at having to approve a truce between the people of Shropshire and 'the land of Wales', because the lord of Powys was in a similar position. Nothing could illustrate the ascendancy of Owain Glyndŵr at this time more conclusively than this humiliation of the King of England and his council: they were unable to rule Wales, and were forced in effect to recognise her independence.[27]

We have to rely on Adam Usk for one of the most important events in Owain's career:

> Owen, in his wretchedness, held — or rather aped, or mimiced — parliaments at Machynlleth, and in the mountains, where he would usurp rights of combat and other royal privileges, although it did him no good.[28]

Machynlleth was well placed in the centre of Wales and in the area which Owain controlled; it was also near one of his newly-won castles, Aberystwyth, and within reach of the other, Harlech, which he had made his capital. With his experience, Owain based his state on the English pattern, with his own chancery and seals.

Meanwhile, in Rome, Adam soon gained contempt for the venality of the Curia, and the brutality and profanity of the Romans, but found himself regarded as untrustworthy by the English in Rome because of his Welshness. Letters indeed show that Adam was under suspicion of collusion with the Welsh rebels. Thus, when he attempted to gain papal provision to the see of Hereford in the summer of 1404, it caused a real rift with the king: 'The English', he claims, '... wrote letters to the king and poisoned his mind against me, so that, far from being promoted, I was humiliated, and spent the next four years undergoing dreadful hardships, condemned to suffer like an exile by land and sea, stripped of all my benefices and goods, reduced to the depths of poverty, and forced like Joseph to live amongst strangers whose language I did not know.'[29] Hyperbole aside, there is some rhetorical licence here; in fact several years were to pass before Usk was stripped of his benefices. His epistolary plea to the king, dated 12 September 1404, not to 'lend your ears to those who speak ill of me' (which was coupled with a request for 'some further promotion') apparently brought no comfort, while his next attempt to gain a see, that of St David's in October-November 1404, drew forth unrelieved fury from Henry, seemingly including even the threat of the gallows.[30] Was his failure really due to the 'slanders of my enemies' about his political sympathies, or might it be that, contrary to his own self-estimation, he was simply not regarded as a serious candidate for a bishopric? The reasons for professional disappointment are subject to all kinds of self-delusion, and his Welshness certainly provided him with a convenient excuse. More ominously, however, it also provided him — or at least soon would — with an alternative route to a see.

By early 1406 he had probably heard of a meeting which had taken place in Paris a few months earlier between the French king and the envoys of Owain, the result of which was the declaration, on 31 March, at Pennal near Machynlleth in north Wales, of the obedience of the Welsh church to the Avignon papacy.[31] Whether it might ever be implemented was, of course, a quite different matter, depending as it did upon Glyndŵr's ability to achieve Welsh independence from England, but it should be emphasised — for it was without doubt crucial to Adam's thinking — that in the summer of 1406 the latter must have seemed far from unattainable. Here, then, was Adam's alternative route to the episcopacy. On 11 June 1406 he left Rome and crossed the Alps to France.

For two years he 'wandered through the lands of Flanders, France, Normandy and Brittany, making enough to live on from the payments which various bishops, abbots and noblemen gave me for my counsel'. In so doing he would have acknowledged the Avignon allegiance. In these wanderings he met the earl of Northumberland and Lord Bardolf, who were seeking French help against Henry IV after the failure of their own revolt in 1405. He refused their offer of promotion to high office if he accompanied them back to England — and when he heard of their death at Bramham Moor in February 1408, he 'gave thanks to God, the great seer, for having stayed behind'.[32]

Instead he sought the help of the 'lord of Powis' (Edward Charlton), in seeking 'a pardon from the king and the kingdom'. Sometime in the summer of 1408 he met Richard del Brugge, Lancaster king at arms (one of the four main heralds of the crown), in Paris, who explained to him that, 'partly because of my contact with the earl of Northumberland, and partly because of smears written by my enemies at Rome and sent to the king', no pardon would be forthcoming for the moment. He therefore 'swore an oath to this king at arms that I would pretend to be one of Owen's supporters, and that I would take my men and make my way to Wales to join him, but that once there I would, when an opportunity presented itself, secretly slip away from him and go and stay with my lord of Powis, hoping thereby to gain the king's pardon. And that is what happened; and it was this promise which saved my life.' This is indeed what happened. Despite various alarms on the way, Usk succeeded in landing at Barmouth and joining up with Glyndŵr's supporters. However, when they discovered that he had written for a safe-conduct to Edward Charlton, lord of Powis, he was 'placed under close restraint by pledges'. Nevertheless he managed to obtain his safe-conduct from Charlton, whereupon he 'secretly slipped away by night' to join him at Welshpool. Here Usk spent the next two years or so, 'a poor chaplain in the parish church, not daring to venture beyond (Charlton's) lands, receiving no food except what I could earn for saying masses, and shunned by my ungrateful kinsmen and former friends'. In the end, however, relief was forthcoming: at the request of Charlton, Henry IV finally relented and, on 20 March 1411, granted

Usk a full pardon. He returned to south Wales, and thence, 'with a trembling heart but a cheerful demeanour', to England, where, 'like another Job, I began once more to acquire servants, and books, and clothes, and a home; for which God be praised for ever and ever'.[33]

From his tale of woe, Adam omits one crucial fact. According to an enquiry of April 1408 into his tenure of the rectory of Castle Combe, which he still held in 1407, when Adam left Rome in June 1406 he had 'joined the antipope (Benedict XIII), who within half a year had conferred the bishopric of Llandaff on him. For this he had been excommunicated by the pope and deprived of all his benefices since (8 September 1407)'.[34] This is confirmed by Pope Benedict's register, which states that permission for Usk's installation to Llandaff was issued by Griffith Young (Glyndŵr's choice — and Benedict's appointment — as bishop of Bangor); the date given there is 26 April 1407.[35]

It would seem that Henry IV's fury with Usk in 1407 was initially due to his contact with Northumberland and Bardolf, and it was not until some months later that the king learned of his provision to Llandaff. This may help to explain Henry's apparent change of heart. Having at first (in the winter of 1406-7) been told that he would not be pardoned, Adam was later (in the spring or summer of 1408) told that he might be, but only under certain conditions. Yet why should the English king have been prepared to allow Adam to join the Welsh rebels? There is, surely, only one likely answer: he was going to betray, or at least to spy on, Glyndŵr. As Henry must have realized by now, Adam was in an ideal position to do this; so far as the rebels knew, he had thrown in his lot with them, and suffered mightily for it. Why should they mistrust him? Only once they realized that he was in communication with Charlton did they begin to suspect and attempt to restrain him. Adam's plan, presumably, was to barter what knowledge he could acquire of Glyndŵr's operations in return for his own freedom to resume his life in England. In the winter of 1406-7, embittered by English hostility and frustrated ambition, when he may well have truly believed that Glyndŵr would shortly be prince of an independent Wales, he evidently reckoned that support for the Welsh cause was his likeliest route to advancement. By the summer of 1408, however, the tide had turned: Glyndŵr had been pushed on to the defensive, his ally Northumberland was dead, and the Franco-Welsh alliance had been rendered virtually impotent. Realizing the magnitude of his error, Usk set about repairing the damage. It says much for his instinct for self-preservation that if the only way in which that could be achieved was through the betrayal of his own countrymen — to whose cause he had so recently adhered, and with whom, at heart, he surely sympathised — he nevertheless did not demur.

So how had Owain's fortunes been turned on their head between the winter of 1406/7 and the summer of 1408? Events had, in fact, started to go against him even earlier. The signs are that Prince Henry, after his reappointment to overall command in January 1404, was determined to take the offensive and wrest the initiative from Owain. This could explain a serious Welsh defeat which occurred at about this time, and of which the only evidence we have is provided by Gruffydd Hiraethog:

> In the same year was the slaughter of the Welsh on Campstone Hill [Camstwn], and another of the English at Craig y Dorth, between Penclawdd and Monmouth town. Here the more part of the English were slain and they were chased up to the town gate.

Campston Hill is near the Lancastrian castle of Grosmont, whilst Craig y Dorth lies in the Trothy valley near Monmouth. There is every reason to think that the English were led by Richard Beauchamp, Earl of Warwick, who had impressed the Prince of Wales so much with his well-armed men, and was in the area at about that time. It is possible that he almost captured Owain himself, and seized his banner from its bearer, Ellis ap Richard. A picture which may represent this feat is in an illustrated biography of Earl Richard, who was to become one of the most distinguished Englishmen of his time. The Welsh

then avenged this bloody defeat by the English with a pursuit and a massacre of their foes.

In March 1405 the Prince of Wales wrote exultantly to his father from Hereford, at last announcing a major victory:

> On 11 March your rebels from the districts of Glamorgan, Morgannwg, Usk, lower and upper Gwent assembled to the number of 8,000 men, by their own account. They advanced the said Wednesday morning and burned part of your town of Grosmont in your lordship of Monmouth. I at once sent my well-beloved cousin Lord Talbot and a small detachment of my household. They were joined by your faithful and valiant knights William Newport and John Greyndor, who together were but a small force ... And there, by the aid of the blessed Trinity, your people won the field and vanquished all the said rebels.

It should be noted that this victory was won by mobile companies acting in concert, under orders from the prince's headquarters at Hereford. Talbot was in charge of the household troops; Greyndor and Newport were leading a separate company. The dead were reckoned at 800 to 1,000, in both the battle and the pursuit.[36]

Worse was soon to follow for Owain's cause. Gruffydd Hiraethog writes:

> A slaughter of the Welsh on Pwll Melin Mountain, near Usk, where Gruffydd ab Owen was taken prisoner. It was now that the tide began to turn against Owen and his men. At this time Glamorgan made its submission to the English, except a few who went to Gwynedd to their master.

Walsingham gives the date of the battle of Pwll Melin (Yellow Pool) as 5 May, which is usually accepted. We rely largely on Adam Usk for the details:

> Griffith, the eldest son of Owen, attacked Usk castle with a great host on the feast of St Gregory [12 March] — an evil hour for him; however, the defences there had been considerably strengthened, and Lord Grey of Codnor, Sir John Greyndor, and many more of the king's

soldiers were there, and they made a sortie in force from the castle and captured him and his men, driving them relentlessly through the river Usk, where many of them — most notably the abbot of Llantarnam — were killed either at the point of a sword or by drowning in the river, through Monkswood, where Griffith himself was captured, and on to the mountains of Upper Went. Of those whom they took alive, three hundred were beheaded in front of the castle, near Ponfald, although some of the nobler ones, including Griffith, were sent as prisoners to the king. This Griffith remained in captivity for six years, eventually dying of the plague in the Tower of London.[37]

If Adam was correctly informed, the battle ended in a cold-blooded massacre worse than any other known atrocity in the Rising.

Abbot Walter Bower's account of Pwll Melin is of great interest; he first confirms what Gruffydd Hiraethog says about the submission of Glamorgan, and then the successful direction of strategy by the prince:

> When Henry prince of England, who still held the title of Wales, aimed to attack with a large army and totally destroy Wales, he sent Lords Cobham and Grey of Codnor, and David Gam, to exterminate them.

Fig. 9.2 The victors of the Battle of Pwll Melin, 1405. Sir John Greyndour is on the left, bearing his arms on jupon, trapper and shield (Or, a Fess between 6 cross crosslets gules), following the commander, Richard de Grey, Lord Codnor wearing his coat armour (Barry of 6 argent and azure).
The de Grey banner borne by the esquire would have served as a rallying point for his detachment.
The cross of St George and other national banners would have been carried in a major engagement.
The Welsh army would also have taken the field with their personal banners, but Glyndŵr carried the
Golden Dragon, not the one familiar today which arrived with Henry Tudor

Bower seems not to have realised that Henry was responding to another Welsh assault on Gwent, but he agrees with Adam about Grey, who with Greyndor would have been commanding the Brecon and Radnor troops. Bower may well be right about Cobham, the future title of Sir John Oldcastle, one of the prince's most trusted knights; perhaps he and Dafydd Gam were in charge of some household troops sent by Henry from Hereford to join Grey and Greyndor, as on the previous occasion before the battle of Grosmont. Bower goes on to say that many were killed, and that the prisoners included Gruffydd ab Owain.[38]

At first it seemed to the English that their greatest enemy had also fallen. According to Ellis,

> among the dead bodies was found one much like unto Owen, whom they supposed, and gave out, to be Owen that was slain; but upon further enquiry, it was found that it was not Owen, but his brother Tudor, who very much resembled him, and was often taken for him being hardly distinguished asunder, only Owen had a little wart above one of his eyebrows, which Tudor had not. The report of Owen's overthrow and death disheartened the Welsh exceedingly; insomuch that the people of Glamorgan submitted unto the king, save some few, who went unto Owen, when they understood he was alive.

The tide had certainly now turned against Owain. Despite armed intervention by the French with a fruitless chevauchée of their own in the late summer of 1405, re-embarking for France before winter, Owen's position gradually worsened. In part this was due to war weariness and the impoverished state in which most of Wales found itself after three years of major conflict. Yet, considering that Owain's hold over Wales was beginning to crumble, it is remarkable that he was able to go on fighting for another six years.

In 1406 Gruffydd Hiraethog wrote: 'Gower and Ystrad Tywi and Ceredigion yielded and took the English side', meaning the loss of all of south-west Wales. Ystrad Tywi was the valley of the River Towy, the greater part of Carmarthenshire. On St George's Day, 23 April, Walsingham records the severe defeat of a Welsh army, in which a son of Owain was slain, though we are not told which son, where this happened, or who the English commander was. In June Northumberland and Bardolf were defeated by Edward Charlton with troops raised in Shropshire and Cheshire, and driven from Wales. They went to Paris, where Orléans refused to help them, and were seen by Adam Usk: 'because I was frequently in contact with them, King Henry was stirred to even greater fury when he heard about it.'[39] Such remarks make one wonder whether Adam had an inflated sense of his own importance; he cannot have been one of the king's major worries.

In April 1406 the king formally notified Lord Grey of Codnor, responsible for the defences of the southern border, that the Prince of Wales, his lieutenant in Wales and the Marches, was now given full discretion to grant the royal grace and pardon to all rebels who submitted. John Bodenham, previously sheriff of Herefordshire, was appointed receiver of all fines, fees and payments for the redemption of confiscated lands. War weariness and the sense of impending defeat soon made the new policy effective. This was demonstrated in what can best be called a public ceremony at Beaumaris in November; in growing numbers, the Welsh were coming to realise that Owain's cause was doomed, and it was time to make terms with the enemy.

As already recounted, in February 1408, Owain's last English allies, the Earl of Northumberland and Lord Bardolf, were defeated and killed at Bramham Moor by the sheriff of Yorkshire. Within a year Owain had lost Aberystwyth and Harlech castles and the rising was effectively over, even though he managed one last raid into the borders in 1412 — and then effectively disappeared.

In the meantime, Adam's standard of living had improved, though never to the extent that he would have liked. With his pardon, his old patron Thomas Arundel was prepared to be forgiving. Usk was reappointed as an advocate in the Court of Arches (he was still acting as such in October

Fig. 9.3 The inscription on the memorial brass of Adam Usk in Usk Priory

1419),[40] and he says that he 'sat in parliament with other doctors' — probably the parliament of May-June 1413. Arundel also gave him 'the fine church of Merstham' (Surrey), as his living, though he did not regain any of the benefices of which he had been deprived in 1407, nor is there any indication that he regained the status that he had enjoyed in *c*.1395-1402.

Arundel died in February 1414. That Arundel's death was a personal blow need not be doubted, but Usk was well aware that it was also a blow to what small chance remained of salvaging his career. After 1414, the autobiographical element which is so prominent in the earlier sections of the chronicle largely disappears. In 1418 he was still seeking preferment, but soon afterwards, and well into his 60s, he sought instead a corrody (the right of board and lodging) at a religious house.[41] These were granted by the patron of the house or the king and would have enabled Adam to live out his retirement enjoying the income from his benefices. It may be that he obtained his wish at St Augustine's Abbey in Bristol.

His will, however, was dated at Usk, on 20 January 1430, and he must have died within the next two months, for it was proved on 26 March.[43] It reveals a man of some wealth, and strong local attachment. He left cash bequests to the vicar of Usk, to each nun of Usk Priory, and to Llandaff Cathedral, and 'trentals' (sufficient money to pay for 30 masses for his soul) to the Dominican and Franciscan friars of Cardiff and the Austin friars of Newport. A further 21 individual legatees are named or specified, all of them Welsh. They included a brother and sister, and several others may well have been kinsmen too. The total value of these bequests was something over £30. Apart from the *Polychronicon* which he left to Edward ap Adam, the only book which he bequeathed (to the church of Usk) was the encyclopaedic *Rationale*

diuinorum officiorum of Guillaume Durand, bishop of Mende, a further indication, perhaps, of that interest in ecclesiastical liturgy and protocol which surfaces on a number of occasions in Usk's chronicle. His soul he bequeathed to God and the Blessed Virgin, and his body to the parish church of Usk, to be buried before the statue of the Virgin.

He was interred in accordance with his wishes, his grave (which was probably in the Lady chapel) being marked by a memorial brass strip containing an epitaph (Fig. 9.3) which is now riveted to the north-eastern side of the 15th-century choir screen. This is in Welsh, and for long defied all efforts at either transcription or translation, until in 1921 Professor Morris-Jones supplied the following, which subsequent scholars have had no hesitation in accepting:

> After fame, to the tomb, from on the bench,
> The most skilled advocate of London,
> And judge of the world by gracious privilege,
> May the heavenly abode be thine, good sir.
> Lo! a Solomon of wisdom, Adam Usk, is sleeping
> here,
> Wise doctor of ten commotes,
> Behold a place full of learning![42]

Basing his analysis on the orthography of the couplets, Professor Morris-Jones concluded that while it is unlikely that Usk composed his own epitaph, he may well have been the one who actually wrote it down before passing it to the engraver.[43] He was, after all, almost certainly a Welsh speaker. His failure to join the ranks of the episcopate, the great disappointment of Usk's life, naturally remains unvoiced.

What of Usk's feelings towards Glyndŵr? As recorded above, these were mixed, for although Usk was a Welshman, he was a south Welshman, and from a lordship that was anglicized almost to the point of schizophrenia. In the sections that he wrote before he left for Rome, it is hard not to detect a note of sympathy for Glyndŵr and his followers: he says pointedly that the king regarded them as (rather than that they were) traitors and outlaws, noted with disapproval the brutality and sacrilege of Henry's invasion of Wales in 1401, and supplied a generous epitaph for Llywelyn ap Gruffydd Vaughan, who suffered a gruesome death 'because he had supported Owen'.[44] Not that Glyndŵr's own brutality escaped Usk's notice, but the detail is less graphic, the tone less bitter.[45] By 1414, his experiences during the intervening years had evidently persuaded him of the need to redress the balance: he speaks now of Glyndŵr's 'unprecedented tyrannies', adding that 'nor did he spare even the churches, which ultimately was to lead to his downfall', and that 'the people silently cursed his flagrant barbarities'.[46] When he came to record Glyndŵr's death in 1416, however, he passed no comment except to remark that he had to be re-interred because his enemies had discovered the location of his grave.[47] Given what we know of Usk's experiences in 1406-11, all this is rather strange. It is actually difficult to believe that he did not, at heart, sympathize with Glyndŵr's cause, but perhaps he was too cautious to say so.

CHAPTER X

The Gwehelog pottery kiln and brickworks
by Geoffrey Mein

One of the most productive local rural industries for something over a century from the end of the Civil War in 1648, the Gwehelog kiln had been all but forgotten until its rediscovery by Rudge Humphreys and the publication in 1980 of the work of Richard Hughes and Stuart Wrathmell in the now sadly defunct bulletin of the Welsh Medieval Pottery Research Group.[1] What follows is an attempt to throw more light on the period of activity of the kiln, and on its owners, the Progers from the results of recent excavation work at Trostrey Castle near Usk.[2]

It was as a result of initial small scale excavations by the late Rudge Humphreys of the pottery kiln, leading to his loan to the National Museum of Wales of the 'Stag plate', one of its finer products (Fig. 10.7), that Hughes and Wrathmell became aware of the site. The adjacent brick works, a later affair exploiting the same good potting clay of the Raglan Marl Group of the Old Red Sandstone was identified by Wrathmell as having lain some 350m north of the kiln and immediately east of the 1930s bungalow Camp Wood Lodge. The relationship of pottery kiln and brick kiln is shown on Wrathmell's Fig. 1, reproduced here, with some additional information, by his kind permission (Fig. 10.1).

The clay pits and possible buildings of the Camp Wood pottery kiln (SO 3793 0365) are dug partially into the south-eastern bank and ditch of the annex of the Iron Age hillfort of Camp Wood, whilst the nearby waster heap and the base of the kiln itself are shown in Wrathmell's Fig. 2, also reproduced here (Fig. 10.2). A clay pit converted by Henry Humphreys into a duck flighting pond is shown in Figure 10.3.

This is not the only kiln recorded in Gwehelog parish, for, following a suggestion by Wrathmell that others might exist, documentary research by Paul Courtney identified another 'Pott Killn' shown as being in ruins in the 1776 survey by Joseph Aram for the Earl of Worcester of his newly purchased lands in Usk lordship. The 'ruins' were on a piece of pasture just under half an acre (0.2ha) in extent, now part of Ty Gwyn Farm, Gwehelog Common (SO 3895 0450) shown on Figure 10.1.[3] Together with my late wife I carried out a field survey of the farm, but failed to find any sign of potting activity. We concluded that the most likely site for the kiln is under the cattle shed south-east of the farmhouse, whilst depressions around the nearby spring could have been its clay pits. Shown examples of pottery wasters from the Camp Wood kiln, the owners, Mr and Mrs Arnett, confirmed that they had found nothing similar.

Courtney also recorded a third kiln in the parish from a Badminton Estate map of 1765, together with a field called Kiln Field.[4] This lies south-west of Coed y Brain Farm (SO 3970 0195). In field walking I have found no trace of this kiln, nor of pottery wasters. A kiln here could have been used instead for corn drying or for malting, as was another kiln excavated at the Trostrey Castle site and dated by the pantiles built into the kiln structure to some years after their introduction in 1761. Excavation of the area around it provided a possible terminal date of 1780-5, whilst there is a firm terminal date of 1799 for the occupation of the castle area, for in that year Archdeacon William Coxe visited the nearby Trostrey Church and noted its isolation from any sign of human habitation.[5]

Among the finds from the Gwehelog kiln was an Edward VI shilling of his 'fine silver' issue of 1550-53. This cannot be used however to date the beginning of the kiln's production, since hammered coinage of this type remained in circulation until the great recoinage of 1696. The kiln produced 'tygs' (drinking mugs) and floor and roof tiles which were in use during the occupation by a blacksmith of a house built on the ruins of Trostrey Castle.

Aram's survey also recorded that part of Ty Gwyn Farm with the ruins of its 'Pott Killn' was held in 1776 by John Proger as part of his scattered lands, totalling 26 acres, in Gwehelog. It is not known how long he had been living there when Aram conducted his survey, but clearly the remains of the kiln were sufficiently obvious for him to note them, suggesting that it had ceased to be fired only a few years previously. Recent research by Jan Barrow further suggests that the Gwehelog industry was for part of its later history a family business of the Proger family. The excavations at Trostrey suggests that some of the occupants of the post-medieval house built on the ruins of the castle were employed by the Progers or their predecessors. It is not known who ran the pottery and tile business between the

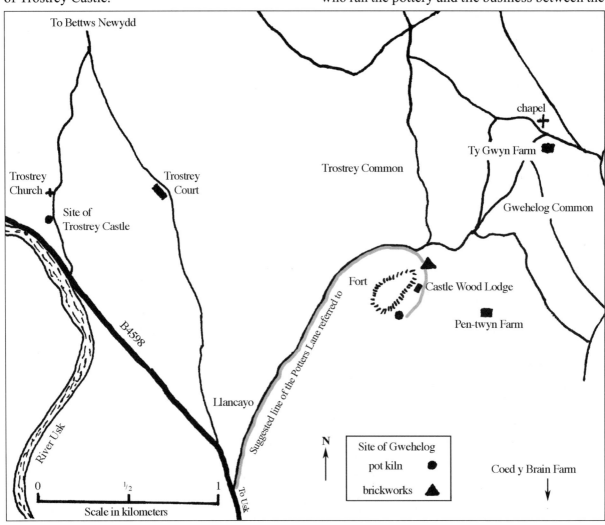

Fig. 10.1 Plan of the area showing the relationship of sites mentioned in this chapter

Civil War and the mid 18th century, but the Proger connection with the business is worth recording.

Several members of the family lived in Gwehelog between 1743 and 1812, with another in nearby Llandenny. Two of the Gwehelog Progers were recorded on their burial records as having been potters: George, who died in March 1759, according to the burial register of St Mary's Church in Usk, and Philip, who was buried there two months later. Unfortunately we do not know their ages at death, or their relationship, but perhaps they were brothers. Equally unfortunately, no Proger wills survive which might have made up for lack of other records of the Gwehlog pottery. Although it is not known where George lived, Philip is recorded at Pentwyn Farm, only a few hundred yards east of the Camp Wood kiln. He was an active member of the Usk community, being town bailiff in 1731 when he was assaulted by a labourer, Morgan Lewis. Any charge he may have made against Lewis was withdrawn.[6]

The John Proger who held the old kiln on Ty Gwyn Farm on the edge of Gwehelog Common in 1776 could have been George's son, still living where his father, and perhaps he, had operated it, possibly together with the Camp Wood kiln along with Philip. The timber supply for the kilns would have come from the renewable coppice of the local woodland, and even the brash from the hedgerows, whilst both kilns were in the immediate vicinity of good potting clay. It seems possible that it was the temporarily available supplies of wood which decided which kiln should be fired that year and for how long. The coppice cycle recorded for the neighbouring Kemeys

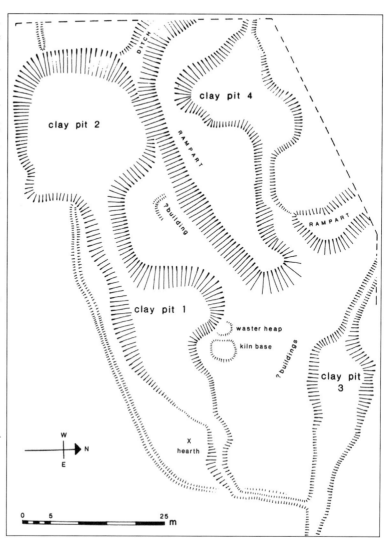

Fig. 10.2 The earthworks of the Iron Age defences and the Gwehelog kiln site

Fig. 10.3 Clay Pit 1 converted to a duck flighting pond

103

Fig. 10.4 The pot kiln site seen from Philip Proger's Farm

Inferior woods varied between 9 and 32 years.[7] It was presumably the Ty Gwyn John Proger who married Margaret, and whose daughter Ann was baptised in St Mary's Church, Usk in May 1764, perhaps named after the unmarried Ann Proger of Gwehelog who died in April 1759. The deaths at the same time of George and Philip Proger may indicate an unrecorded outbreak of some endemic disease such as cholera.

Philip Proger owned Pentwyn Farm, Gwehelog (SO 383 036) some time before 1750, by which time he had become so well known that, though it was then owned by John James it was still known as 'Philip Proger's Farm'.[8] Philip was married to Susan, and their son Henry was baptised in St Mary's in October 1743. It seems likely that the Camp Wood kiln was worked by Philip, for his farm is only 250 yards to its east. Figure 10.4 shows the view from the farmhouse to the kiln. The west elevation of Pentwyn is seen in Figure 10.5, added perhaps in the early 1800s to 'gentrify' the older farmhouse to the rear. The house is now a children's home. It stands within the enclosure of an Iron Age farmstead, part of whose ditch is visible to the north, over the garden wall.

It is not known where the family lived between selling Pentwyn and Philip's death in 1759. Could the Progers by then have started the brickworks adjacent to their pottery kiln, and if so, were they living in one of the three houses which now form the site of Camp Wood Lodge (Fig. 10.6)? These houses were still present in 1830 when they appear next to the still operating 'Brick Kiln' on Greenwood's map of Monmouthshire.[9] Significantly this does not show the pottery kiln, which must have ceased working and been forgotten by 1830.

Another local Proger was William Proger of Llandenny, two miles to the east. William predeceased his wife, who was buried in Llandenny churchyard in 1740 aged 63.[10] We do not know his age or occupation and cannot relate him to the pottery industry, any more than we can the otherwise unknown Edward Proger of Gwehelog, married to Ann and father of Mary Ann, baptised in St Mary's in 1812. He may have been a contemporary of John Proger the younger, 'yeoman' in 1792. Another John Proger, perhaps his father,

*Fig. 10.5 Pentwyn Farm, Gwehelog
— the 'new' house*

104

Fig. 10.6 Camp Wood Lodge, behind which is the quarry for clay for the brickworks

was the gamekeeper for Usk Manor from 1788.[11] The younger John was involved in the assignment of a lease from the Henry Duke of Worcester to William Andrews on 15 June 1790 of some 4 acres of land fronting on to the Gwehelog-Trostrey road,[12] the road leading to Llancayo and once known, according to my informant, the late Mr James, farmer, of Llandenny, as 'Potters Lane'. A name now forgotten, its top end leads to Camp Wood (Fig. 10.7).[13] This leased land could have included the area of the brickworks.

Whoever owned and ran the Gwehelog business over the years, their employees would have been local people who were probably seasonally employed at the kilns in the periods when they were not busy with agricultural jobs. This in turn would make the potting business a seasonal one.

The only site where the evidence shows that some of them lived, was in the post-medieval house erected over the ruins of the castle at Trostrey. The castle may have been demolished by Owain Glyndŵr's forces, possibly in 1405.[14]

That the employees were partly paid in kind is suggested by the considerable quantity and variety of ceramics from the Camp Wood kiln found at Trostrey, including a large proportion of 'seconds'. Many of these had been overfired, spoiling the glaze or producing cracks in the fabric. Others had been badly 'blunged', the clay

Fig. 10.7 The course of Potters Lane leading down from the kiln towards the brickworks and the tree-hidden Camp Wood Lodge

being so poorly prepared as to include air spaces, and so fractured in use. The impression gained by the excavators was that much of the ware was not good enough for sale in local markets in Usk and elsewhere.

However, one well glazed and handsome vessel that I found in Maryport Street, when working in the trench for the re-laying of Usk's main sewers, showed that the Gwehelog potters sold wares in which they had covered up faults. They had plugged with plaster a small hole in the side of a pot caused as a result of faulty 'blunging' in the first firing, and covered the plug with the glaze so as to make it invisible after the second firing. The pot broke in use, and the plug only came out when I was washing the broken fragments.

The products of the kiln were domestic and utilitarian. A more unusual vessel was a goblet or lidded sugar pot found by one of the Humphreys family and retained in their collection of sherds. This rare attempt at an elegant form would post-date 1684 if inspired by one of the large ring-handled lidded urns from the Pontypool Japanware works, or after 1763 if based on one produced at Usk.[15] Alternatively, in the latest phases of the Gwehelog industry, when the market was being flooded by the products of the midland and north-eastern potteries, the potters might have seen one of the pink lustre ware forms produced in Sunderland from 1720, but in particular from 1762 when the Maling family went into large scale production and export.

The domestic wares from Gwehelog were clearly intended for lower and middle income families (Fig. 10.8). The bulk of its production comprised utilitarian kitchen ware: large cylindrical storage jars with opposed horizontal strap handles (Fig. 10.8 top), jugs (Fig. 10.8 middle) and large ceramic bowls or 'panshions' (Fig. 10.8 bottom) used for raising bread dough or for rising the cream from milk. All these types had handles with hollowed cross-sections and pairs of bold thumb impressions. Similar wares were produced in a number of local rural kilns, though the Gwehelog products have distinctive features, such as the thumbnail handles and slip decorated 'stag' plates. Other vessels, steep-sided with flattened rims and one handle, were chamber pots, including at least one which was clearly a second

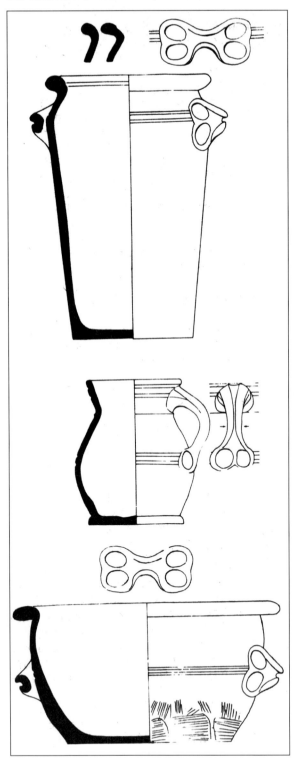

Fig. 10.8 Examples of Gwehelog ware

due to gross over-firing. Other larger bowls had pouring spouts and external decoration usually of finger impressed reinforcing strips just below the rim. Some had horizontal strip handles around the vessel, decorated with rouletting added by the use of small carved wooden rollers or with raised convoluted decoration (such as sherds coded T/29/1 and T/81/1 (7)). Most vessels were glazed overall.

Dishes and platters were plentiful, many with a yellow-green glaze and others with applied white trailed slip in a variety of geometric decoration around the flattened rim. The designs were not standardized and were the product of extempore fancy by the individual potter. None from Trostrey carried animal decoration, like Rudge Humphreys' 'stag dish' (Fig 10.9).

Basting or dripping pans and fish dishes appeared at Trostrey with the base of a poorly made watering pot found in field walking (T/ 102/ I(14)). A very badly made slab-built shallow dish (T/100/E and W/(4)) may have been the work of an apprentice. Trostrey also produced much other Gwehelog ware, including four types of the small handled drinking mugs or tygs, known to the diggers as 'coffee mugs', a small handled jug, one of the few Gwehelog pieces with true sgraffito decoration, and the rim of a black glazed chamber pot. All were dateable to 1625-80.

Another piece of Gwehelog graffito ware came from the post-medieval fill of the northern ditch of the medieval castle at Trostrey (T 33/Va (2)). This fill also included a tripod based handled skillet, surely a faulty design as it would be risky to pour out any heated liquid as the spout was opposite the handle (T 33/V/(8)). Keeping these and other pots warm on the table was achieved by placing them on top of chafing dishes (from the French *chauffer*, to warm), into the base of which glowing charcoal was placed. Fragments of these were a common find at Trostrey, the heat of the charcoal fracturing the base frequently. Out of normal use now in Britain, they can be purchased readily in Holland where they are used to keep the coffee pot warm by means of 'nightlight' candles. These were some of the Gwehelog products which presumably sold well, for they

Fig. 10.9 The Gwehelog pottery 'stag dish' now in the National Museum and Art Gallery of Wales, Cardiff (Accession no.57.115)

turn up in Usk in every excavation in the town, and I have found them as far away as Llantarnam Abbey, in the post-medieval excavation levels.

In addition to the kitchen wares, both roof and floor tiles were produced in the pottery or in the brickworks, mostly finished with the typical dark purple glaze, although some floor tiles were left unglazed, examples of the latter varying in thickness. The roof ridge tiles were being produced by 1650 and were brown glazed, lacking the ridge crests of medieval examples. The kitchen floor at Trostrey was tiled with Camp Wood products. The building's collapse was dateable to soon after 1777 from a forged George III halfpenny found amongst the debris.

Whilst it is impossible to identify the owners of the brickworks, it is possible to suggest its period of life. The evidence from Trostrey suggests that the bricks, reminiscent of Elizabethan bricks in size at 4.5 inches wide by only 2 inches thick and poorly made, were in production by the very early 1700s. Greenwood's map shows the pottery kiln forgotten, but the brickworks working in 1830, whilst the 1841 census shows no bricklayers and not a Proger in sight. With no sign of coal firing, the works had by then been open to ruinous competition from more up to date works for many years.

The lives of both pottery and brick industries seem therefore to have been roughly 150 years, though with a considerable overlap, the pottery perhaps dying out with the Progers and the brickworks because of competition, perhaps from the castle brickworks in Usk.

CHAPTER XI

Religious Conflict and Religious Toleration in Usk

by Jeremy Knight

In retrospect, 17th-century Britain seems dominated by religious conflict and civil war, but it is far from certain that contemporaries would have seen things in this way. Usk played little part in the Civil War. The castle, save for its gatehouse, was long in ruin, and partly dismantled. There was one skirmish near the town and local people would have grown familiar with bodies of troops passing through. The demands of local garrisons at Llangybi or Raglan would certainly have been tiresome, particularly to landowners and farmers whose hay crops were burnt and stock seized by the soldiers of both sides, as the diaries of Monmouthshire people who lived through the experience show. Yet for Usk major events like the siege of Raglan took place offstage. At other times in the century, national events impinged: local catholics were fined as recusants, whilst the vicar of Usk was deprived of his living by the Cromwellians.

The one memorial to 17th-century conflict in Usk is the grave of St David Lewis in the priory churchyard. His execution was a deeply divisive event which caused bitter divisions. Yet it needs to be asked whether the event reflected longer standing religious conflict in the town or was an almost fortuitous event, reflecting external politics, and of limited relevance to the longer term history of Usk.

Catholic recusants

On 13 May 1588, a few months before the Spanish Armada appeared in the English Channel, 11 Roman catholics from Usk, led by their priest, George Morris, appeared before the authorities to be fined for their non-attendance in the parish church. Morris had graduated M.A. from Oxford in 1553, the year of the catholic Queen Mary's accession. Unusually, *Alumni Oxoniensis* records neither his parentage, age or college.[1] Later, when catholics were barred from Oxford by religious tests, they sometimes attended without entering a college, so avoiding such tests. This may already have been the case with Morris under Mary's brother, the protestant King Edward VI. Recusants (non-attenders at church, which in practice at this date meant catholics) had been subject to fines since Elizabeth I's accession in 1558. However, it was unusual for a group of recusants to appear headed by their priest, and for him to be accorded the title *clericus*, particularly since it was a capital offence to exercise the functions of a catholic priest. This suggests that George Morris was a well known figure in the town. He may have been vicar of Usk under Mary. In 1577-8 Bishop Blethin of Llandaff had described him as 'a preacher in Queen Mary's days' (1553-8) 'who did forsake his living for his Romish religion' and as 'a great preacher in the Popish time, who refused his living because he would not subscribe' (to the Elizabethan church settlement). He was then chaplain to Rowland Morgan of Machen.[2] Catholic priests at this time often acted as chaplain to a gentry household (giving them cover) and as a parish priest elsewhere.

Between 1588 and 1623, over 50 recusancy fines were inflicted on a total of 39 Usk people, mostly styled 'yeoman' or 'spinster', with the occasional gentleman and a few craftsmen — a tiler, two sawyers and possibly two carpenters, if Carpenter and Saer were occupational surnames.[3] It was a bilingual community. Rice David ap John and Margaret David ap John also appear as Richard David John, Gentleman and Margaret David John, spinster. Welsh language poets writing in the traditional metres found ready local patronage. One dedicated a poem to St Mary Magdalene of Usk Priory. Under Edward VI a *marwynad* or elegy was written on two brothers from Usk, whilst catholic poets like Philip Ieuan of Tredunnock made plain their dislike of the new age. There may well have been a connection between the old faith and the old language.[4]

The simple statistics hide the spasmodic nature of the prosecutions, coinciding with periods of social tension. After the fines of Armada year, Usk catholics were left in peace until the tense early years of James I, which culminated in the Gunpowder Plot of 1605; in 1603-4, 16 fines were inflicted.[5] However, there were only four fines imposed between 1607 and 1620, all on women. For some reason there was then a sharp renewal of prosecutions between 1620 and 1623, with 21 fines and some people picked out several times. Some catholics may even have moved out of Usk itself to Gwehelog, Glascoed or Monkswood to escape notice.[6]

The Church by Law Established 1621-60
Possibly these moves were connected with the appointment of a new bishop of Llandaff, Theophilus Field (bishop 1619-27), who had a puritan background. It is unlikely to have been connected with the arrival of the new vicar of Usk, Moore Fortune (1584-1640), in September 1621 (before that date, the list of vicars of Usk is fragmentary).[7] Fortune, from a well established local

family, was a graduate of Jesus College, Oxford.[8] He was appointed vicar of Panteg in 1612, a living in the gift of the University of Oxford and of Jesus, 'the Welsh College'. At Oxford, Fortune had been the tutor of the writer and scholar James Howell, who in 1621 wrote sending his respects to his 'Master' and to Sir Charles Williams of Llangybi, who had just presented Fortune to the living. Fortune was succeeded in Usk in 1633 by Michael Hughes and retired to Panteg, where he was buried, near the pulpit, in 1640.[9]

Michael Hughes was a Merionethshire man, from Machynlleth. Vicar during the Civil War, Hughes was accused of having 'promoted the late tyrant's service' and of 'publishing the declarations of the late king', as well as using the prohibited Anglican Book of Common Prayer instead of the Parliamentarian Directory of Worship.[10] The latter was not easy to obtain (a special trip to Bristol would probably have been needed) and only a minority of churches had managed to do so. However, the Parliamentarians had plans to install puritan ministers in the main towns of the county, perhaps with wider jurisdiction, like an Anglican archdeacon. Michael Hughes was accordingly deprived of his living and replaced by Walter Cradock.

Walter Cradock was a local man, born about 1606 at Tre Bela, Llangwm. There is no record of his University career, but from 1633 he began a series of short-lived curacies — sometimes short-lived because of his controversial views. In 1634 he and his vicar, William Ebery of St Mary's, Cardiff, were denounced by Bishop Murray of Llandaff to the king as 'very disobedient to your Majesty's injunctions'. Cradock became curate at the puritan stronghold of Wrexham and then vicar of Llanfair Waterdine in Shropshire, a living in the gift of the presbyterian Sir Robert Harley. In 1639 he returned to Monmouthshire as assistant to William Wroth at the newly established separated chapel (the first in Wales) at Llanvaches. When Wroth died in 1641, Cradock succeeded him as minister.[11] Harley presented a petition to Parliament on behalf of people, possibly at Llanvaches, fined for 'gadding to sermons' instead of attending their parish church.[12] The following year, at the outbreak of war, he led his flock to Bristol and, when Bristol fell to the Royalists, to London. Here he was preacher to All Hallows the Great and sometimes to Parliament. He also served as chaplain and war correspondent with Fairfax's New Model Army and was almost certainly the 'W.C.' who was author of *A Letter from His Excellencie's Quarters* (1646) describing the siege of Raglan.[13]

In 1645 Parliament allocated £300 a year from the revenues of the bishoprics of St Davids and Llandaff to the support of Henry Walter, Richard Symonds and Walter Cradock 'to go into Wales, to preach the Gospel there'. The following year they were told 'with all convenient speed to proceed thither'.[14] Cradock was a believer in religious toleration, wary of over-rigid church government. 'Where God hath left a latitude,' he wrote, 'let us take notice of it'. He was involved in Cromwell's readmission of the Jews to England (though there were sound commercial as well as religious grounds for this) and once told a scandalised puritan, 'There is many a man that may be in the Ale-house, a drinking and swearing and whoring and his quean with him, that may be in heaven before thee.' In 1658 he retired to his native Llangwm. Parliament granted him a salary increase of £100, since the living there was of small value.[15]

William Jones and the Committee at Usk

After the Dissolution of Usk Priory in 1535, its buildings were sold by the crown to the Earl of Pembroke, who sold them to Roger Williams, who in turn sold them to his brother-in-law, William John ap Jevan, founder of the Jones family of Usk Priory. The Joneses of Usk Priory were thus distant cousins of the Williamses of Llangybi, and bore their arms.[16] William Jones (1577-1658) was a Parliamentary supporter. On the outbreak of war, like a number of Monmouthshire Parliamentarians, he removed to puritan Gloucester. He joined the Parliamentary Committee for South Wales, an offshoot of the County Committee for Gloucester, and for most of the war a committee in exile.[17] When Massey

captured Monmouth for Parliament in September 1644, its members were able to set up shop there, but when the Royalists retook the town in a surprise attack that November, Jones, with several other committeemen, including the lawyer Christopher Catchmay of Trellech, was taken prisoner. Five months later Jones, together with a fellow committeeman, Colonel Thomas Stephens of the Gloucester garrison, was exchanged for the Royalist Earl of Cleveland, who had been unhorsed and captured at the Second Battle of Newbury.[18]

As a County Commissioner, Jones was present at Raglan Castle after the surrender. War had not destroyed all good-neighbourliness. Among the civilians who fled into the castle was the vicar of Bryngwyn, Robert Frampton, clutching his parish register for safe keeping. At the surrender, this got left behind and 'was all torne in pieces' by the soldiers. A remnant was rescued by William Jones and passed to his kinsman David Pritchard of Bryngwyn. 'One poore leaf' survived to be included in a new church register after the Restoration. It is now safe in the County Record Office.[19]

At the end of the war, the Committee for south Wales established itself at Usk and became known as 'The Committee at Usk', just as that for the neighbouring county was known as 'The Committee at Hereford'.[20] Its members were mainly from the Usk and Trellech lordships of the Earl of Pembroke. Two colonels, Broughton and Stephens, may have been only wartime members. Civilians included William Jones, Christopher Catchmay, John Walter of Piercefield, William Blethyn of Dinham, Roger Williams and Rice Williams, William Herbert and Edward Morgan. Two MPs and Parliamentary colonels, Henry Herbert of Coldbrook and Thomas Hughes of Moynes Court may have been *ex-officio* members. By September 1645, Williams and Catchmay were actively raising taxes for the British army in Ireland.[21]

Jones became a leading figure on the Committee. He was Sequestrator General for the county, responsible for overseeing the sequestrations of the lands of former Royalists, a

Commissioner for the Propagation and Preaching of the Gospel in Wales and for Ejecting scandalous, ignorant and insufficient ministers and schoolmasters. In the latter role he was responsible for removing from their livings clergymen unacceptable to the new regime. In 1647 the county bench of magistrates was made up in numbers, replacing excluded Royalists. Of the seven new JPs, all save Henry Baker of Abergavenny were members of the Committee. Jones and Roger Oates of Cefntilla were also the two Chief Constables of Usk Hundred. This post bears no real relationship to its present day namesake, but they were responsible for the vital task of overseeing the array of parish constables and petty constables on whom local administration depended.[22] When Royalists in Glamorgan staged a rising that summer, alleging maladministration and corruption, the Usk Committee were anxious to rebut the charges and to demonstrate their zeal in restoring order. They issued a pamphlet setting out their defence.[23]

Religious Conflict Under Charles II

William Jones died in April 1657 and was buried under an altar tomb in the chancel of Usk Priory. His epitaph was recorded in 1683.[24] Walter Cradock, in retirement in Llangwm, died on Christmas Eve 1659. The two main figures in Cromwellian Usk had thus both left the scene before the Restoration. Michael Hughes, the expelled Anglican vicar, outlived both Jones and Cradock and was restored to his living at the Restoration, before returning to his native north Wales in 1664 as vicar of Chirk.[25]

Dissenters and former Parliamentarians were subject to harassment for much of the reign of Charles II. The so called 'Popish Plot' of 1678-9 enabled them to turn the tables. There were very real fears, exploited by the parliamentary opposition, that the heir to the throne, Charles's catholic brother James, duke of York, would restore Britain to catholicism on his accession. This raised memories of Mary's burnings of protestants, but nearer at hand was Louis XIV's vicious persecution of French huguenots, which was to culminate in the revocation of the Edict of Nantes

in 1685, in which the Jesuits played an active role. This seemed a foretaste of things to come.[26]

Sir Trevor Williams of Llangybi was patron of the living of Usk, and we may assume that the religious views of Phineas Rogers (vicar 1664-82) and Thomas Tyler (vicar 1682-95) were in accord with his own. Some Usk people may have attended the nonconformist cause at Llangybi, but unfortunately the returns for Usk in the 1676 Compton census, listing the numbers of catholics, 'conformists' (Anglicans) and nonconformists in each parish are lost.[27]

St David Lewis

David Lewis's martyrdom at Usk was a chance happening in several respects. Usk, unlike Abergavenny or Monmouth, was not a catholic stronghold. Lewis had been chaplain to the Morgans at Llantarnam and priest in Thomas Gunter's house in Abergavenny. He had no particular association with Usk. Also, until the paranoia of the so-called Popish Plot, the execution of catholic priests for their religion had seemed a thing of the past. Cromwell, who, like Walter Cradock, believed in religious toleration, had with great reluctance executed two priests, but otherwise there had been no executions nationally during the 30 years of Lewis's ministry in Monmouthshire.

Lewis was born in Abergavenny about 1616, the son of Morgan Lewis, headmaster of Abergavenny Grammar School, and his wife, Margaret Pritchard. Abergavenny families at this time often had both catholic and protestant branches and the two faiths seem to have lived together without undue conflict, save when outsiders muddied the waters.[28] Lewis and his parents were initially protestant, though a great uncle had become a Benedictine monk under the name Augustine Baker. Many of his mother's family were also catholics and his uncle, John Pritchard, a Jesuit.[29] About 1635 Lewis spent three months in Paris as companion to a young nobleman, the son of Count Savage. I owe to Dr Michael Siddons the suggestion that this may have been one of the Savage family of Rock Savage, Cheshire, perhaps the John Savage who succeeded his father as Viscount Savage in 1635.[30]

Fig. 11.1 The Gunter house in the High Street, Abergavenny, c.1907. This was the seat of the catholic branch of an important Abergavenny family. St David Lewis ministered in the chapel behind the second-floor window in the right-hand gable

Whilst there he converted to Rome, as did his parents at about the same time. He then returned to Wales and lived for two years at home.[31] When his parents died of fever about 1638, he left Britain and travelled to Rome, where he entered the English College. He was priested in 1642 and became a Jesuit in 1645. The following year he was sent to join the Jesuit Mission in south Wales, but was soon after recalled to Rome as spiritual director of the English College. However, at his own request he returned to south Wales in 1648. He was the Superior of the Jesuit College of St Francis Xavier at the Cwm, Llanrothal from 1667 to 1672 and from 1674 until his arrest in 1678.

The Popish Plot, though part of national politics, had many of its roots in Monmouthshire. John Arnold of Llanvihangel Court had been a personal assistant to the Sergeant at Arms at the trial of Charles I.[32] Initially friendly towards Lewis, it is unclear whether he was motivated more by religious hatred or by political opportunism. He collected a bulky dossier of allegations against various Monmouthshire gentry and their priests, which was presented to parliament through his ally Sir Trevor Williams, an MP with a long record of anti-papist activities and membership of anti-catholic committees in the Commons.[33] Two of the Jesuits singled out for attack were the future martyrs David Lewis and Philip Evans. Of the principal accusers during the London trials of the alleged plotters to assassinate the king, Titus Oates was a disreputable member of the Oates family of Cefntilla, though unsurprisingly his exact relationship is not recorded in the family tree. The confidence trickster and petty criminal William Bedloe, originally from Chepstow, provided, after suitable prompting, the second witness needed in cases of capital treason.

After his arrest in November 1678, Lewis was held in Monmouth Castle until the following January, when he was transferred to the new gaol at Usk. On 28 March he was back in Monmouth for trial before a single judge, Sir Thomas Atkins, who was seemingly a kinsman of Arnold. Arnold sat at the judge's right hand and challenged any jurors of Lewis's 'neighbourhood or acquaintance' (of whom, said Lewis, there were many), until a jury acceptable to Arnold had been chosen. There was no mention of any plot. The only charge was that of being a catholic priest. The outcome was inevitable. Lewis was sentenced to be hanged, drawn and quartered for treason.[34]

In the month after his trial, Lewis and other condemned priests were taken to London to Newgate and interrogated by Oates and others in an attempt to shore up the plot. They were then returned to their 'home prisons' by coach. In some towns, there were hostile crowds, but in Usk there

Fig. 11.2 Saint David Lewis, an engraving by Alex Vost from Brevis Relatio Felicis Agonis quam pro Religione Subierunt *(Prague 1683)*

was much sympathy for Lewis. 'The townspeople stared and pitied me', he wrote, 'thinking I came there to dye, and my executioner with me'. It was still far from certain that the sentence would be carried out. Many, from the king downwards, were delaying matters in the hope that the hysteria would blow over (as Oates and Arnold feared). However, Shaftesbury, puppet master of the plot, was now Lord President of the Privy Council. Parliament was forcing the king into a corner, in an attempt to exclude his brother James from the throne. They ordered the Assize judges to confirm the sentences and see that they were carried out. Early on 16 July, word was brought to Lewis's bedside that the judges were on their way. 'The next approaching Assizes will clear the matter' he wrote. On 31 July Judge Atkins signed the death warrant. The High Sheriff, James Herbert of Coldbrook, found reasons to delay the execution, and Arnold sent messengers posting after Atkins to Shrewsbury and Worcester, complaining of the delay.[35]

On 27 August 1679, Lewis was taken from the prison near Usk bridge and transported on a hurdle to the place of execution at the Island, near the site of the present catholic church of St Francis Xavier and St David Lewis in Porth Y Carn Street. The execution had been moved from the normal venue at Monmouth, perhaps because it was thought that popular sympathy in Usk would be less than in the catholic stronghold of Monmouth. If so, it was a mistaken hope. The change in venue meant that the scaffold was an improvised affair. There were rumours that no local carpenter was willing to do the work. Lewis had to stand on a stool in a trench dug under the scaffold beam, which was supported on two forked posts. Here, the 63-year-old Jesuit, who had preached before Pope Urban VIII at Rome, gave his last and most remarkable sermon. His text was from I Peter 4, vv. 15-16: 'Let none of you suffer as a murderer or thief, but if as a Christian, let him not be ashamed.'

'Here is a numerous assembly I see,' he began. 'The Great Saviour of the World save every soul of you. I believe you are here met not only to see a fellow native die, but ... to hear a dying fellow native speak.' He asked why he was 'thus sledg'd to this country Tyburne'. He denied all knowledge of any plot, but readily admitted the charge for which he had been sentenced: 'A Roman Catholick I am, a Roman Catholick priest I am, a Roman Catholick priest of that religious order called the Society of Jesus.' He had been condemned solely for exercising the functions of a priest. He declared the malicious tales circulated about him by the spin doctors and tabloid journalists of the day to be false and forgave his enemies 'especially ... my Capital Persecutor [presumably Arnold] who hath been so long thirsting after my blood'.

He gave the Benediction, at which many in the crowd are said to have knelt. 'Sweet Jesus receive my soul,' he concluded. 'And so was executed', ended the pamphlet describing the trial and execution, though the crowd refused to let him be cut down until he was dead.[36]

An anonymous local Welsh poet described the scene in an elegy in Gwentian dialect:

> Creaduried Duw nefol
> pawb eraill daearol,
> gwrandewch fi'n bresennol,
> yn traethu fy nghwyn,
> am golled a gawsom,
> waith difa gwr gwirion,
> nid oedd dan y goron mwy mwyn ...
> Pan oedd ef yn pregethu
> oedd Saeson a Chymry
> a phawb yn rhyfeddu
> gwroldeb y sant
> heb atal heb unwaith
> colli gair trwy'r holl bregeth
> daeth deigre gwyr, gwragedd a'u plant

> Creatures of heavenly God,
> and all others on earth,
> Listen to me now
> Giving voice to my lament
> For the loss we have suffered
> With the destruction of that innocent man
> Under the crown, none was gentler
> When he preached,
> Both Welsh and English
> All were filled with wonder
> At the courage of the saint

> Never faltering or once missing
> A word of his entire sermon
> Tears flowed from men, women and children[37]

The bitter divisions in Usk following the execution were seen the following February, when Arnold accused Thomas Herbert, Steward of Usk and a former High Sheriff who lived in Usk Castle gatehouse, of seditious libel. Herbert was a former parliamentary supporter, but his wife Mary was the widow of James Gunter of Abergavenny, the protestant branch of the family whose catholic cousins maintained the chapel in the Gunter House at Abergavenny served by David Lewis and his fellow martyr Philip Evans. Herbert had presumably opposed Arnold's persecution of Lewis. As was often the case, ties of kinship were stronger than political or religious allegiances.

The quarrels within the town over the execution seem to have escalated and Arnold later accused John Giles, the catholic chief constable

Fig. 11.3 The grave of St David Lewis is thought to lie close to the west porch of Usk Priory, where a modern memorial marks the spot

Fig. 11.4 Plaque on the Gunter house in Abergavenny commemorating St David Lewis

of Usk, of a probably fabricated assault on Arnold in Jackanapes Lane off the Strand in London. Arnold claimed to have been stabbed by three hooded men and only saved by his whalebone corset. Giles had dipped cloths in Lewis's blood at the execution as relics, and had publicly rubbished the idea of any 'Popish plot'. These activities drew Arnold's paranoid anger upon him. Giles was alleged to have taken a broken

sword to an Usk cutler for repair whilst those who gave sworn evidence that he was in Usk at the time of the alleged assault were dismissed as 'for the most part Welsh'. After an orchestrated pamphlet campaign he was sentenced to be pilloried in London. Unable to pay a heavy fine, he was still in prison three years later, whilst in Usk his wife's possessions had been seized by the sheriff for her catholicism.[38]

The inscription on Lewis's grave 'Here lies the body of Edward [*sic*] Lewis who was condemned for a priest and a Jesuit and executed the 27 of August 1679 *Beati mortui qui in Domino Moriantur*' (Blessed be the dead that die in the Lord), was recorded by a friend of the Oxford Jacobite antiquary Thomas Hearne in 1734. It was said to have been visible until about 1830.[39]

The historian John Morrill once wrote: 'Religious commitment is best observed in conditions of persecution'.[40] Persecution, like other forms of violence, makes good headlines and generates the source material on which historians depend. David Lewis ministered in Monmouthshire for over 30 years. It is a sobering thought, however, that if it were not for the partly fortuitous circumstances of his martyrdom, he would today be almost as obscure a figure as the vicars of Usk who were his contemporaries.

CHAPTER XII

Some Buildings of Usk

by Geoffrey Mein

The town contains an appreciable number of buildings of both architectural and historical interest. Over the centuries virtually all have undergone alterations which hide features which can tell one something of their origin and history, and the object of what follows is to describe some of them and attempt to fit them into the story of Usk.

The building that caused the greatest surprise when its original function was revealed was the large Mulberry House which stands behind its wall and trees on the north side of Twyn Square in the shadow of the castle (Fig. 12.1). Now looking for all the world like a late Victorian vicarage, in the print by G. Samuel published in 1801 it appears rather as a possible 17th-century town

Fig. 12.1 Mulberry House from Twyn Square

house (Fig. 12.2). However, it proves to have been many centuries older as shown by the Royal Commission on Historic and Ancient Monuments of Wales (RCHAMW).

Their inspection revealed that in its earliest phase it had been a large hall-like building and not a dwelling. It retains its vaulted undercroft which was reached via a stair from the rear garden, meaning that the building stood not within the bounds of Usk town but, like the castle, on land which had been the property of the lords of Usk. It appears to have been the town's original market hall, its position suggesting that it was added to the town as an afterthought, rather than having been included in the original planning and layout, and that it was built for the town by the then lord of Usk. The upper part would have been used by the burgesses as their town hall, presumably on their promising to keep it in repair, while the undercroft below would have been available for use with the market in the square outside.

The income from its letting is mentioned in the accounts of 'Nicholas T. reeve of the borough of Usk'.[1] For the quarter October 1294 to the following January, there is an entry for the market and fair day of 18 October 1294 of '5s From the seld [from *selda*, a shop] under the hall in the market place hir[e]d the same day'. As five shillings was then a very large sum of money, the period of the let was presumably for the whole quarter, not simply the day of that market and fair. Whatever its use, it was clearly of considerable

Fig. 12.2 Samuel's print of Mulberry House in 1801

value when compared with the rent for the whole quarter of '2s 2d for the cheese house', wherever that was, though considerably less than the astonishing '44s 6d of prisage of beer expended on the garrison of the castle' — presumably also for the full quarter.

The burgesses clearly did not keep the market hall in repair and it had to be replaced by what they later built on 'a piece of unbuilt upon land in the street of the New Market'. This plot, which equals in size that of the original town hall, was given to them in 1598 by the then lord of Usk, the Earl of Pembroke, and is now the site of the British Legion Club (Fig. 13.3). The long blocked arches on the east side where the present front door is to be seen, along with those on the south and west elevations, show that it originally had an open undercroft, like the original building in Twyn Square, again with the hall above. The outside stair on the west end of the building is clearly a replacement for a stair up through the hall floor from the open market area. This arrangement can still be seen in some of the surviving market halls in Britain, for instance that

of Ross-on-Wye. Used for the meetings of the burgesses in council and for the various courts until replaced by the Sessions House in Maryport Street, the hall was also the scene of some major events in the town, including two visits by King Charles I. The first occurred during his period of personal rule (1629-1640) after he had dissolved Parliament, when he was raising money for his wars with Scotland by reviving long abandoned taxes and extending others to new taxpayers, as with Ship Money. He also made considerable use of the sale of honours, a form of revenue-raising which remained popular at least until the days of Lloyd George. His second visit took place during the succeeding Civil War, when he was again attempting to raise more money from a then war-weary population.[2]

Mulberry House was for many years the vicarage, as befits its current appearance, although the present vicarage is to its rear in what used to be part of its garden. The parish hall was until 1900 the small building alongside the main house. When it became the vicarage is unknown, but until the Dissolution of the monasteries and

Fig. 12.3 Black Friars from the south, showing the two stairlights

the winding up of Usk Priory, the priest in charge of the town's church may have lived in part of the Black Friars, the fine early building in Four Ash Street. The two small stair lights in its south elevation disclose the original existence of two staircases, showing that the original building had been in two separate parts (Fig. 12.3). Its name and the fact that on the Dissolution the building, along with much of the rest of Usk Priory's property, was acquired by the local entrepreneur Roger Williams, indicates its earlier dual purpose, for the other half would presumably have been occupied by the priest serving the nuns of the priory (see chapter V). As a man, he would not have been permitted to live in their enclosed monastic community.

A few yards from the Black Friars is the attractive Vine Cottage alongside the gate into the churchyard (Fig. 12.4). It is one of the few remaining examples of Regency Gothic in the county, one of the others, a small farmhouse alongside the A449 to Usk from the Coldra roundabout, having been lost as a result of a fire a couple of years ago. Vine Cottage was the house of the head gardener for the estate of Robert Rickards, Usk's late Victorian philanthropist and historian, the garden then extending to include what is now the almost full 'new' churchyard.

When it ceased to be a garden it became the site of a motor garage, the construction of which revealed the victim of an Usk murder which was never reported and has never been solved. The skeleton of a large man was found by the garage owner when excavating for an inspection pit. Identified by the post-mortem examination as male and negroid, from his teeth, no cause of death or identity was established. The records of the post-mortem have since been destroyed by the police authorities. The garage proprietor had been chief mechanic for the racing driver Mike Hawthorn, killed in a car accident on the Hog's Back in Surrey.

The Rickards lived for many years in The Priory, a house built out of what had probably been the prioress's lodging, and which can be seen from the Garden of Remembrance east of the tower of the Priory Church. Now sadly neglected, it contains internally and on its southern side architectural features indicating its former fine state.

The original line of the street frontage on the town centre side of the Black Friars is preserved in that of the row of cottages which still exhibit the narrow frontages associated with properties nearest to the original market place in Twyn Square. One or two of them have had their frontages slightly altered over the years but the architectural details preserved inside the southernmost

Fig. 12.4 Vine Cottage

cottage in the row, including a wattle and daub wall to the small main room and the style of the stops on the beams of the ceiling, show that in its present form it dates from about 1590 or 1600. Still standing on their original narrow burgage plots, it seems likely that virtually the whole row was rebuilt at about the same time and prior to the construction or reconstruction of the building immediately between the southernmost cottage and the Black Friars. This building is one of several examples in Usk of 'trespass building', for which see chapter VIII.

Opposite Mulberry House on the south side of Twyn Square is the fine Ty Brith, 'the speckled house'. Now divided into apartments (with houses built in its former large gardens to the east), it was for many years one large house. An examination of its plan shows that even earlier the property consisted of shops fronting on to Twyn Square and the present small car park, with one shop in Priory Street to the south of the doorway. The Twyn Square shops extended eastwards along the start of Four Ash Street to include what became the stables of Ty Brith, themselves now a house. Again to the south along Priory Street, excavations I carried out in the garden on that side of the house established the foundations of further small buildings, probably more shops. Some idea of the earlier use of the house can be seen from an examination of the Twyn Square elevation of the property. The fine front door in Priory Street contains one of the only two 'Judas windows' in Usk, the other being in the earlier front gate of Usk Castle. The predecessor of the modern 'fish eye' peephole in a door, they consisted of a small eye-level panel, enabling the occupant of the house to identify callers before opening the door, without being either stabbed or pistolled.

Opposite this entrance is another fine late 16th-century house — The Laurels, 10 Priory Street, noted in chapter VIII as blocking an early street leading towards the river. Newly repaired, it contains, as is normal for Usk, a very thick end wall which includes the stairway approached via a door beside the inglenook fireplace, in this case in the southern wall. As with the Old Maltsters in New Market Street, this house many years ago

suffered the collapse of the outer leaf of another main chimney wall, here the northern wall, presently adjoining the passageway between numbers 10 and 12. The collapse was due to a change in use of fuel from wood to coal. Wood smoke contains little sulphur, unlike coal smoke which can contain a great deal (especially that derived from soft Monmouthshire coal), and the wide and high chimney cooled the coal smoke as it rose, with the result that much of the sulphur content was deposited as soot on the stone of the chimney sides. Being open to the sky and the elements, the rain dropping on to the soot turned the sulphur to sulphuric acid, which eventually ate away the stonework until it collapsed (Fig. 12.5).

The same process occurred, but was detected before it could cause terminal damage, to the chimneys of Buxton House, 39 Old Market Street, and its neighbour on the corner of Mill Street, 35 Old

Fig. 12.5 The rebuilt chimney breast at The Old Maltsters, New Market Street

Market Street, as recently as the 1990s. This was possibly the cause of the damage to the smaller stack between nos. 37 and 35, and is a continuing danger to houses with wide old chimneys, either of stone or brick, which remain unlined and are still used for coal fires.

The remaining properties worth noting are virtually all in either Old or New Market Street. The area now occupied by a large house on the north-west corner of Old Market Street and Maryport Street, formerly the Lamb and Flag Inn (and still locally known as such, despite now being flats) was originally an open space that formed part of the old market that gave its name to the street (Fig. 12.6). This is shown by the garderobe (latrine) chute, which discharged on to it from the still existing medieval latrine half way up the stairway in the thick fireplace wall of the adjoining cottage to the north, 42 Maryport Street (Fig. 12.7). Supporting this evidence is a now blocked stair light a few steps up the same

Fig. 12.7 The garderobe on the stair of 42 Maryport Street

stair. Apart from having one of the biggest stone bressumers in the town in that same wall, no. 42 is notable for having its original and now blocked

Fig. 12.6 The former Lamb and Flag to the left with no. 42 Maryport Street. Of the two doors to no. 42, that on the left is the present front door and that on the right is the door to the original — and still open — passageway between 42 and 40

121

Fig. 12.8 The original front door of 42 Maryport Street which opened on to the still functioning passageway between 42 and 40

Fig. 12.9 The inner end of the passageway between nos. 42 and 40 Maryport Street. Note the partial blocking of the arch

front door, with its fine Tudor style timber door-head (Fig. 12.8), marking the former entrance from the still used passageway between it and its neighbour, no. 40 (Fig. 12.9). The passageway has at some time been reduced in width on the side of no. 40.

Quite when the Lamb and Flag was built is not known but it predates 1800, its site being marked on Coxe's plan of the town. It also predates the development of the rest of the market area on the opposite side of Old Market Street, which was partially occupied by housing by 1846 as shown on the Tithe Map. A sense of the latter area having long been open can still be gained from the rear of the present properties.

The original width of the street is shown by the set-back frontages of the blocks of sheltered housing west of the coach house, and the cottages adjoining the Lamb and Flag. The blocks stand upon land long in the ownership of the Williams family, later the Adams-Williams, who had built two houses to that frontage in about 1620. Excavated in 1979, they proved to have been so badly damaged by subsidence, having been built over the long-forgotten town ditch (Fig. 12.10), that they had to be demolished after not more than 60 years, the site remaining open until the present sheltered housing of Plas Mawr was built following the excavations. Later excavations on the adjoining site to the east revealed the barracks and stables of the Roman auxiliary cavalry unit left to keep an eye on local tribespeople after the legionaries were posted elsewhere.

Fig. 12.10 A section of Usk's town ditch north of Old Market Street, now the site of Plas Mawr

The Usk home of the Williamses was The Great House in Old Market Street, now numbers 17-27 Old Market Street (Fig. 12.11). The earliest document in the family papers referring to plots in this street is of 1521. Whilst not mentioning this house, its architecture supports a date around that period for its construction. It was originally entered from what is now the rear, which then fronted on to large gardens and land running down to the present cricket ground. There are two interesting features on the street side of the house, which is now divided into a number of dwellings. No. 27 has decorated plaster ceilings on both floors. That of one room on the lower floor has a pattern of interlocking pointed quatrefoils with shields, whilst a second room has a ceiling of thistle decoration, suggesting a date after the Union of the crowns of England and Scotland in 1603. The ceiling on the upper floor is even more elaborate, with sprigs of flowers, shields and wyverns.[3] The second and more enigmatic feature is the outside chimney stack on the street frontage of number 19, the house at the eastern end. Supported on three corbels, the fireplace of which this could be the chimney must either have been a late addition or more probably the conversion to a fireplace of what had been the rear elevation and chute of a garderobe or latrine, similar to that at 42 Maryport Street. The Williams family, having become increasingly wealthy and influential through property transactions, soon moved to Llangybi,

Fig. 12.11 The Great House, Old Market Street with (right) no. 19 showing the external first-storey chimney stack, since converted to provide a window

the castle there having been purchased from the Earl of Pembroke by Roger Williams, who in 1562-3 was the steward of the lordship and his agent.[4]

Opposite the Great House is Ty Mawr, the three storey house now owned by Steve Musto of the King's Head and intended for conversion to additional hotel accommodation, along with the row of intervening small houses already so incorporated. Previously the offices of Monmouth District Council, it was owned in 1818 by the Addams-Williams family and occupied in 1851 by William Evans, the vicar of Usk.[5] He married Louisa Caroline, daughter of William Addams-Williams who then owned all the land down Old Market Street as far as the coach house.

Ty Mawr was originally thought to be Georgian in origin, but Steve Musto's architect, Philip Musker, has shown by a detailed measured survey that the house is much older, being probably yet another of Usk's buildings of the very early 1600s. The oddly aligned western end wall is up to 7 feet thick and must hide another of Usk's massive end-wall inglenook fireplaces. That this is the case is clear from the floor below, where two appropriately spaced pillars support the fireplace and chimney breast. There is still the unsolved problem of why the Williamses built it and for whom, and when it underwent its 'Georgianisation'. Was it perhaps in 1818 or thereabouts? It appears on the Usk Tithe map of 1846, but its site was still marked as fields in Coxe's map of 1801. Was it intended for some member of the Addams-Williams family, to replace Great House opposite, which by then had declined into multiple occupation?

Fig. 12.12 The King's Head with, just showing on the right, the start of the row of cottages which has been incorporated with the inn to provide more accommodation

Fig. 12.13 Buxton House, Old Market Street (centre of the photograph).
The house at one time incorporated the properties to either side

The layout of The King's Head shows this to be a building of about the same date as the early phase of Ty Mawr, having not only the large open fireplace at the west end of the building, but another in the east wall of the same bar. What the function of the remainder of the east end of the building was is not clear, but it could have been another shop. The King's Head would seem to have been both contemporary with and about the same size as Buxton House on the opposite side and further along Old Market Street.

Buxton House (Fig. 12.13) is an end-door lower hall house of about 1590, with massive fireplace end walls, the western one once containing a spiral stair and with Type 1 beam stops similar to those in the cottage adjoining Black Friars and indicative of its date. The original owner clearly also owned the adjacent plots each side, for the main door was at its western end, on the opposite side of the fireplace to the stairway, and opened on to a cobbled passageway, rather as did that of 42 Maryport Street. This is now the site of the garage of the neighbouring, and later, no. 41, the passageway leading to the stables at the far end of the garden. Now a house approached by the side turning off Baron Street, at its east end can

be seen the now blocked archways of the original carriage exit for Buxton House stables leading on to Mill Street. The main house was extended both ways, first by a jettied portion over the cobbled passageway and subsequently in the opposite direction in the late 17th or early 18th century. This latter portion is now no. 37.

That house has, upstairs, some early wattle and daub walls and, to the rear, a fine dining room extension, possibly Georgian. There is a box design parapet to nos. 37 and 39, but not no. 41, meaning that it must have been added after the latter had passed into different ownership. This fashion for added parapets was in favour in the south-east of England by 1610 and then spread slowly westwards to Cheltenham and Bath before reaching Usk perhaps as late as 1845.

Another example is to be seen on the frontage of Rose Cottage, 21 New Market Street, which is much older than it might seem. It has two stone fireplaces, the lower another gable-end chimney, whilst the upstairs fireplace bressumer has above it the remnants of an early geometric patterned mural painting. This is reminiscent of that in the upper chamber at Iron Acton, Gloucestershire, of about 1550.

Fig. 12.14 The Royal Hotel, New Market Street

Adjacent to the old town hall is the Royal Hotel, with its two elegant bowed windows (Fig. 12.14). Built in 1839 it was the first Usk home of Edward John Trelawney (1792-1881). A friend of Byron and Shelley, ex-pirate, incorrigible womaniser, traveller, romantic poet and author, he fought with Byron for Greek independence from the Turks. He was with Byron and Shelley in Italy when the latter was drowned in August 1812, and organized, along with Byron and Leigh Hunt, the cremation of his friend on the beach at Viareggio where the body of the possibly murdered Shelley had been washed up. Moving to Usk from London in 1841-2 with his second or third wife, they lived here whilst he built Twyn Bell above Llanbadoc Church. Later, they built the bigger Cefn Ila House, since burnt down, where they entertained guests including the widowed Mary Shelley, author of *Frankenstein*.

Further along New Market Street is the large Ynys Hafod ('the summer dwelling by the water-meadow'), built about 1562 by John Rumsey, secretary to Roger Williams of Llangybi, sheriff of the county. Its original front was towards the river, approached by carriage drives from both sides, that nearest the Royal Hotel now occupied by Riverside House, with its neo-classical façade. It was built in 1844 by the then owner of Ynys Hafod, Illtyd Nichol (1775-1871), for his friend

the barrister and judge, Thomas Falconer. The other, northern, coach drive is still open, flanked by Min-yr-Afon, which, like so many Usk houses is larger and architecturally more interesting than at first appears.

Beyond is Usk's last surviving jettied and half-timbered house, The Old House, at no. 18. Built probably before 1550, Peter Smith, the former secretary of the RCHAMW, reported it as 'a perplexing mixture' of periods, of three portions. The rear, not visible from the street, has the familiar gable chimney and fireplace stairs and a roof containing possible upper crucks, an interesting and important feature. The side wall to the south, now the entrance passage, seems to have been timber framed, while the front section, a cross wing, is mainly half timbered but with the lower portion of the front wall of stone. The four-light, mullioned and sunk-chamfered window in this wall should be of 1600-25 and could be the replacement of a diamond mullioned window, with would agree better in date with the rest of the façade. Part of the portion to the north is probably an added parlour of the 18th or 19th century. Considerably altered over time, there is some fine carved woodwork, including a rounded, bar-stopped main beam (i.e. with a transverse raised 'bar' before the rounded moulding of the stop), unusual but not unique in the county.

Opposite the Old House is The Rosary, no. 23, with its pleasing Georgian front to what may have been a house of the early 1600s, like Rose Cottage next door. In between times it underwent considerable gentrification in the Queen Anne period (1702-14). That this work also included increasing the building's height is suggested by the rear elevation.

Next to the Old House is The Lawns, a fine large house now divided into flats, probably built for the Revd Thomas Addams-Williams just before his marriage in November 1785. He had been appointed vicar of Usk the previous April by his father, the patron of the living.

Opposite is the Rural Life Museum (Fig. 12.17), which with the two houses immediately to the north comprise a particularly interesting group. The Museum has on its north elevation a medieval mullioned window and another of the window lights which we see elsewhere. Internally, visitors can see the remains of pads on the tops of the front and back walls of the main room. These appear to have been the bases for an original arch-braced or even hammer-beamed roof. This has led experts to suggest that the building was a hall house dating from the commencement of rebuilding in the town shortly after the destruction caused by Glyndŵr's attack in 1402. However, it is also possible that these are the remains of a hall house constructed before 1402, but so badly damaged by Glyndŵr's men that it had to be replaced by the house across the open way to the north, later becoming the barn of the maltster living across the alleyway. The plan of the building is basically an E without the central stroke, suggesting a hall with the lord's dais end on the south and the solar and parlour to his right

as he looked down the hall to the kitchen, pantry and buttery. These were in what later became an attached cottage, now the cottage kitchen exhibit of the museum.

Whichever suggestion is correct, it is likely that what followed after 1402 was a single large building, now divided into the Old Maltsters and the Nook (Figs. 12.15 and 12.16) (but not including the museum which was the original hall house). The clue to the original plan lies in the main north wall of the Old Maltsters, the wall on the right as one enters through the present porch. This is pierced by three doorways, the first originally leading to the kitchen, the second to the pantry and the third to the buttery, which lay at right angles to this wall, and comprises the present house known as the Nook. Here again I must thank Peter Smith, who has pointed out that the dais, where the owner and his family would

Fig. 12.15 The Rural Life Museum, New Market Street, with the Old Maltsters on the left

have sat, would have been at the north end of the hall. From here they would have looked down the hall, where their retainers sat 'below the salt' on benches at long tables, the food and drink being brought out through the lower doors from the service rooms. The solar and parlour of the owner were to the rear of the dais, in the projecting wing to the east. This can be seen over the dividing fence from the adjoining car park. This suggests a reverse of the museum's former layout.

But who built and occupied this fine house? I have suggested that it was the townhouse of William ap Thomas, from 1431 until his death in 1445 the royal steward of the lordship of Usk, and I now suggest that the adoption of an architectural design which was by then outdated was due both to the desire to replace a similar house destroyed by the Welsh and to the always tardy adoption of new designs in Monmouthshire.

Finally, there is a building which shows several of the interesting features of the Usk houses considered above, and which is open for our inspection and sustenance — the Cross Keys Inn in Bridge Street (Fig. 13.4). Originally another ground-floor hall house, this was rebuilt in the late 1500s, the time of the 'great Elizabethan rebuilding' which saw the construction or rebuilding of many Monmouthshire farmhouses as well as houses and inns in the older towns of Wales. Here, if one turns into the right-hand bar on entering, one is immediately faced with a familiar massive end-wall fireplace and the original doorway into the building on its right, as in Buxton House, Old Market Street. Here, however, one still has the winding stair to the right of the fireplace, a plan matched in the private Ty Tadcu — 'Grandpa's House' — further down Bridge Street. In that well

Fig. 12.16 The Nook, New Market Street

restored home the stairs are made not of separate risers and treads, but of massive squared pieces of solid timber. Whilst still in the Cross Keys, one can with the permission of the landlord go up the winding stair and view the Jacobean ceiling in one of the rooms facing on to the street, before resting one's feet and quenching one's thirst.

CHAPTER XIII

The 18th-century Market Town
by Jan Barrow

After the Civil War Usk was in a poor state, with a dearth of tradesmen and artisans. The population had shrunk, with only 56 ratepayers noted in the 1664 Hearth Tax return.[1] Trades were dwindling, there were visits from the plague and the stringent years of the Commonwealth had taken their toll. However, by the beginning of the 18th century there was greater stability; there were no invasions by foreigners, no tyrants on the throne, the plague appeared to have been eliminated, there were no political upheavals, and Usk was settling down as a quiet market town.

Three important factors were to affect Wales and Monmouthshire during the 18th century: the period of calm after the upheavals of the Civil War and the Commonwealth in the previous century; the stagnation of the Established Anglican Church in Wales and the resulting rise of Nonconformism, in particular the Methodist church; and the fast-developing Industrial Revolution.

For centuries Wales had been dominated by its princes, Norman and English kings and nobles, and the Church, but 18th-century Wales was dominated by the gentry. Parliamentary elections were often uncontested because the electorate were largely dependent upon the gentry for leases, tenancies, or custom as tradesmen, and were voting out of a sense of loyalty to their employers. It is also possible that voters with less than benevolent employers were considering their positions when they voted. Elections were lengthened to every seven years in 1716 and

seats stayed in the hands of a few landowners and landed gentry for long periods.

In Monmouthshire, politics were dominated by the Duke of Beaufort, whose seat was at Badminton in Gloucestershire; and by the Morgans of Tredegar. In Usk the only parliamentary voters in the borough were the burgesses who were nominated by the lord of the borough and this practice continued until the Reform Act of 1832. In the 1715 Election the candidates were William Bray, related by marriage to Sir Edward Morgan of Llantarnam, and the Hon. Andrews Windsor, youngest son of the 1st Earl of Plymouth. William Bray was elected but died in 1720 and Andrews Windsor became the Member. Some of the voters were described as 'of Badminton' and were obviously in the duke's employ, having been granted burgess status as a qualification for a vote for the duke's candidate.

In the Poll of Burgesses of Monmouth, Newport and Usk at the Election on 12 March 1715[2] there appear the names of some of the influential gentry and professional men of Usk who made up the voting population in 1715. Thomas Jones of the Priory was sheriff (the Jones family had married into the family of Roger Williams of Llangybi in the 16th century); James Davies was portreeve; Edward Rumsey (whose family had owned much property in Usk since the 16th century, in particular Ynys Hafod in New Market Street), and John Williams of The Rhadyr (whose ancestors were the Norman Benet/Williams of

Llanbadoc), were among the burgesses entitled to vote. Very democratically some men with a trade or occupation were included: a tiler, a tailor, a miner, a smith, a shoemaker and a harper.

The gentry and well to do tradesmen of Usk in the latter half of the 18th century were largely represented by the old families of the town and locality. Thomas Prothero, clerk of the peace for Monmouthshire and a well known attorney, was the son of Edward Prytherch or Prothero, a currier (leather dresser), and lived at Ty Brith in Priory Street. The Rumsey family were well represented. Richard Jones the Usk maltster of the Henrhiw (Llanbadoc) family, portreeve from 1759-64 and again in 1774, lived in New Market Street in the house next to what is now the Usk Rural Life Museum. Reginald Williams came from the Radyr (and Cilfeigan) family in Llanbadoc. Knowles Kinsey who died in 1758 was the father of Robert Kinsey the 1775 portreeve who lived in Middle Street for many years.[3] The family of Sheppard (of various spellings) dated back to 1630 in the town and became attorneys, clergymen and inn keepers. Philip Powell, a burgess in 1783, was probably a descendant of the old family of The Ton in Llangybi.

Others of the gentry were relative newcomers: Richard Jones of Dingestow came to Usk to retire after losing the estate and fortune which had been in his family since the 17th century; he built Castle Vale (Porthycarne Street) *c*.1750. David Lewis moved from Llanbadoc into Usk leaving the land and the advowson of Llanbadoc to his daughter, Mary. There were others who styled themselves gentlemen, but those listed above are the ones who cared about their town and its people, and were willing to do public service.

The population was mostly Welsh and bilingual, although English people were gradually coming over the border from England and across the estuary from Somerset. The town at this time must have been almost self-supporting, for every house had a garden and piece of land on which to grow fruit and vegetables and even keep a cow or a few sheep. Employment of some description was there for almost everyone who worked well and behaved themselves, the employers consisting of the gentry of the town and the wealthier tradesmen.

The town and its houses must have been shabby and some even derelict by the beginning of the 18th century, and this gave much incentive to those who wanted to rebuild their homes. This coincided with the English version of renaissance architecture known as 'Georgian'. Eminent architects such as Robert Adam, Robert Wood, William Kent and John Nash (1752-1835) were commissioned to build grand edifices in England. John Nash settled in Carmarthen and designed Carmarthen, Cardigan and Hereford gaols and a market house in Abergavenny (now gone) and the entrance to Clytha Park in 1790; he was known throughout Wales. However, despite Nash and the comparatively nearby fashionable Georgian towns of Cheltenham, Bristol and Bath, there is little Georgian architecture in Monmouthshire. Whilst there are some fine houses in Monmouth, Chepstow and further afield in Brecon, sadly Usk has nothing comparable with them.

Even so the Georgian style was copied in Usk. Pattern books of houses were available by the mid-18th century which could be used by talented master masons and craftsmen. Georgian houses had a central doorway with a room on either side and bedroom windows above to

Fig. 13.1 Georgian house in New Market Street

Fig. 13.2 Row of Georgian houses in Four Ash Street

match; double hung sash windows divided into smaller panes were another important feature of the Georgian house. There are a number of houses in Usk which have been identified by CADW as Georgian or with Georgian frontages. New Market Street, which was a smart area in the 18th century, has the greatest number of such houses, including numbers 7, 9, 10, 29, 31 and 33. In Priory Street, which leads into Twyn Square, numbers 10, 12 and 14 have Georgian façades with no. 10 having important earlier fabric. In Maryport Street, no. 30 is listed as a town centre cottage retaining historic fabric probably of the late 16th and 18th centuries. Next door, no. 32 is an 18th-century town house with classical detail and probably earlier origins. Number 7 Porthycarne Street, once a farmhouse, is another Georgian town house. A pair of cottages at 27 and 29 Four Ash Street have later Georgian features. Opposite the ancient Great House and alongside the Kings Head Hotel in Old Market Street, no. 10 is another listed Georgian town house.[4] The above may explain the large number of men in the building trade in Usk by the middle of the late 18th century, when there were at least five families of masons in the town. Whole families

worked in the building trade in the 18th century as tilers, carpenters, glaziers and nailers.

Much of the stone used for Usk houses came from the Llanbadoc cliffs, but it was porous and had to be plastered and whitewashed. The roofs of the houses were almost certainly covered with stone tiles, for the Usk valley is not an area noted for straw and thatching as is its neighbour the Vale of Glamorgan, and slates were not brought down from north Wales until the early 19th century. The stone used would have been the Old Red Sandstone widely available to the north, south and east of Usk.[5] However, ceramic tiles were being produced at the Gwehelog kilns at this period, so there may have been a mixture of roofing materials used.

One of the most important events for Usk in the 18th century was the building of the New Market House/Town Hall. Henry, Earl of Pembroke had donated the site of New Market House in New Market Street in 1598 and it had been left to the portreeve, burgesses and inhabitants to build and maintain it. But the ravages of wind, weather, and neglect had taken their toll and by the mid 18th century the Market Hall was in a poor condition. The Earls of Pembroke had died out by 1683 and the estates descended through marriage to Viscount Windsor in 1699. His son, Herbert, sold the lordship and castle to Valentine Morris of Piercefield (the Valentine Morris who was responsible for the turnpikes in Monmouthshire), but needing money he sold to Lord Clive of India, who sold it on to Henry 5th Duke of Beaufort in 1772.

Clive clearly gave little time to his Usk estates for in 1771 he was indicted for not repairing Usk Market House and Town Hall, and so the Duke of Beaufort, having bought the lordship of Usk, had to set about repairing the old building. In the event he decided to have another market house erected and during 1774-77 plans, estimates and contracts were drawn up with local builders and craftsmen.[6] The duke was to find 30 tons of rough standing timber which was felled in Great Wood and Coed Cae Wood, for 'There would be deal frame partitions at each side of the Jury Room and the roof thereof oak and a turret for a clock, the top thereof to be covered with lead ... The ground

Fig. 13.3 The Town Hall in 2007, showing filled in arches to the 18th-century Market Hall and the round windows of the extra storey built in 1859 to provide more room for the courts

floor to have oak double doors.' No doubt most of the stone used came from the old building. The project gave much scope to tradesmen in Usk with, for example, the yard at the Market Hall needing pitching (cobbling) at 5 pence per yard. A chandelier was also required and a 10 light branch chandelier with a blue painted chain was sent by the Caerleon boat to be delivered to 'Mr Davies Attorney Usk' for the Town Hall.

The following years saw various maintenance work being undertaken, including whitewashing every few years. Magistrates used the upstairs floor for holding the Sessions and the borough of Usk for meetings. The ground floor was used as the Market House, for which rent was paid to the lord of the manor.[7]

The little market towns of Wales survived for centuries because the lives of country and town were interdependent. The wives of poor country husbandmen arrived in town on market day perched between the packs of their horses, often knitting stockings as they jogged along. These stockings were sold at markets and fairs. Good knitters (men too), could produce a stocking a day, and in 1794 a pair fetched 8d at Brecon Market.[8] The best produce was always brought to the market to raise money for the rent of their often mean dwellings, but country people with skills could also bring their carvings, love spoons, carpentry and needlework to sell for extra cash.

Not all town dwellers enjoyed fairs and markets. Indeed the principal traders and inhabitants of Abergavenny were positively unwelcoming. In a petition to Sir William Morgan in Tredegar in 1730, they requested his support for a Bill for Suppressing Hawkers and Pedlars the pest of the Nation.[9] However the only complaints registered by the inhabitants of Usk seem to have been about brawls and assaults on market day. The markets and fairs had changed little over the centuries, certainly in the manner of goods sold: sheep, cattle, and horses were sold in the Twyn and nearby streets; other goods included wool, corn and hides, pottery (see chapter X), ironware, fabrics, trimmings and ribbons, all manner of domestic articles, feathers for beds, tobacco, honey, rabbits, goose eggs, butter and cheese — brought in on market days by cart or packhorse along the country roads.

These roads in the 18th century were nightmares to travel after rain or in winter. They were narrow, and overtaking a slow cart or string of pack horses meant clambering into a muddy ditch to get past. The roads were often flooded, or had enormous potholes into which horses stumbled, tipping over their loads and their passengers. Even the streets of small towns like Usk, some of which had a hardcore base, a legacy from the Roman occupation, had only a cobbled pathway each side with ditches for surface water, and were muddy or dusty depending on the season.

But the roads linking the markets and post towns were to undergo a dramatic change. A great (although gradual) improvement came with the introduction of turnpike roads. Turnpikes were introduced early into Monmouthshire largely through the efforts of Valentine Morris of Piercefield[10] (and for a short time the owner of Usk Castle). He promoted the Monmouth Turnpike Act of 1755, and in 1758 an Act for Repairing the Road from the village of Magor to the footbridge of the town of Chepstow, which created seven turnpike areas in Monmouthshire and Gloucestershire. Usk had its own district which covered the area from Clytha to Trostrey through Usk; through the parish of Gwernesney to the Four Ashes towards Monmouth; from Cross Lane at Llantrissant; through Usk via Llanbadoc and Llangybi to Court Bleddyn; and from Monks Wood House Gate through Usk to the high road leading through Raglan from Chepstow to Abergavenny.

Morris was also on the Turnpike Trust for Usk, which had the power to widen roads and take in more land near an existing road. In the early days the trustees of the Usk Turnpike met in private houses or in the Town Hall.[11] Although streets in a town were still in the care of the surveyors of highways appointed by the Church Vestry, the Turnpike Trusts were allowed to ask parishes for six days' labour from each (able) parishioner. The turnpike made sure that a toll was extracted from the traveller before the gate was opened,

thus ensuring a revenue for the maintaining of the roads. Roads gradually improved and for 18th-century traders and travellers it must have been like having motorways today.

The stone bridge over the Usk was built at this time too, but it was done as a result of private enterprise rather than by a Trust. By 1750 the old wooden bridge crossing to Llanbadoc was in a ruinous state. Heavy carts, coals, stones, animals and the seasonal floods had done their worst and the bridge, although many times repaired in the past, was becoming dangerous. A long and complaining petition was sent to Sir Charles Hanbury Williams from the inhabitants of the town and borough:

> A Survey of the state and condition of the bridge was to be made by some experienced workmen who reported it was impracticable and beyond skill to keep, support and amend the same, and that a new bridge must be built. Your petitioners were advised to have a stone Bridge built … but were quite unable to do so without the kind assistance of some generous, well dispo'sd and benevolent persons …

The estimated cost of the bridge was £980 and contributions were received from the Duke of Beaufort, Lord Windsor, Capel Hanbury, Sir Charles Hanbury Williams and others. The bridge was built by William Edwards, a well known south Wales bridge builder who built the famous bridge over the Taff at Pontypridd, three bridges over the River Towy, and bridges at Bettws, Llandovery and Aberafon.

These improved roads and bridges in Monmouthshire obviously speeded up contacts between towns, and by the late 18th century many Welsh towns had post offices. From the middle of the 17th century Usk had been on the mail road from Monmouth to Newport, Cardiff and west Wales, but when the mail coach started running from the New Passage across the Bristol Channel near Chepstow in 1787, Usk was taken off the mail road and had its letters brought from Caerwent via Raglan, coming to Usk via St Arvans, Devauden and the Star at Llanfihangel Torymynydd.[12]

The growing population of Usk and the increasingly polluted drinking water put the Usk maltsters into a good line of business. For centuries ale had been brewed in the home by alewives, and in the inns if their husbands were inn keepers; unless one was lucky and lived near a pure spring or well, drinking water was a hazard. By the 18th century there was much demand for quality ale and so the maltsters with their larger premises gradually took over from the medieval alewives. There were five malt-sters in Usk: one in Bridge Street, now probably part of the back buildings of the Spar; another in Porthycarne Street near Castle Vale; a third along the street leading to the Priory and next door to no. 10 Priory Street; the fourth was tucked away in Baron Street, now no. 11, on the left-hand side behind the houses of Old Market Street; and the fifth and most important was in New Market Street, in premises which today house the Usk Rural Life Museum.

Another drink much favoured in Wales was cider. It was originally brought to Britain by the Norman de Clares, whose apples from their Gloucestershire estates were sent to Usk and 'Llantrissent' during the reigns of Edward I and Edward II. Monmouthshire and the Usk valley made the best cider in Wales. Four cider mills have been noted in Usk over the centuries; in 1771 the mill was in Porthycarne Street at Castle Vale.

The good ale and cider produced pleased not only local inhabitants but also those who travelled through Usk, for the improved turnpike roads greatly increased the flow of people through the town. The town had four inns (as opposed to the more numerous alehouses) from earliest times. The first to offer hospitality to travellers as they

Fig. 13.4 The Cross Keys, the first inn to greet travellers as they cross Usk Bridge

came over Usk Bridge was the Cross Keys, near the site of the medieval hospital, first recorded in 1322.[13] The King's Head in Old Market Street was a well known coaching inn as was the Nag's Head in Twyn Square, which from its position in the main square and market place must have had centuries of bustle and trading. It is remarkable for being the only inn in Usk which also has a Welsh name — Pen Cefyl is the literal translation of the Nag's Head. But the Three Salmons was the most famous of the coaching inns in the town in the 18th century. Stage coaches called regularly on their way to Abergavenny, Brecon, Bristol and Chepstow; it was a big inn and could cater for all kinds of events. In 1793 it was even hired by the legal profession for the spacious room it offered in which to interrogate those making depositions in the High Court of Chancery.[14]

Perhaps the downside of the good supply of alcohol was the increase in crime more than likely to have been caused by over-indulgence in strong ale. There were numerous assaults recorded in the Quarter Sessions Process Books. Many of these were directed at the petty constables who had a thankless task in bringing the offenders to the justices. Other drink-related crime centred on the alehouse keepers themselves, who sometimes sold ale without a licence or kept a disorderly house. Felons were sent to the Assizes, but there was yet another corrective for petty offenders — including those who gave false measures and weights, created nuisances, left dunghills outside houses or wagons and carts in Bridge Street, or who built a pigsty in the street. This was via the Court Leet which met every month under the auspices of the portreeve, who could commit such offenders to the House of Correction. But not all crime could be blamed on alcohol.

As a market town Usk benefited from the trade generated by local inhabitants and those coming in on market and fair days. The markets were held on Mondays and Fridays in 1742,[15] whilst fairs were held on 1 May, St Luke's Day (18 October), and the Monday after Holy Trinity.[16]

Usk had a thriving leather trade with a tanyard near the back of the churchyard and the ancient upper mill which had a good supply of water from springs above the castle and leats from the River Olway. There were at least five tanners during the 18th century and they were all men of property and standing in the community. Leather was especially important before the days of domestic metal goods, when everything was made from leather and wood. The rough roads before 1750 soon reduced leather shoes to a state of disrepair in spite of hob nails; there were at least 38 corvisors (cobblers) in Usk in the years between 1742 and 1792.

Although itinerant tailors travelled from farm to farm in remote areas of Wales, Usk men and those from nearby parishes came into town for their clothes. As a result there was a good number of tailors in Usk in the 18th century, for making men's coats, waistcoats and breeches needed more skill than housewives generally possessed. Often the poor would wear clothes handed down from their employers, but women's clothes were cheaper and easier to make than men's and a length of cloth could easily be bought at a fair or market, or from a pedlar if there were no spinning or weaving facilities at home.

Charles Heath, the Monmouth printer, wrote about the town at the end of the 18th century and described the farmers and their wives on market day:

> they wore a drab cloth coast, velveteen waistcoat, corduroy breeches, blue woollen stockings and a silk handkerchief for a neck cloth. Their wives wore a black fur hat, a stuff or cotton gown, a mob cap, silk handkerchief, check or woollen apron and a blue cloth coat.

Later, the Usk printer J.H. Clark included in the *Usk Gleaner* for 1878 an article which described the dress of the people of Newport in 1780: 'The town was occupied by natives of the Principality or their families of Welsh extraction — customs, dress, habits essentially Welsh. Grey flannel entered largely into the clothing for men. The attire was homely.' It is very probable that this was the way Usk people dressed too.

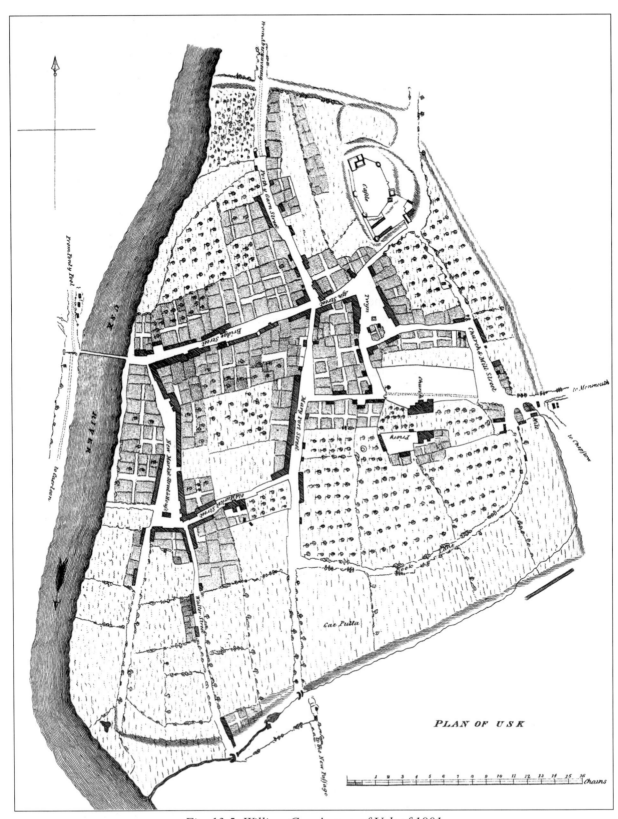

Fig. 13.5 William Coxe's map of Usk of 1801

Men appeared in black beaver three-cornered hats perched on top of their wigs, but wearers of very tall wigs usually had to carry their hats! Three-cornered hats were worn throughout the 18th century, cocked into different shapes. There was a peruke (wig) maker in Usk in 1762 called John Wiggington, but the large periwigs which had been worn since the restoration of Charles II in 1660 went out of fashion by 1760,[17] and Wigginton's son then described himself as a hairdresser.

An indispensable tradesman was the chandler; he had the means and skill to produce the candles which for many were the only source of illumination during the hours of darkness. Poor people made their own rushlights, dipping rushes into tallow (bacon or mutton fat skimmed from the cooking pot). Candles were made in the same way, and had been for centuries, but only the rich could afford wax candles. By the late 18th century lighting became easier with the use of whale oil from the east coast of America which did not cause smoke and smell, and by the end of the century the use of oil lamps was increasing.

Usk had professional fishermen who fished from coracles — shallow, flat-bottomed boats about 6 feet long and 4 feet wide. Today coracles can only be found on the Teifi and the Severn at Shrewsbury.

By the 18th century townspeople were demanding more sophisticated remedies for their ailments than the old cottage potions and poultices. There were no doctors or surgeons recorded as such in the town in the 18th century, but apothecaries were recognised as pharmaceutical practitioners.

Wales had no newspapers in the 18th century, but papers were brought in from over the border and the *Gloucester Journal* and *Bristol Journal* were the ones preferred in Monmouthshire. Naturally many of the gentry and well to do tradesmen who had benefited from an education could read, but there were many who remained illiterate and could only make a mark for their name. There had been a grammar school in Usk since Roger Edwards had endowed it in 1621,[18] which had a grammar master (usually a cler-

gyman) who was able to teach classics to bright boys. But the 18th-century parents who were skilled merchants and tradesmen wanted their boys to learn 'useful' things, like writing and mathematics, so a writing master was appointed in 1769 to teach 55 boys.

Eighteenth-century Wales was much influenced by the religious zeal of a group of young preachers and teachers — young men who were fired with a consciousness of piety and strict morality. Much inspired by Howel Harris, a preacher of Trefecca in south Wales, these men played an important part in the emergence of a non-conformist Wales. Methodism was greatest in south Wales; in the north the Established (Anglican) church remained strong and resisted Methodism. In south Wales the dioceses of Llandaff and St Davids were impoverished and their clergy too poor to carry out their duties. Church buildings were crumbling, damp and neglected; in the Priory Church of St Mary the nave and the north aisle appear to have been closed in by a masonry screen, blocking the western arch of the tower. The crossing under the tower remained open, and at one time was said to have formed a shelter for cattle.[19] The Roman Catholic church too was at its lowest ebb in Wales since the Reformation, though it recovered somewhat at the end of the century when public feeling became more tolerant.

The Methodists sought to evangelise and save souls and, often without a church or chapel to house the clergy, gave spirited open air sermons to the hundreds who came to listen. John Wesley was one of these and there are records of his preaching at Chepstow, Devauden, Monmouth, Newport, Pontypool and Usk.

On 17 October 1739 about noon I came to Usk, where I preached to a small company of poor people on those words 'The son of man is come to save that which is lost.' One grey haired man wept and trembled exceedingly and another who was there … are gone quite distracted.[20]

Undoubtedly the biggest influence on Monmouthshire in the 18th century was the quickening of the Industrial Revolution. But Usk was left out of the industrial age because there were no coal measures nor iron deposits in the Usk Valley.[21] In 1761 John Bedford started a forge at Trostrey on Valentine Morris's estate, probably on the site of an old corn mill with good water power. But it was short lived and closed down in 1820.[22]

However Usk was not left completely out in the cold, for in 1763 the Allgoods brought the japanning trade to Usk from Pontypool. Japanning was a form of varnishing and ornamentation which could be applied to metal or wooden surfaces. The original oriental Japanwork dates back at least to the 12th century BC and came originally from the east, mainly China, India and Japan. It was produced by the use of natural lacquers which would take a very high polish. By the 16th century, the Japanese had developed the art to perfection and the best work came to be associated with Japan, hence the term 'Japanning'. The method used in Pontypool was perfected in the mid 18th century by the Allgood family, using smooth, very thin black iron sheets covered with a film of tin and then treated by varnishing with oxidised linseed oil and hot stoving.[23]

The Usk japan works started when the founder of the business died, resulting in a squabble within the Allgood family over the secret of the 18th-century japanning method in Pontypool. Work started in 1763 when one branch of the family came to a little factory in New Market Street next to the George inn. There was intense rivalry between the two branches of the Allgoods, the one at Pontypool and the one at Usk, some of their quarrels spilling out into the local newspapers, the *Gloucester Journal* and the *Bristol Journal*.

The Usk japan works were to continue well into the next century and the wares were bought by the well to do who wanted what was then a very desirable acquisition. The 20 or so japanners and the japan works were the nearest Usk ever got to the Industrial Revolution.

Life in 18th century Usk would have been neither exciting nor particularly comfortable. There was no sewerage (families had cess pits in their gardens); water was not tested or purified; babies and toddlers died of gastroenteritis; tuberculosis was still rife; houses were lit by candles and rush lights; the rivers flooded homes in winter; manual and agricultural work was still the order of the day; and women, even in the wealthier groups, were still tied to the home and supporting their husband's business or trade.

By the end of the century Monmouth had become the county town, Abergavenny was still important, Chepstow was expanding and Newport was still small. Usk had lost all its medieval importance and settled into a quiet agricultural market town. The 18th-century traveller and historian Archdeacon William Coxe wrote in 1801: 'Usk has 166 houses, about 700 inhabitants, a manufactory of japan, and no commerce.'

CHAPTER XIV

The Garden at Usk Castle
by Rosemary Humphreys

To write about the garden at Usk Castle is to write about the man who made it. Rudge Humphreys was born at The Castle House (the castle's gatehouse) in 1911. His father, John, had moved to Usk from Leicestershire as agent for the Perry-Herrick estate, based at Penhow Castle. He initially rented Castle House when he married Kitty Eddowes in 1908, and then bought it in 1921 from Albert Addams-Williams. (At that time the castle ruins were owned separately.)

Watercolour sketches by Kitty and early photos show Rudge in the garden, invariably with a watering can or hoe, so it is hardly surprising to find that the first entry in his garden diary records: 'Oct 1926. Made my Herb Garden'. He was 15 at the time and studying horticulture at Rhadyr College, Usk. Though not his favourite subject, this was, he later said, the only exam he ever passed.

His diary contains detailed lists of all the plants he bought, the suppliers, and where they were planted. The number of plants ordered is astonishing: old and unusual varieties of roses, cob nuts, cherries, peaches, vines, herbs, fruit bushes and trees, flowering shrubs and forest trees for the paddocks. In 1928 he ordered from Bowell and Skarrat of Cheltenham 26 types of herbs for £1 8s with which to further stock the new herb garden, and he later added the sweet briars Med Merrillies, Annie of Gernstein, Amy Robsart, Brenda and Mac Iron. In 1929 Clibrans of Altringham supplied black, red and white currants and some special berries: King Acre

Berry, Veitchberry, Japanese Wineberry and Laxtonberry. Alas, none of these have survived to the present time. The pomegranate tree and a banana tree from Warwick Castle (to be over-wintered at The Mayfield) only appear once so presumably died within the year, although the date palm, bought for 3s 6d from Treseder and Co in 1934 thrived, and is still with us.

Fig. 14.1 R.H.J. Humphreys as a boy (watercolour)

Fig. 14.2 Usk Castle in the 1920s. On the left is the north tower, in the centre the chamber block, and on the right the domestic block

The front garden in the 1920s was simply a lawn at the south front of the gatehouse, with an immaculate vegetable garden below the barn and a lawn to the north of the house. At the west end of the lawn was a vegetable plot, with a long row of glass for tomatoes on the former site of a second large barn, shown in a 19th-century watercolour by Michael Angelo Rooker. Today it is the site of the herbaceous border. There were remnants of a fine fern collection, part of which still exists, and a glass fernery that was replaced by the Oak room built in 1923 to house panelling from the Old Mansion, Shrewsbury, when it was demolished. To the east of the castle was a large potato patch which Rudge turned into a tree nursery and vegetable garden. It was only given up and turned into paddock in the 1970s.

Over the next few years, Rudge put in place ideas probably gleaned from other Monmouthshire gardens, such as those designed by Avray Tipping and Gertrude Jekyll. The herb garden is a separate 'room', to be discovered by the curious. A central path leads past a mulberry, with the broken cauldron for distilling alcohol from Still House Farm (smashed by Customs) to the well head under the medlar tree. The well is in fact a cistern ingeniously fed from the barn roof by

a pipe under the lawn which in turn supplies a dipping well by the barn greenhouse.

By 1932 the garden must have been much as it is today in plan, as Rudge was turning his attention to trees. From 1929 until 1931 he was a student at the Royal Agricultural College, Cirencester, where he was inspired by several people, including Jimmy James, an authority on forestry who founded a trust for the Royal Forestry Society, and later Richard St Barbe Baker. St Barbe became a lifelong friend and it was at his suggestion that Rudge went, after Cirencester, to Hargham Hall, Sir Hugh Beaver's estate in Norfolk, to work as a student and learn about large scale forestry.

St Barbe was born in 1889 and founded the 'Men of the Trees' society in 1924. It is now the International Tree Foundation. He foresaw the devastation of the world climate that would ensue if the deforestation that he had witnessed in the African Sahara and in America were to continue. He started the campaign to save the giant Californian redwoods (*sequoia sempeviens*) from logging in the 1930s. His work in conservation helped lead to the establishment of the American National Parks and his many books earned him a worldwide reputation. St Barbe's far-sighted work made him an important forerunner of the 'Eco' movement of the 21st century. Rudge's son, Henry, remembers him as a charismatic figure leading tree-dances on the lawn at Castle House, whilst his conversations were spellbinding even to the next generation. He gave Rudge a grove of redwoods for the Castle Chase woods as a wedding present.

So tree planting became a passion, filling the winter months. '12th January 1932, plant 150 Scots Firs and 8 rows of Hazel to make a real windbreak in the paddock. 7s 6d from Clibrans', the first of many such orders, was proudly annotated in the diary with red stars for a job well done. This day was soon followed by planting four hundred larch in the paddock, and a lifetime of tree-planting, both at home and for friends, was launched. There is hardly a scenic group of trees on a hilltop in the county that was not planted by Rudge. He established a tree nursery with 700 larch from Hargham and for the paths around Castle House he used river cobbles hauled up in a vast, heavy wooden barrow.

The garden continued to gain treasures. 'September 2nd 1932, get an old cider mill from The Hill Farm, Trostrey, and put it up on the rockery'. A cider-press stone and an old whisky still from Still Farm joined it, with more planting, this time green and golden yews for the terraces below the house: 'Nov. 9th, plant for my 21st birthday, present from Mother. 22 all told as one sent for luck.'

Rudge had boundless enthusiasm and energy. The vineyard was started in 1931 with 13 vines on poles (12 stars in the diary), a rose garden with flagstone path, stone steps down to the lawn from the herb garden, and a herb house on the terrace above the herb garden with 'red tiles from Powel's for the roof ... windows from the church, oak door made by Windows [Mr. Windows, a carpenter], so it looks really old already'. This gem, disappointingly, did not survive, being deemed too

Fig. 14.3 Usk Castle in the 1920s. On the left is the Keep with the gateway to the inner ward on its right, with the North Tower on the right. The main lawn is shown before the magnolias and yew hedges were planted. In the right foreground is the stable

conspicuous by general consensus. Today, the 'Temple of Peace' stands in its place, named after the two shellcases supporting the roof truss.

A new challenge came in 1933: 'May 20th. Mother buys Usk Castle for £525 in my name'. The bill included a flag and a donkey. The ruins of Usk Castle, lately in the ownership of D.E. Thorn, had overlooked the family home in the gatehouse since the Humphreys had lived there and had now been offered for sale. John Humphreys had recognised the difficulty of owning such a ruin and always refused to purchase it. However, there had been talk of unsuitable developments — a private house to be built for a rich American, a hostel for hikers. Finally Nan (Mrs Poiser), who had looked after the family and continued to live with them until after the war, said 'Master Rudge should have his castle' and paid for it out of her savings. She was promptly reimbursed and it was a matter of some pride that Kitty Humphreys could say that she had covered the cost in just a few years with sixpences from the entry tolls and the sale of lavender sticks, made as she chatted to visitors.

Rudge was eager to start on his next project. 'The dear old place was in a very bad state of neglect. We spent many weeks getting things cleared up.' Ownership of the castle was soon celebrated:

> May 21st, Empire Day. Our first chance to fly the flag on the castle. I break it at the top of the mast at 8am. The Main Gates. These were the first things we started to mend ('We' consist of myself and Windows). Put iron plates and handles on them. Give three coats of paint (red) and pick the iron studs out in black. They look like lasting for years now. Also paint west door and put hammocks up under trees in courtyard.

The castle gates were not replaced until Rudge died in 1985, the new ones being made by Hugo Egleston and dedicated in Rudge's memory.

The castle also experienced its first cannon firing for a very long time. 'Got Savery of the Nag's Head to lend me an old signalling gun taken off a Russian boat in the Crimea, to fire in the castle for the king's birthday. Windows and I put four egg cups full of powder and rammed well with paper. Fired three good shots.' Things didn't always go to plan and after one misfire both Rudge and Windows found themselves tattooed on the cheek for life by the black powder smuts. However, cannon salutes have become something of a tradition since then.

There followed years of excavations, often 'navvy parties' of up to 30 friends. Spoil was carried out of the Inner Ward on a truck made by Windows and named 'The Flying de Clare' in honour of the castle's original builder, which ran on iron rails from the Albion Works in Cardiff. Over a hundred loads were taken in a donkey cart to make the terraces in the lower vegetable garden. The excavation in the Garrison Tower revealed another floor, well below ground level, and the beautifully preserved stonework of its doorway. The well, a potential treasure trove for historians and archaeologists, has never been found, but the chapel was: 'May 1935. Dug out between hall and W. Tower. Find chapel, at all events what H.M. Office of Works says is a chapel ... to date only remains of altar and altar step, very much damaged.' And again: 'April 1936. Put up altar rails in the chapel, also have a slab of Forest stone cut for altar top ... this is in readiness for St George's Day and as a memorial to father.' The service on 23 April was taken by Revd W.M. Davies and attended by some 30 people, as reported in the newspapers. The tradition continues to this day, with the cross of St George flown on the North Tower.

The Laburnum Avenue dates from 1935, planted either side of the path leading up to Castle Parade, in line with Church Street and St Mary's Church. 'The doorway on to the street finished. It has taken 3 weeks and 20 tons of stone from Llanover House, which is being pulled down. Cost £5 for 20 ton.' Llanover House, built by Lady Llanover, champion of the revival of Welsh literature and music, had lasted hardly one generation, being built of unweathered sandstone which was impractically porous. The Llanover stone was also used for a new garage and tack room in the stable yard. Seeing the fine new red doors and Gothic arches, the late Lord Raglan is said to have asked 'Rudge, why have you built a fire station?'

The construction of the Laburnum Avenue was followed by the building of St George's Gate in 1936, which visitors to the castle walk through today, with the ancient-looking wisteria trailing over it and clambering high up into the nearby spruce.

The lawn between the house and castle was extended, with a path of cobbles and flagstones laid in 1936. The finishing touch was the purchase of an Atco 17 inch motor mower which was only retired 50 years later, still in good working order. It took four months to excavate the 6-feet deep 28 by 10 feet pool at the end of the lawn, which was walled using the old bricks from a tomato house and cost £23 10s. The shallow curved centre portion is now ideal for growing water lilies. The whole project was much helped by the arrival of an itinerant Irishman, Flanagan, who had been found sleeping in the wash house and given a job. The iron bar used for breaking the rock needed sharpening daily. Dubbed 'Queen Anne's Pool', it was ready for 'May 29th, Oak Apple Day. Have my first dip, well worth all the trouble of digging it out.' He marked this day with three ticks. Until the Second World War, Oak Apple Day was a national holiday which commemorated the restoration of the monarchy under Charles II. Rudge always delighted in celebrating the day with a party in the Oak Room, which was decorated with large sprays of oak leaves. In 1937 the pool was stocked with goldfish and Golden Orfe.

In honour of the coronation of George VI, Rudge started a pinetum to the south-east of the house in November 1937. Many of these trees tower over the gardens today, a spectacular variety not only of pines such as Silver Fir, Monkey Puzzle, cedars Atlantica and Deodar, Japanese

Fig. 14.4 Excavation Usk-style of the chapel in the 1930s

Cedar, Redwood and Wellingtonia, but also the large Catalpa, Tulip tree and Magnolias. It makes a good example of 'Dinosaur-era' trees to show the next generations. The orchard was planted in the paddock next to the road early the next year with two dozen cider apples, the varieties being Frederick, Kingston Black and Sweet Alfred.

Events in the outside world were almost portended when, on 19 February 1938 'Usk Town Council send large German gun up after some divided opinion. They have fixed it in the top Paddock on concrete blocks and have given it a coat of paint.' Rudge was still working on the castle and ordering more shrubs to plant right up to the start of the Second World War. He had enlisted in the Territorial Army and found that being posted to different parts of the country was a good opportunity to source more trees: the Bog Cypress and Tulip Tree come from Dartington Hall and stone ornaments for the terraces from Glamorgan. In a letter to his mother in October 1941, Rudge sent a list of 40 shrubs, along with cuttings grown in the mess garden and wild rhododendrons fom the foothills of the Mountains of Mourne in Ireland to be dug in and overwintered so that he could plant them when he got home. He was slightly apologetic about the extra work.

One army exercise was held on Dartmoor and involved motorbikes. Rudge was never one to enjoy working with machines and his bike soon disappeared into a bog, whereupon he was offered the choice of court-martial or going with the mule companies to the North-West Frontier of India. After a final leave spent at Portmeirion with his brother and mother, Rudge embarked on the *SS Ormonde* for Bombay on 8 May 1942. Never one to be idle, he had found time whilst at the transit camp to dig the Mess garden and do 'a bit of gardening for a farmer near the camp'. Hating to leave Britain, believing he might never return, Rudge never forgave the dockers of Liverpool for herding them up the gangway 'as cattle to slaughter' in their haste to get off from work. Once on board, he planted mustard and cress in his boots. This story must have amused Brian Johnstone when he visited Usk and met Rudge almost 40 years later for the radio programme 'Down Your Way', as he mentioned it in his anthology years later. The seed planting continued throughout the ten week journey, to cheer him up. 'Sorry not to have land to look at, these endless wastes of sea are chill to a landsman ... mustard and cress planted Sunday ... showing green.' He then asked for beans to grow in his cabin. The head waiter thought this a great joke and produced a 'catalogue' drawing of a plant: 'Height: anything from 2 miles upwards, Bloom: sky-blue pink'. Rudge stayed in India with the 76th Mule Company on the North-West Frontier in Waziristan, where he became known as 'Mafeking' (due to his signature moustache), until the end of the war. Unsurprisingly, he left his mark on a desolate and barren country. The area he planted with trees around Wana flourished, prompting the government to write and thank him after the war. One entry in his diary in May 1945 reveals his dreams for the future. 'Read St Barbe's book *I Planted Trees* which makes me all the more sure that the rest of my life is going to be spent planting trees, God willing.'

Returning to Wales in 1945, Rudge wasted no time in getting back to work. Within a month, a thousand Scots Pines had been ordered for the tree nursery, and he was negotiating to buy the woods and land at Baldwin's Farm (now Cwm Cayo Farm) from the timber merchant Gwyn Davies. This was commemorated by a light-hearted military operation:

Orders for Flagstaff Hill Date of Attack June 6th 1946

Information Usk Castle Garrison have taken green hill half mile north of Usk

To show the flag in tribal territory

Intention To erect flagpole on same hill, to be known from now on as 'Flagstaff Hill'

Method Tractor belonging to the enemy to report at Usk castle gates by 8.30 a.m..

The following load will be transported to Flagstaff Hill:

1 Flag Pole
4 short handled pickaxes
1 coil of wire
16 larch rails
9 larch posts
5 larch rails

6 pickets for seat, date stone 1946
3 struts

This also signalled the beginning of his life's major work, the results of which are enjoyed by all who walk in the Castle Chase woods. Two hundred acres of trees were planted in orderly compartments, each one bounded by lines of hardwoods along avenues laid out on the lines of the great estates that Rudge had visited and long admired. Any good excuse to plant an avenue meant that the woods are criss-crossed by rides to celebrate births in the royal family and also his own family, and, most importantly, the coronation of Elizabeth II. This was the most splendid of all, with a jumping lane and double rows of red oaks on either side, ending at the Coronation Gate. Whilst this may seem a little whimsical, it does mean that every part of the woods can be easily identified, and adds to the special character of his planting.

Rudge was used to the austerity of the war years and found post-war life claustrophobic. He sold the car and had the telephone removed from Castle House, lived in a small, isolated cottage on the farm and devoted himself to planting trees. One wonders how Kitty had managed to maintain the garden during the war, with very little help and many shortages. There was, however, a national ethos, a 'British bulldog' spirit, that nothing should change or be given up just because of events across the Channel, and everything must be in good order for when the 'boys' came home. Kitty was best remembered for her creative contributions to the garden — watercolours that give a fascinating record of pre-war days, and china mosaic figures in niches — but her determination was remarkable. Apparently she managed to keep the lawn mown using a push mower to do a bit each day, with one day off a week, starting again the next week! There were also lodgers at Castle House who had come to Usk to work at the Glascoed munitions factory, and were looked after by Nan, who kept chickens in the paddock and black ducks on the pond.

However, things were about to change. The diary notes 'Anne for tea at Castle House' several times. This was Anne Laybourne, one of six sisters from The Firs at Malpas. Rudge had helped the family with tree planting schemes in the 1930s, and after the war planted the Graigwith Beeches. These were to be in memory of Anne's only brother, Richard Laybourne, who was killed in a flying accident in 1939, just before the war. Today this clump of beeches makes a distinctive Monmouthshire landmark above Llangybi. Before too long (but seemingly long enough for Anne to have to given a determined hint), another clump of beeches was planted above Cwm Cayo to mark the spot where they had become engaged while out hunting.

This was the beginning of the next chapter in the story of the gardens at Castle House. '1949 Feb: Candlemas day, Anne and I plant 9 yews around the sundial (in the castle) to commemorate our engagement, 5 gold ones @ 12s 6d each, 4 green ones, 7s 6d ... Sept: plant 300 narcissus, present from Phil Laybourne, around the sundial. From Ballymena, Ireland. Very good bulbs.'

With Rudge devoting his time to the planting of the woods, Anne took over much of the garden, though she also helped in the woods and would often take the children for a picnic, cooking 'bangers' over the fire on a shovel if the frying pan was left behind. Hunting filled many winter days, come rain or shine, and Anne knew the countryside as well as anyone, having looked after the Llangybi hounds and worked in the hunt kennels during the war. Many a time the Field, breathless and muddy after a fast hunt across hill and dale, would catch up with the hounds to find Anne waiting for them, having known which way the fox would run and quietly made her own way there.

Anne had a gift for growing seeds — the large airing cupboard at Castle House was always full of seed-trays — and the greenhouse was her bolt-hole from the busy household full of fairly eccentric family characters. This, luckily, came to be run by Mrs Crawshay, queen of cake-makers, who once found herself entertaining Hattie Jacques to tea!

Rudge had always longed to have a walled garden, and in 1970 began work to realise his dream: 'The Matthews brothers finish pillars

The gardens bloomed in Anne's sole care and were opened to the public under the National Garden Scheme in 1976. The display of annuals was her particular pride, and filled the garden with colour when the many flowering shrubs planted by Rudge were over. Gardening was becoming a subject of increasing interest by this time, and Anne's garden was much written about in the press. She had no secrets for her success, it was simply honest hard work and unceasing care, but she must have been quietly pleased when Monty Don wrote in 1990 that it was his favourite garden:

> Castle House garden is not like anywhere else. It is quirky, grand, very private yet always full of bustle and guests ...When changes come they are dramatic, creative and always true to the spirit of the place. ... This, I suppose is

Fig. 14.5 R.H.J. Humphreys at Cwm Cayo, September 1977

in the castle green for the Fig yard. Stone from Rose Cottage, pulled down for new road (into Usk) and iron balls from Croesonnen. They make a good set off for my new garden ... Old St Barbe Baker plants the 1st Fig Tree in the new Fig yard ... The start of my dream garden.' The finished garden had four square vegetable plots, with two gateways in the larch-lap fencing made from home-grown timber, and was surrounded by figs, vines and roses. The fencing lasted until 1989, four years after his death, and the two pillars now stand alone, sometimes used for an entrance to the marquees put up in the summer for wedding receptions.

Fig. 14.6 Rudge and Anne Humphreys in the herbaceous border

what all good gardening is about ... People, plants and buildings coming together through passion, dreams and sheer hard work to create a garden.

Anne died in 1991 and is buried in the chapel vault beside Rudge (dug out by them together in 1954), she under the vine, he under the fig, and their garden lives on for the next generation. Some things never change. The collecting of interesting artefacts continues, for instance, sometimes in cast iron, as with the remnants of a riveted pressure tank used in the steel works at Port Talbot for bitumen. One end of it is now a fountain bowl and the other a Golden Jubilee tempietto. Downpipes from the Isca Foundry of Newport (once owned by the Laybourne family) support the vines over the bandstand. Also in iron are the sea-mines guarding the drive entrance, and the two horseshoe gates welded by Henry

Humphreys using old horseshoes from the forge at Llangybi.

The legacy of gardeners like Anne and Rudge is a garden where there is something to see all year round, to delight or to surprise. Snowdrops light the path to the castle on dark winter evenings, Mahonia Charity and Witch Hazel scent the short March days, those engagement daffodils still flower in the castle in spring as the gilly flowers and Arabis decorate the crumbling walls. Magnolias often blossom to the end of April. The magnolias Rudge so loved, and often propagated, provide much of the spectacle in spring:

1960 - March 11th. The Duke of Edinburgh in Usk to visit the Borstal. Mother plants a Metasequoia on the Lower Lawn to mark the occasion. A cutting I have grown myself. Aunt Doll plants a dark magnolia and I put in two pink ones on the site of the old Cedar tree.

A St George's Gate	E Herb Garden	I Gatehouse
B The Keep	F Well	J Laburnam Avenue
C Castle Gateway	G Pool, Bridge & Bandstand	K Pinetum
D Chapel	H Vegetable Garden	L Yew Terrace

Fig. 14.7 Plan of the Garden

These still astonish us each spring with their abundance of blossom below the window of the kitchen. In May, Paul's Himalayan musk rose climbs high up the castle walls, as the *hydrangea petiolaris* hangs its heavy white flowers over the gateway, and the herbaceous border moves on from the brilliant red Beauty of Livermere poppies to the succession of colourful hardy perennials that fight each year to get to the front. Catmint, anthemis, phlox, delphinium, day lilies, and penstemon have all survived from Anne's day, amongst their more recent companions. Few annuals are sown these days, but in the herb garden, now planted to remind us which plants would have been cultivated when the castle was last lived in, the old-fashioned roses of York and Lancaster, *Rosa Alba* and *Rosa Gallica*, together with *Rosa Mundi* flower above the mass of herbs and columbine. Apple and medlar trees blossom behind the tall yew hedges which are cut in July to give hundreds of kilos of clippings for the production of an anti-cancer drug called paclitaxel.

With the end of summer the Clerodendrons scent the whole garden. Autumn colours begin with creepers festooning the walls in a deep red, the large leaves of *Vitis Coignetiae* scramble over the sumachs, and the grand old beech and acacia drop their golden leaves. Full of variety and invention as it is, the garden never fails to charm and surprise, a gentle reminder of how much we owe to Rudge and Anne, who created this lovely place.

CHAPTER XV

Usk's Secret Army: The Wartime Auxiliary Units and the Defence of Monmouthshire

by Peter Rennie and Henry Humphreys

Introduction (Henry Humphreys)

Having been born at Castle House, in my present bedroom, I became the third generation of my family to live in the gatehouse. 2008 saw the centenary of the Humphreys family living here. Being brought up with the ruins of a castle in one's front garden was a great privilege. My earliest memories are of going up the Garrison Tower at the crack of dawn with my father on royal birthdays to fly the Union Jack. The geese kept me from playing in the Inner Bailey when I was very young, but later on there were always work parties clearing ivy off the walls. Thus a happy childhood was spent conserving the ruins of an old castle, but the castle was not the only military installation that I grew up with.

At the outer end of the Castle Chase lies the very fine Iron Age Camp of Llancayo in the parish of Gwehelog. An impressive earth bank and deep ditches encircles some 5 acres. My father had planted walnut trees on the encircled land, and I remember well Lady Raglan planting a ceremonial tree in memory of her late husband, Lord Raglan, the renowned historian and author of the Fox and Raglan books.

In contrast to this, but widening the range of military installations, there is also an Auxiliary Unit operational base. It is hidden in a bank with an entrance pipe facing out towards the Usk/Raglan road, once the gateway in and out of Wales. With the completion of the Glascoed ordnance factory just before the Second World War, Usk had a network of defences in place — the many pill-boxes on the perimeter of the ordnance factory, five others guarding the railway crossing and tunnel, and the anti-aircraft observation post in the centre of the Conigaer field on Castle Farm. There were also in Llancayo Wood underground reserve stores for weapons and food of similar construction, albeit smaller, to the operational base on Little Castle land.

This base was a marvellous place for a child to go exploring. It had two well-concealed entrances leading down large pipes to a double-roomed underground chamber. I remember it contained the rusting remains of iron beds and wall shelving. The Auxiliary Units which operated such bases should not to be confused with the Home Guard, though their uniforms were similar. It may seem strange to have such a facility on the Welsh Borders, rather than in eastern or southern England, but there were fears that the Germans might occupy Ireland and invade Britain through Wales. In the event of such a German invasion the men of the Auxiliary Unit would take to their operational base subsequently to emerge behind German lines and cause havoc to the rear of the invaders.

By the time that we took over the land in 1991 the structure had all but collapsed after a massive

Fig. 15.1 Exploded view of the operational base of the Usk Auxiliary Unit

tree had been uprooted, leaving the metal roof exposed to the elements. The hole in the ground was a danger to stock, but I did not want to fill it in (with happy childhood memories of exploring), so contacted Cadw, who knew me as the owner

*Fig. 15.2 The Usk operational base
in course of restoration*

of the castle, and asked them if they were interested in protecting a more modern military structure. To my surprise and delight they agreed to help save it. With the help of a grant from them, I purchased heavy galvanised iron sheeting. I then undertook the work of restoring the base by digging down to the brick structure, cleaning out the entrance shafts with the help of my slim son Adam who, with his friends, removed the debris in real Colditz style. Peter Morgan of Morspan supplied the iron sheeting, which needed bolting together and placing over the brick ends, then topping with a plastic sheet membrane. Finally it was buried, becoming part of the field once more. It is still a damp dark place, as it would have been when first built.

I'm glad that it is now protected for another generation to enjoy. I'm always happy to show people around it. Living on the Welsh border, I've grown up with these defensive structures of different ages and am proud to have been able to protect them for posterity. But to tell the story of the operational base, there is no one better than Peter Rennie, who has lived in Usk all his life and whose brother was a member of Usk's Auxiliary Unit.

Usk's Secret Army and its base (Peter Rennie)
Britain's first line of defence had traditionally been the Royal Navy, but from the late 19th century, Britain felt less secure in the face of powerful European powers. The Victorian Rifle Volunteer movement (from which later sprang the Monmouthshire Regiment) reflected this, before the Luftwaffe finally destroyed Britain's feeling of island security. By the summer of 1940 a German invasion seemed probable. Second World War pillboxes are a reminder of those days, but less familiar and much hidden from public view were other defence structures, though their story was not revealed for many years.

My knowledge of the Auxiliary Units in Monmouthshire began when I was conscripted, on a sunny Sunday when on leave from the army, by my elder brother who was the Sergeant commanding the Usk patrol, to help work on the patrol's base. There was much shovelling of earth and rock required over the completed bunker (there were no JCBs in those days), whilst its Royal Engineer builders moved on to the next one. The Auxiliary Units remained a secret to the public at large for 20 years or more after the war. The first book on the subject, *The Last Ditch*, by David Lampe, was published in 1968. Other writers and commentators, television and radio programmes soon followed. Many of the Auxiliers, as they called themselves, nevertheless took their oaths of secrecy very seriously, and never referred to their involvement.

In about 1975, in the course of my work, I found myself in the vicinity of the Usk operational base (OB) and had no difficulty in finding its entrance tunnel. In 1985 the Imperial War Museum and other bodies launched the Defence of Britain Project to record all military and civilian structures connected with war effort still existing before they disappeared. As part of this, and for an exhibit on the Usk Civic Society stand at Usk

Fig. 15.3 The base's secondary entrance (on the right on Fig. 15.1)

Show, I photographed and measured the Usk OB, which by then had collapsed, along with another that had survived intact on the west end of the Wentwood ridge overlooking Caerleon, whose patrol leader, Alan Hollingdale, was a personal friend. My brother-in-law, a farmer, had been patrol leader of the Chepstow patrol, a secret I had been let into since I already knew about the unit at Usk. However, I did not discover the location of its OB until many years after his death, and that of his comrades. Similarly, I found the location of the OB at Llanarth via possibly the patrol's last survivor, and that indirectly.

Fig. 15.4 The base's secret trap door exit (on the left on Fig. 15.1)

In the summer of 1940 high level military thinking on the probable invasion accepted that our extended coastline could not all be defended and the invader immediately thrown back into the sea. It followed that a mobile reserve should be used to counter the threat once its actual point of arrival was known, and that plans must be laid both to prevent its advance too far inland and to counter the effects of paratroops and diversionary attacks. Within the territory that might be occupied before the mobile forces could be brought to bear, it was planned to create as big a nuisance to the invaders as possible, even though open warfare would have ceased in that area. The planned stabilization, or stop, line at which an initial German advance would be halted ran from south of Bristol towards Reading, south and east of London and northwards to Yorkshire. It was known as the Ironside or GHQ line, General Ironside, the Chief of the Imperial General Staff, then being Commander of Home Forces. Similar plans were laid in case of an invasion via the Severn Estuary or through Wales which aimed to knock out the heart of British military manufacturing capability in Birmingham and the Black Country.[1]

Certain men in British Military Intelligence had in the 1930s given thought to the possible future need for less traditional forms of warfare. Guerrilla warfare had played a large part in both the Spanish Civil War and earlier in Ireland and in north Russia during the Bolshevik Revolution. Leading plans for irregular warfare were Major Colin Gubbins and Colonel Joe Holland, both later Major Generals. By late 1938 they had been instructed to bring together these plans within Military Intelligence (Research). These involved an underground movement of armed civilians and/or military personnel disrupting invaders. The fact that the former would not have been covered by the Geneva Convention on the treatment of combatants and would have been subject, at best, to being shot out of hand when captured seems to have been ignored.

In May 1940, at about the time of the setting up of the Local Defence Volunteers (later called the Home Guard), but quite independently of it, such an underground movement was set up under the leadership of Gubbins, Holland and other like-minded officers, in what became known as the Auxiliary Units. In addition, a Home Defence Organization had been created by Section D of MI6 in 1939 or earlier, with stockpiles of military material across the country to carry out 'obstructive activities' — a euphemism for guerrilla warfare. The combatant aspects of this section were ended in July 1940, leaving the stockpiles in the hands of the new Auxiliary Units, but retaining its 'stay behind' intelligence gathering and communications roles in its Special Duties Section. This was under the overall administrative umbrella of the Auxiliary Units, though on the ground, for security reasons, they had no contact with or knowledge of each other. The birth of the Auxiliary Units was thus a very complicated affair.

Initially, these cells or units were set up in south-east England and East Anglia, the regions most liable to invasion, but they quickly spread as far as west Wales, Cornwall and up the east coast to Scotland. The name Auxiliary Units may have been deliberately vague to confuse German Intelligence into thinking that it was something like the Auxiliary Fire Service, another wartime creation. Later they came to have a second, unofficial title, the British Resistance Organization.

From the beginning, secrecy was paramount, recruits being required to swear on oath to that effect, even before they knew what they were letting themselves in for. This included secrecy between husband and wife, no doubt awkward when the husband had to find an excuse for being away from home for several nights on training. Matrimonial breakdowns are not recorded and in practice the degree of secrecy seems to have varied. The wife of one member recalled many years later that an airing cupboard made an excellent store for plastic explosives, but another, less in the know, found a hidden cache of tommy guns and thought that her husband and his friends had taken up bank robbery. There was also the embarrassment of being unable to explain to friends in the regular forces why these often young and fit men were still, as they thought, in the Home Guard.

Intelligence Officers (IOs) were appointed on roughly a county basis. They were originally 12 in number and their role was to set up cells or patrols in their allocated areas. They were detached from General Duties units for the purpose and had no connection with the Intelligence Services as such. They reconnoitred their areas, identified the location for each patrol and selected the patrol leaders, later to have the rank of Sergeant. Recruitment was obviously a secret matter, relying on the patrol leader's local knowledge and personal contacts. Intellignce Officers had their own methods of approach. That of Captain Todd, IO for Monmouthshire, Herefordshire and Worcestershire as well, was extremely individual, to judge from a post-war BBC interview with Alan Hollingdale. He had been summoned by a phone call to a pub opposite Newport station by a mysterious army officer, sworn to secrecy, and then apprised of the Secret Army and asked for his help in organising it. Possibly lord lieutenants and sheriffs, as the king's representatives in conditions of the breakdown of traditional authority, were a source of guidance independent of local authorities; IOs did not necessarily have previous knowledge of their area, though Todd did of Monmouthshire.

Recruits were drawn from people exempt from military service, being in reserved occupations, important to the war effort, or under or over the age for military service. Some were poached from the Home Guard. Most patrols were based in rural areas and drew on farmers, poachers, gamekeepers, landowners and other countryfolk. The Llanwern patrol was largely recruited from ex-Newport Rover Scouts, who had camped and hiked in Wentwood for many years and knew it intimately. The structure of the Scout movement, with its own patrol leaders, made it ideal for the job in hand, for it was essential that members of the patrols were familiar with the countryside in which they were to operate, and with each other.

The patrols were soon in being, each numbering seven or eight men, and being trained for their task. Combat training was given by Regular Army instructors and colleagues who had gone on training courses at Coleshill near Swindon,

the administrative and training Headquarters of the Auxiliary Units. They were trained in the use of weapons and explosive devices and these were soon supplied in seeming abundance. For security reasons, there was no chain of military command in the usual sense and there were only limited training exercises with neighbouring patrols, so that if one cell was captured, it could not compromise or betray others. Each leader was to be autonomous, deciding on his patrol's objectives and methods within the overall philosophy of guerrilla warfare — disruption of supply lines, destruction of the transport system, railways, bridges, military installations and headquarters, airfields and aircraft, as spelt out by the training cadre. An early project for each patrol was to identify likely targets and reconnoitre them, and thus be ready when the time came for mobilization.

Fundamental to the operational thinking was that each patrol would have an underground secret operational base or OB, stocked with arms, ammunition and explosives, survival material and food. As soon as a patrol's territory had been overrun by an invader, the members would abandon their homes and civilian occupations and go to ground in their OB, from which they would emerge to carry out their tasks and, hopefully, return. As their name implies, OBs were not intended as combat or defensive positions, though their sites were often in elevated positions from which, or from nearby, good observation of the surrounding terrain could be maintained. Proximity to potential targets such as main roads or railways and to large houses likely to be taken over as German headquarters was also desirable. Each patrol's territory seems to have been about 20 square miles in extent.

In Monmouthshire there were eight patrols, each with a Biblical codename. These were based on Usk (Esau); Chepstow (Abraham); Newport East or Llanwern (Jonah); Newport West or Bassaleg (Moses); Cwmbran (Absalom); Abergavenny (Jephtha); Llanarth (Noah) and Glascoed (Lucifer). Lucifer only had five members, three at least being employees of the Royal Ordnance Factory and one an employee of the railway serving it. Could their job have been to blow up the factory as a last resort? Wooded land or rough countryside was helpful in camouflaging or hiding OBs and if on private land this helped to deter snoopers.

The design of OBs was fairly standardised, with a concrete base, brick end walls and some, as at Usk, with a central dividing wall. Overall was a curved roof of heavy gauge corrugated iron, strong enough to carry the backfilled earth and rock. They all had hidden trap door entrances, leading either to a vertical shaft or to a long tunnel depending on the ground contours and situation. They also had a secondary tunnel as an emergency exit. One East Anglian unit, based on an RAF airfield, found, the only time they had to use it, that someone had parked a lorry on the trap door.

Unlike pillboxes, which were usually built by local contractors, the OBs were constructed, for reasons of secrecy, by Army engineers. Similar structures, of smaller dimensions, were built as reserve stores for war material. These could be close to the OB or half a mile away, as at Usk. Very few of the instructions for Auxiliary Units were committed to paper. One manual had a completely bogus cover in the form of an agricultural catalogue, to deceive the casual observer.

As for the Units' potential usefulness, Major Gubbins, who led the creation of the Auxiliary Units from the earliest days, later moving to the Special Operations Executive, summed it up thus:

> They would have justified their existence, but to what degree would have been entirely dependant on the circumstances. But my judgement is based heavily on the fact that they were costing the country nothing, either in manpower or in weapons. These patrols in their left behind missions [bases], out of all contact, entirely on their own with their caches of arms and stores would have given some account of themselves in the invasion areas, but their usefulness would have been short lived, at the longest until their

stocks were exhausted, at their shortest when they were caught and wiped out. They were designed and trained for a particular and imminent crisis — that was their specialist role.

Under the same administrative umbrella as the Auxiliary Units, but operationally separate and even more secret, was the Special Duties Section (SDS) referred to earlier. Similarly deriving from the assumption that significant parts of the country would be overrun, but that resistance would continue from unoccupied Britain, the SDS was a communications and information gathering network intended to operate in the occupied area and pass intelligence material by radio to the military command headquarters. The radio stations involved needed top secret hidden underground bases, some very similar to the Auxiliary Unit OBs, including one in the Catsash area. Short range links fed more powerful transmitters linked to the military headquarters carrying on the war.

Though not part of the Home Guard, the Auxiliary Units wore a similar uniform and were formally disbanded, along with that organization, in 1944. Alan Hollingdale became, in effect, Secretary of an Auxiliers (of Monmouthshire) Old Comrades Association which maintained an annual reunion supper at the Greyhound Inn, Llantrisant, until reduced numbers through death and age made it unviable. The Greyhound had previously been their home from home after strenuous exercises at Glen Court Mansion, just up the road. This had been dilapidated and unoccupied since 1905 and further damage from explosives and bullet holes was hardly noticeable.

A museum of the Auxiliary Units has been established at Parham in Suffolk, where a replica OB has been built, but above ground so that it is accessible to handicapped visitors. The Usk OB may be one of the few still in existence *in situ*.

Thankfully, the Secret Army was never called upon to carry out the role for which it was set up.[1]

CHAPTER XVI

Challenges to the Future of Usk

by John Barrow

(The views expressed are entirely those of the author, a former Director of Planning and Property Services in Local Government, and a Planning Inspector)

A brief history

In the conclusion of his book *Early Victorian Usk*[1] David R. Lewis discusses why Usk failed to develop over the preceding centuries as a significant centre of population, despite the town's strategic location, river crossing and large catchment area distant from other Monmouthshire towns. He suggests that poor communications were important and that the absence of a navigable waterway played a part. Problems of flooding and possibly the diversion of entrepreneurial skills and investment to the iron and coal fields also contributed. Also, unlike the Valley towns of south Wales, Usk does not lie in an area where there were minerals to be exploited, and allied factories built and raw materials and manufactured goods exported. These factors remain relevant to discussions of the town's future.

The town retained the layout and physical extent of the planned Norman town for at least six centuries. Only in the 17th century did westward expansion occur towards the river, with houses built along New Market Street. In 1801 Coxe[2] estimated Usk's population at not more than 700, with 160 occupied houses. However, another source of the same year gives a figure of 734 people in 306 households, with houses built

in frontage gaps of the historic street pattern. This gradual expansion of the built-up area through Victorian times and into the 20th century may have been stimulated by improved communications (notably the Turnpike roads and then the railway from the 1850s), notwithstanding periodic flooding from the River Usk and the Olway brook. However, population increase through the 19th century lagged behind Monmouthshire's overall growth rate in every decade. Numbers actually fell in the period 1871-91 and by 1901 the town accommodated fewer than 1,500 people due to the agricultural depression.[3]

The railway and improved roads (as Monmouthshire County Council took over responsibility) ensured slow but steady expansion thereafter, giving credence to the theory that improved communications contribute significantly to urban growth. The risk of flooding (probably more frequently than records attest) did not deter house building, for this peripheral expansion was at the whim of the landowner and builder and it was not until the 20th century that some sort of control operated.

All developments since the late 1930s have operated under planning legislation. A draft map of April 1939 of the East Monmouthshire Joint Planning Committee,[4] proposed minor development and an eastern bypass from Glen Oak House on the Gwehelog road approximately on the line of the Olway, to Llanbadoc Island. The war years prevented construction and the scheme was left in abeyance. The Monmouthshire County Development Plan of 1954 rehearsed the familiar problems,[5] notably that of flooding, but also noted the lack of landowners sympathetic to making land available for development.[6] This, the plan suggested, had retarded the natural development of 'this strategically located centre'.

The planning authority had contemplated major expansion in house building from the 1950s onwards due to the proximity of Usk to the nylon factory at Mamhilad, the Royal Ordnance Factory at Glascoed and the heavily industrialised area around Pontypool, but the designation of Cwmbran as a new town in 1949 was to have a far-reaching effect on the settlement pattern. By 1954 it was concluded that only a limited expansion was needed 'to meet the needs of those persons who are likely to desire to erect their houses in this area,' as the report accompanying the plan somewhat naively puts it. To be precise, Usk was saved by Cwmbran!

The Usk Town Map of 1959[7] was based on a planned population of 2,135, some 291 more than the estimated population of 1,844 in December 1949. New housing was proposed along Monmouth Road and in the area of Black Barn Lane. The proposed bypass north-east of the town (as in the East Monmouthshire Joint Planning Committee's proposals of two decades earlier) was included,[8] and a site for a secondary school defined at Priory Gardens.[9]

In the 1970s Usk experienced some relief from through traffic en route between the Midlands and Newport/South Wales with the opening of the new A449. This dual carriageway was built in stages from the end of the M50 near Ross-on-Wye with the last section from Usk to Newport being opened in 1972. However, an interchange connecting the A472 at Usk meant that traffic to and from Pontypool and Cwmbran would still pass through the town, even if signs encouraged truck drivers to take the trunk roads linking Raglan/Abergavenny/Little Mill to Pontypool.

By the time of the Gwent Structure Plan of 1977-8 [10] land for 100 houses had been committed. It rehearsed a need for a further 500 by 1991 and, taking into account existing commitments,

proposed allocations for about 400. Usk would retain its functions as a retailing and service centre. The lack of drainage capacity had hindered development before 1977, but the Water Authority now had a five-year improvement programme. Taking into account existing planning approvals, new houses were not to exceed 300, mostly by peripheral expansion, and some infilling. The rate of growth would be similar to the 1960s and, with household sizes expected to fall, the net increase would be 500 people by 1991.

The survey document that accompanied the structure plan discussed the problems of through traffic, especially on the A472, and referred to a line reserved for an Usk bypass 'to the north of the town'. It suggested that industrial development at Mamhilad created a long-term need for improved access to the A449 east of Usk, but favoured the more immediate benefit of major improvements to the A40 (Raglan/Abergavenny) and the A4042 (Abergavenny/Newport). It proposed the prohibition (as an experiment) of heavy traffic on the A472 and A471 except for access; out of a total of about 470 heavy lorries then using the A472 daily, approximately 82% was through traffic. In the long term, construction of an Usk bypass was considered desirable, but deemed not possible to include within the plan. The matter was to be kept under review! The Traffic Orders excluding heavy goods vehicles without access needs from travelling through Usk were put into effect in 1985 and enhanced in 1995. They have been periodically enforced by Gwent Police, who stop vehicles to enquire about origin and destination. The majority prove that they need access to the former Royal Ordnance Factory at Glascoed, to Woodside and to other locations west of the River Usk. However, as noted later in this chapter, recent legal opinion has expressed doubts about the enforceability of the wording of the Orders and the road signs!

The structure plan was then translated into detailed proposals.[11] Room at Woodside was found for 240 houses,[12] the developer being required to finance a roundabout junction on the A472, north of the railway embankment. A town development boundary was drawn to prevent expansion outside this 'envelope'.[13] As for a bypass, the local plan[14] summed up the position thus: 'There is no definite proposal as a final decision by the Council will be subject to the outcome of detailed discussion with interested parties and the views of the general public.'

The Unitary Development Plan (UDP) adopted in June 2006 after a public enquiry into objections, led to the town development boundary being extended at Castle Oak to allow for the construction of about 100 houses. This was made necessary by the lack of suitable development sites around Usk,[15] with 'the northern limit of the allocation set at approximately the 30 metre contour to limit its intrusive impact'.

The subsequent planning application resulted in permission for 115 houses off the Gwehelog / Old Monmouth Road with no alteration proposed to the existing road junction on which long traffic queues occur at peak hours. The UDP references to Usk (and Little Mill) bypasses remain long term aspirations of the county council, but are unlikely to be implemented during the plan's life (to 2011). It notes that the Welsh Assembly Government's trunk road programme for 2002 adds the A472 from Usk to Pontypool to the trunk road network.[16]

Fig. 16.1 *Vehicles sometimes have to mount the pavement in order to pass each other in the narrowest parts of Bridge Street. Deliveries to premises in this street cause vehicles to queue, further contributing to pollution levels*

In the meantime, areas within the original town have been built upon, as the various plans surmised. The small groups of houses of the inter-war and post-war years in Mill Street, Conigar Crescent, Abergavenny Road, Priory Gardens and Porth-y-carne Gate, along with minor infillings on street frontages, have all been constructed within the historic street pattern. There have been minor additions to the road system in some places, *eg* Priory Gardens; but other than the Turnpike road eastwards in the 1850s (Castle Parade/Monmouth Road), since enlarged and realigned as the access to the dual carriageway A449, no significant new roads have been built. Meanwhile the town has grown to over 1,000 households with consequent increases in car ownership. Previous development plans have aired the need for a relief road to the town centre and at least two (pre-war and 1959) have shown a proposed alignment northeast to south-west. Traffic volumes have reached an annual average daily flow in Bridge Street of over 1,100 cars, 1,443 light goods vehicles, 100 rigid heavy goods and 18 articulated heavy goods vehicles, and 10 buses and coaches,[17] with all the concomitant problems of noise, fumes and pedestrian fears.

Usk has therefore developed from a Norman planned town to one with accretions and peripheral development; but with no substantive recent improvements to its road pattern.

The Future

If a bypass is to be built, there is a need to define an acceptable new route. The alignment proposed in the 1930s and 1950s, north-east and south-west from Gwehelog Road to Llanbadoc Island, would not deal with the principal direction of traffic to and from the A449 towards Pontypool and Cwmbran. A new road on such an alignment, however well designed, would also intrude into the tranquillity of the Olway valley and the unspoilt countryside near Llanbadoc Island.

A route hitherto favoured by the county council but never safeguarded in a development plan, would use the line of the disused railway from east of Usk Primary School via the cutting, tunnel and river bridge to join the Pontypool Road north of Woodside. This area has been for the past few years the subject of environmental work by volunteers — planting, conservation and promotion as a local scenic walk. In addition, the physical effect of this route on adjoining houses and on Usk Castle (a Scheduled Ancient Monument) through noise and vibration, must make its acceptability highly questionable. It would certainly be the subject of strong local opposition. Whichever authority is to be responsible for improvements to the A472, if the road is to be brought up to trunk road standards it will have to announce a preferred route selected from various options, and justify the selection and the need, almost certainly in a public inquiry. If an acceptable route for a relief road and improvement of the A472 cannot be found, is there a greater role for traffic management?

As noted earlier, traffic orders came into effect in 1985 and 1995.[18] Both orders prohibit commercial vehicles over 7.5 tonnes gross metric weight from using the specified roads in the restricted area. There are, however, exceptions. The most significant is for vehicles accessing premises situated on or adjacent to the specified roads, mainly the Woodside Industrial Estate and Usk Garden Centre at Llanbadoc, and the former Royal Ordnance Factory at Glascoed. This exemption allows vehicles over that weight to deliver to, or collect from, such premises.

To ensure compliance, the police are obliged to prove that a vehicle above that weight (laden or not) entered and left the area without stopping for one of the specified purposes. Although shoppers, shopkeepers and residents often see vehicles over 7.5 tonnes in Bridge Street, including large tractors pulling heavy loads, the police find that all but a small minority are not breaking the order. There have been, however, several recent prosecutions.

Before making a traffic order, a highway authority seeks the chief constable's views. Consultation with local councils, organisations and the public at large are also part of the procedure. Unresolved objections may require the holding of a public inquiry from which an independent inspector reports his findings and recommendations. Recent legal opinion (June 2008) on the doubtful legality of the existing traffic orders,

notably of the signs, has prompted the commissioning of consultants by the county council to undertake a full traffic survey to provide the basis of a new order. To comply with the procedures outlined above, it would probably take at least six months for the order to come into effect. In the absence of new road proposals such an order must have the aim of diverting more traffic away from Usk.

Recent reports on the level of exhaust pollution in Bridge Street add further weight to the need for action.[19] There is a duty under the Environment Act of 1995 to carry out tests where levels of nitrogen dioxide are suspected as being above a certain limit, and as a result of these tests the county council concluded that an air quality management area (AQMA) order would have to be made for Bridge Street and parts of Castle Parade. The draft order came into effect on 1 November 2005 and the council were then required to carry out a further assessment to validate the first survey and supplementing the data already collected.

This found that the declaration of the AQMA was justified and the boundaries of the area substantially correct. The next stage is the drawing up of an air quality action plan (AQAP), which would include all possible actions that could be implemented to improve air quality. Perhaps surprisingly, the main pollutants are exhaust fumes from cars and light goods vehicles rather than from heavy goods vehicles, buses and coaches — the vehicles usually perceived to be the main cause of the problem. Table 1 below shows the percentage[20] of the annual average daily flow of vehicles in Bridge Street and Castle Parade. Cars and light goods vehicles contribute 94% to the former and 96% to the latter.

	Bridge Street	Castle Parade
Cars	41	40
Light goods	53	56
Rigid HGVs	> 4	4
Artic HGVs	> 1	>1
Buses/coaches	> 1	>1

Table 1 Percentage of annual average daily flow

More survey information, notably surveys as to the origins and destinations of vehicles, would be needed to illuminate the full traffic picture and to help decide on a course of action. One certainty, however, will be the need for greater enforcement of parking restrictions and stopping on double yellow lines in the shopping streets, along with the consideration of limiting delivery times to off-peak hours.[21] Other areas for examination might well include:

The introduction of 20mph speed limits associated with the widening of pavements and other physical measures to reduce speeds and divert traffic;

Diverting through traffic so as to reduce the number of vehicles trying to pass through the centre;

Carrying out traffic control experiments to ascertain origin and destination and advising drivers on alternative routes;

Publicity to reduce car use through town;

Discussion with parents about alternatives to using a car to ferry children to the Primary School;

Consideration of the opportunities for relocation;

Minimising developments that would give rise to greater car use and traffic through the town centre.

Car Parking

Coupled with the traffic problems is that of the stationary car in the town streets and car parks. On a typical mid-week day, there are 190 cars parked in the streets of the town centre conservation area. The car parks at Twyn Square, Maryport Street (north) and Maryport Street (south) have spaces for about 210 cars.[22] All car parks are free and largely unregulated. Pressure on spaces varies, depending on events (*eg* the Farmers' Market on the first and third Saturday morning of each month), the weather and the time of year. Anecdotal evidence suggests that there are an increasing number of occasions when drivers cannot find a space in which to park. Consequently the driver tours the car parks and nearby streets until a space is vacated.

Complaints are becoming more strident about all day parking. These involve town centre employees leaving a car all day in the car park. The county council's attempt to introduce charges in 2006 in Usk and elsewhere was withdrawn[23] as a result of the vigorous opposition of several local councils who proved in the High Court that the county council had a case to answer. Put simply, this was that the proposals were finance led and had not been justified by the needs of traffic management and highway requirements.

The current households in Usk (over 1,000) and the several hundred in the surrounding villages will have within the next 5 to 10 years the addition of 115 households at Castle Oak/Burrium Gate. The majority of these will own at least one and probably two cars. Pressure on car parking space and the use of the highway for parking will gradually increase. The following can be envisaged:

Demands to minimise the long stay use of car parks as unsuccessful searchers spend more and more time frustrated by the lack of space;

Shopkeepers and businesses concerned by falling customer numbers as a result;

Residents' reactions to the use of frontages by shoppers unable to find car park spaces;

Requests from residents in and around the town centre that space be reserved for them to park.

It is possible that there will be fresh attempts to introduce charges and residents' parking schemes.

Physical constraints on development
Flood risk

One of the reasons, albeit the lesser, for the move by the Romans from Usk to Caerleon[24] was the propensity for the River Usk to flood. Clearly the Normans some 600 years later were not deterred from building a castle and a planned town (perhaps there had been fewer recent occasions when flooding occurred as a result of a drier climate?) Throughout the following centuries peripheral expansion, especially westwards, was sometimes into the flood plain. Perhaps the medieval householder had a stoical outlook and simply swept out the floodwater. Reports of floods are sparse and were rarely recorded until the 18th century.[25]

One physical consequence of the calamitous floods of 1979 was the construction of flood protection banks. These were built, then enlarged, to protect Usk from a once-in-a-century flood event. Notwithstanding their presence, housing proposals at Woodside, Llanbadoc, were refused by the county council as local planning authority. The developer appealed, claiming the houses would be protected by his drainage scheme and the existence of the flood banks. After a public inquiry, the inspector recommended refusal and the Welsh Assembly Government refused the application as the site lay on the flood plain. This first occasion of a local refusal for such a reason coincided with the introduction of national policy[26] and subsequent local policy in the county council's UDP.[27] These effectively rule out residential building on the flood plains (except in very limited circumstances), a policy that has been enforced in and around Usk when appeals have been dismissed on the flood plain even for barn conversions to domestic use. The extent of the flood plain defined by the Environment Agency is viewable on the

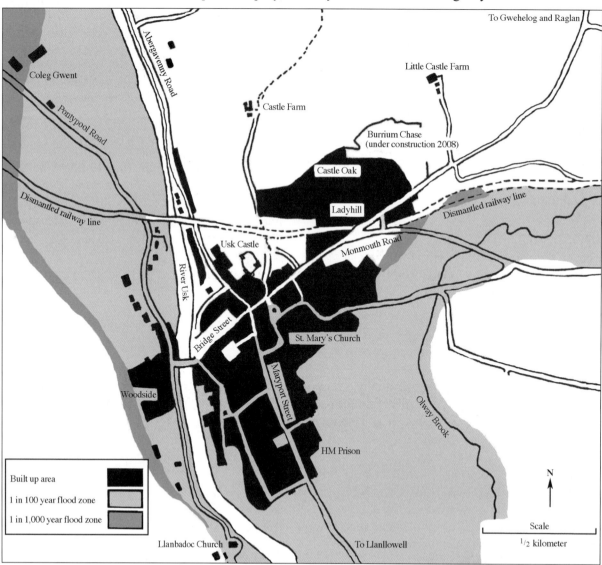

Fig. 16.2 The Extent of the Flood Zone. (This map is based on information supplied by the Environment Agency, © Environment Agency copyright and/or database right 2008. All rights reserved)

160

Fig. 16.3 The churchyard and eastern end of St. Madoc's Church, Llanbadoc: floods of February 2002

Fig. 16.4 View upstream from Usk Bridge adjoining Usk Bridge Mews: floods of February 2002

agency's website and is shown on Figure 16.2. The general effect is to include almost the whole of Usk except the higher ground around and to the east of Usk Castle. This, together with the policy of preventing building on high ground where it would be conspicuous, limits significantly the potential for further urban expansion.

High Ground

The UDP map for Usk (as amended) and the Proposals Map for the county show the extent of the Special Landscape Area (SLA) around Usk, illustrated on Figure 16.6. In effect the SLA policy[28] applies to all the higher land west of the escarpment overlooking the town; the countryside north and east of the new housing allocation at Castle Oak (Burrium Gate) and the countryside east of the Olway Brook.

The large areas not included comprise the former Woodside housing allocation, land along

Fig. 16.5 'The Island' recreation ground on the west bank of the River Usk: floods of February 2002

the Pontypool Road and the fields east of Usk extending into the valley of the Olway Brook. All of these areas omitted from the SLA are on the flood plain as defined by the Environment Agency. The SLA policy was refined in drawing the limits of the new development of Castle Oak (Burrium Gate), using the 30 metre contour as the upper limit for development so as to minimise the effect on the landscape.

Taking these two physical 'constraints' together it is difficult to see where in and around Usk further housing development can be located. The contribution that Usk can make to meet county/ regional housing demand may therefore be very limited. Sites may be small and result from redevelopment. This could create a related problem — the provision of affordable housing.

Affordable Housing

A policy to provide for affordable houses[29] on all sites of 10 or more dwellings in the five Monmouthshire towns, including Usk,[30] is contained in the UDP. This policy enables the county council to negotiate the provision of an element of at least 20% of the total number of houses on a site; the housing provided to be always

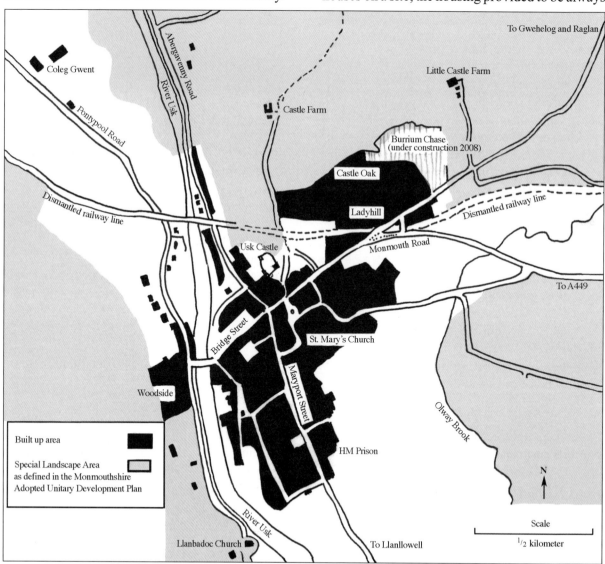

Fig. 16.6 The extent of the Special Landscape Area

available for local people.[31] Housing surveys indicate that this provision is unlikely to be sufficient. Indeed the UDP acknowledges that if the county council were to set its affordable housing target to meet demand, all new housing sites would have to be restricted to affordable housing (some 900 homes being required), which the council deemed unreasonable.

At present the only site approved for new houses is that at Burrium Gate, where only about 20 affordable dwellings are to be provided with an estate of 116 houses. The scale of the problem is such that 150 houses a year would have to be built in the remaining years of the UDP, simply to meet the 20% target, a near impossibility not simply due to the limited availability of land, but also to the financial capacity of the housing associations (as owners and managers of affordable housing) which would have to fund their construction.

One way of aiding the supply of land would be to extend the use of the 'exceptions' policy for rural areas to Usk, under which land outside the agreed development boundary could be released for the specific purpose of building affordable housing for local people. Such a change lies in the hands of the Welsh Assembly Government. Consideration may also have to be given to the purchase of existing houses by the county council, given the necessary funding and arrangements for equity sharing schemes, as is being proposed in England. Once again such changes lie in the hands of the Welsh Assembly Government. Without a solution many local people will find it hard to obtain a home in Usk in the years to come.

Listed Buildings and Conservation Area

More than eight centuries of building, from the Norman planned town to the expansions in the 18th and 19th centuries, have left a legacy of historic and architecturally important buildings, many of which are listed. Of its total stock of 1,092 buildings, 158 are listed (together with 16 structures such as railings, walls and churchyard tombs). Usk Castle, Castle House, St. Mary's Priory Church and the Priory Gatehouse are listed as Grade 1*, the highest category of buildings

of 'exceptional interest'. Grade 2* buildings (of 'particular importance') in Usk are Usk Bridge, the Sessions House, Usk Prison, Old Maltsters, Ynys Hafod, Min-Yr-Afon, Henllys, 27 Old Market Street and Porth y Carne House. All but two of the listed buildings and structures are in the town centre which has been designated a Conservation Area. This designation means that the local planning authority has a duty to pay special attention to the desirability of preserving or enhancing the character and appearance of that area.

Most of the listed buildings appear to be in a reasonable state of repair, such repair sometimes being part funded by the Historic Buildings Council, as advised by Cadw, or the Lottery Heritage Fund. Those perhaps at greatest risk of deteriorating are those along Bridge Street (where somewhat under half of the buildings are listed) due to the physical problems caused by traffic (damage by vibration and the accumulation of corrosive soot and dirt). This threat is enhanced by potential loss of trade as pedestrians find the street unpleasant to visit and shop elsewhere, so reducing shopkeepers' income and the finance available to spend on the buildings.

Festivals and Events

In recent years many organizations and individuals have worked hard to promote the town and encourage people to visit and enjoy it. A Victorian day, a weekend festival, Usk in Bloom and Usk Garden Open Days, the latter attracting several thousand visitors each year, all serve to help bolster trade for hotels, restaurants and shops.

International and National Problems

The foregoing discussion about the identified problems for the future of Usk presume that the extreme effects of climate change in the next ten to twenty years will not render the Usk valley uninhabitable from complete inundation.[32] That would subsume all the issues discussed and does not bear contemplating.

Speculation about the possible effects of the construction of a Severn Barrage is perhaps premature. The Sustainable Development Commission in examining the potential for tidal power in the estuary has stated that the scheme would work it is provided compensatory habitats elsewhere for the bird life affected. On the other hand, the chairman of Natural England has argued that the area is very special, that alternative tidal schemes would be better for the environment and a massive tidal barrier could not satisfy European Union habitats regulations.

Notwithstanding these fears, the government has appointed consultants Parsons Brinkerhoff to carry out a feasibility study. If the outcome is in favour, the effect on the ecology of the estuary would be probably be far more serious than any on the Usk area, the Royal Society for the Protection of Birds having estimated the loss of 50% to 60% of the tidal mudflat habitat of thousands of wading and diving birds.

A new Local Development Plan

The county planning department has recently (July 2007) announced work on a new Local Development Plan to replace the UDP. This will extend the planning period to the year 2021 and no doubt new challenges and issues will be identified and addressed. Arrangements have been published to involve as many organisations, groups and people as possible[33] in an attempt to reach a consensus on them and on potential solutions.

It is doubtful whether this new plan will produce solutions to Usk's traffic problems unless a line for a bypass is identified for safeguarding, which as discussed earlier, is very doubtful. The new plans in Wales are to be wholly concerned with land use and, unlike present UDPs, exclude traffic management which, it is assumed, feature in Regional Transport Plans. Details for the latter for the county have yet to be announced at the time of writing. In light of this, the major challenge for the new LDP is — should further allocations be made for more development (assuming sites can be found) before achievable solutions to the traffic problems are in place.

Abbreviations and References

AC   *Annales Cambriae* ed. John Williams (London 1860)

Alumni Oxoniensis   J. Foster *Alumni Oxoniensis : The Members of the University of Oxford 1500-1714*
                     (Oxford, 3 vols 1891-2).

ANS   *Anglo Norman Studies*

Antiq J   *Antiquaries Journal*

AOI   C.H. Firth and R.S. Rait (eds) *Acts and Ordinances of the Interregnum 1642-1660*
                     (London, 3 vols 1911)

Arch Camb   *Archaeologia Cambrensis*

Archaeol J   *Archaeological Journal*

ASC   *Anglo Saxon Chronicle*

Avent 2003   Avent, Richard 'William Marshal's building works at Chepstow Castle, Monmouthshire, 1189-1219'
                  The Medieval Castle in Ireland and Wales ed. Kenyon, J.R. and O'Conor, Kieran
                  (Dublin), 50-71

Avent 2006   Avent, Richard 'William Marshal's castle at Chepstow and its place in military architecture' in
                  Chepstow Castle 81-90

AW   *Archaeology in Wales*

BAA *CT*   British Archaeological Association, *Conference Transactions*

BBCS   *Bulletin of the Board of Celtic Studies*

BAR   *British Archaeological Reports* (Oxford)

Biographical Register   A.B. Emden *A Biographical Register of the University of Oxford to 1500* (3 vols, Oxford 1955-9)

BL   British Library

Boon 1962   Boon, G.C. 'Remarks on Roman Usk' *Mon Ant* I, part 2 (1962), 28-33

Boon and Hassell 1982   Boon, G.C. and Hassall, M. *Report on the Excavations at Usk 1968-1976, the coins,*
                  inscriptions and graffiti (Cardiff)

Bradney, *Hundred of Usk*   J.A. Bradney *A History of Monmouthshire 3.1. Hundred of Usk* (1921)

Bradney *Hundred of Raglan*   J.A. Bradney *A History of Monmouthshire 2.1. Hundred of Raglan* (1911)

Brewer 2002   Brewer, Richard J. *The Second Augustan Legion and the Military Machine* (Cardiff)

BSNAF   *Bulletin de la Societé Nationale des Antiquaries de France*

By.T   T. Jones (ed) *Brut Y Tywysogion or the Chronicle of the Princes* (Cardiff 1955)

C. Anc. Pet.   *Calendar of Ancient Petitions Relating to Wales* ed. William Rees (Cardiff 1975)

CChR   *Calendar of Charter Rolls*

CCR   *Calendar of Close Rolls*

Chepstow Castle   *Chepstow Castle, its History and Buildings* ed. R. Turner and A. Johnson (Logaston 2006)

Children and Nash   Children, G. and Nash, G. *Prehistoric Sites of Monmouthshire* (Logaston, 1996)

CIPM   *Calendar of Inquisitions Post Mortem*

Courtney 1986-7   Courtney, P. 'Documentary notes on the Gwehelog pottery industry' *Medieval and Later Pottery in*
                  Wales 9, 71-3

Courtney 1994   Courtney, P. *Report on the Excavations at Usk 1965-1976: Medieval and Later Usk*
                  ed. W.H. Manning (Cardiff 1994)

Cowley   Cowley, F.G. *The Monastic Order in South Wales 1066-1349* (Cardiff, 1977)

Coxe *Historical Tour*   William Coxe *An Historical Tour in Monmouthshire* (London 1801, 2 vols)

CPR   *Calendar of Patent Rolls*

Crouch 1985   Crouch, David 'The slow death of kingship in Glamorgan 1067- 1158' *Morgannwg* 29 (1985) 20-41

Crouch 1988   Crouch, David *Llandaff Episcopal Acta 1140-1287* (Cardiff 1988)

Crouch 2002   Crouch, David *William Marshal: Knighthood, War and Chivalry 1147-1219* (2nd ed 2002)

CRR   *Curia Regis Rolls*

CSPD   *Calendar of State Papers, Domestic*

CYS   *Canterbury and York Society*

Davies 1957	Davies, E.T. *Monmouthshire Schools and Education up to 1870*
Davies 2004	Davies, Jeffrey 'Soldier and civilian in Wales' in Todd 2004, 91-113
DB	*Domesday Book* ed. Farley 1783
DNB	*Dictionary of National Biography*
Erlande-Brandenberg	Alain Erlande-Brandenberg 'L'architecture militaire au temps de Phillipe Auguste: une nouvelle conception de la défense' *La France de Phillipe Auguste* 595-603
Evans and Metcalfe	Evans, D.R. and Metcalfe, V.M. 'Excavations at 10, Old Market Street Usk' *Britannia* 20 (1989), 23-68
Evans and Rhys	Evans, J.G. and Rhys J. *The Text of the Book of Llan Dâv* (Oxford 1893)
Foley	Foley, Henry *Records of the English Province of the Society of Jesus* (8 vols, 1877-9)
GEC	Cokayne, G.E. *The Complete Peerage* ed. V Gibbs, H.A. Doubleday *et al* (13 vols, London 1910-59)
Gl. C.H. III	*Glamorgan County History Vol 3 The Middle Ages* ed. Glanmor Williams (Cardiff 1971)
Gray 2002	Gray, M. 'Women of holiness and power: the cults of St Radegund and St Mary Magdalene at Usk' *Mon Ant* 18, 3-11
Griffiths Davies	Griffiths Davies, J.D. 'The Catholic nonconformists of Monmouthshire' *Monmouthshire Review* 2.1 (January 1934).
Gwent C.H. I	*Gwent County History Vol 1 Gwent in Prehistory and Early History* ed R.A. Griffiths, M. Aldhouse Green and R. Howel (Cardiff 2004)
Gwent CRO	Gwent County Record Office, Cwmbran
HMSO	Her Majesty's Stationery Office
Hughes	Hughes, R. 'Pottery from the Post-Medieval kiln at Gwehelog, near Usk' *Medieval and Later Pottery in Wales* 3 (1980), 21- 9
Jarrett	Jarrett, Michael G. 'Early Roman campaigns in Wales' in Brewer 2002, 45-66
JBAA	*Journal of the British Archaeological Association*
JSAH	*Journal of the Society of Architectural Historians*
Kenyon and O'Conor 2003	Kenyon, J.R. and O'Conor K. (eds) *The Medieval Castle in Ireland and Wales* (Dublin)
Kienzle and Walker	Kienzle, Beverley Mayne and Walker, Pamela J. *Woman Preachers and Prophets through Two Millenia of Christianity* (Berkeley, Los Angeles and London, University of California Press 1988)
Knight 1977	Knight, J.K. 'Usk Castle and its affinities' *Ancient Monuments and their Interpretation – Essays Presented to A.J. Taylor* ed M.W. Thompson, A Saunders and M.R. Apted (Chichester 1977), 139-45
Knight 1987	Knight J.K. 'The road to Harlech: aspects of some early thirteenth century Welsh castles' *Castles in Wales and the Marches: Essays in Honour of D.J. Cathcart King* (Cardiff 1987), 79-88
Knight 2005	Knight J.K. *Civil War and Restoration in Monmouthshire* (Logaston)
Manning 1981	Manning, W.H. *Report on the Excavations at Usk 1965-1976 The Fortress Excavations 1968-1971* (Cardiff)
Manning and Scott 1989	Manning, W.H. with Scott, I.R. *Report on the Excavations at Usk 1968-1974 The Fortress Excavations 1972-1974* (Cardiff)
Manning, Price and Webster, 1995	Manning, W.H. with Price, Jennifer and Webster, Janet *Report on the Excavations at Usk 1965-1967 The Roman Small Finds* (Cardiff)
Manning 2002	Manning, W.H. 'Early Roman campaigns in the south-west of Britain' in Brewer, 2002, 27-44
Manning 2004a	Manning, W.H. 'The conquest of Wales' in Todd, 2004
Manning 2004b	Manning, W.H. 'The Roman conquest and the army' *Gw. C.H.* I, 178-204
Marvell	Marvell, A.G. 'Excavations in Usk, 1986-1988' *Britannia* 27 (1996), 51-110
McNamara	Jo Ann McNamara et al. *Sainted Women of the Dark Ages* (Durham and London, Duke University Press 1992)
Mein 1986	Mein, A.G. *Norman Usk; The Birth of a Town*
Mein 2000	Mein, A.G. 'St Mary's Church at Usk: some recent work and new theories *Mon Ant* 16 68-73
MLPW	*Medieval and Later Pottery in Wales*
Monasticon	William Dugdale, *Monasticon Anglicanum* 6 vols ed Caley (London 1818-30)
Mon Ant	*The Monmouthshire Antiquary*
Mont Coll	*Montgomeryshire Collections*
NA	National Archives

Newman   Newman, John *The Buildings of Wales: Gwent/Monmouthshire* (London/Cardiff
                                     Penguin/University of Wales Press, 2000)
NLW   National Library of Wales
OED   *Oxford English Dictionary*
Olding 2000   Olding, F. *The Prehistoric Landscapes of the Eastern Black Mountains* (*BAR* 297, Oxford, 2000)
Olding 2006   Olding, F. '"Some Welsh Popish Books"; Recusant Literature in Monmouthshire 1550-1781'
                                     Mon Ant 22 (2006), 19-37
Orderic Vitalis   *The Ecclesiastical History of Orderic Vitalis* ed. M. Chibnall 6 vols (Oxford 1969-80)
Oxford DNB   *Oxford Dictionary of National Biography*
Peterson and Pollard 2004   Peterson, R. and Pollard, J 'The Neolithic – the first farming societies' *Gwent C.H. 1*, 56-83
Phillips 1874   J.R. Phillips *Memoirs of the Civil War in Wales and the Marches 1642-1649* Vol 1 narrative,
                                     vol 2 sources (1874)
Pitts and St Joseph 1985   Pitts, Lynn F. and St Joseph J.K. *Inchtuthil. The Roman Legionary Fortress*
PPC   *Proceedings and Ordnances of the Privy Council of England.*
PR   *Publications of the Pipe Roll Society*
PRO/NA   Public Record Office/National Archives
Priestley and Turner   S.G. Priestley and R.C. Turner 'Three Castles of the Clare family in Monmouthshire during the
                                     thirteenth and fourteenth centuries' *Arch Camb* 152 (2005 for 2003), 9-52
Probert   A.L. Probert 'Twyn Y Gaer hill fort: an interim assessment' in G.C. Boon and J.M Lewis ed.
                                     Welsh Antiquity: Essays Presented to H.N. Savory (Cardiff 1976), 105-120
Pugh   Pugh, F.H. 'Monmouthshire Recusants in the reigns of Elizabeth I and James I from the returns in
                                     the Public Record Office' *South Wales and Monmouthshire Record Society* 4 (1957), 57-110
RCHME   Royal Commission on Historical Monuments (England)
RCAHMW   Royal Commission on Ancient and Historical Monuments in Wales and Monmouthshire
Rees   Rees, William *South Wales and the March 1284-1415* (1924, re-issued 1974)
Roger of Wendover   *Chronici Rogeri de Wendover* ed. H. Hewlett (R.S. 1889)
RS   *Rolls Series*
Siddons   Siddons, M.P. *Visitations by the Heralds in Wales* (Harleian Society, new series 14 1996)
Taylor   Taylor, A.J. 'Usk Castle and the Pipe Roll of 1185; with a note on an expenses account of 1289'
                                     Arch Camb (1947), 249-55
TBGAS   *Transactions of the Bristol and Gloucestershire Archaeological Society*
THSC   *Transactions of the Honourable Society of Cymmrodorion*
Thurlby   Thurlby, M. *Romanesque Architecture and Sculpture in Wales* (Logaston 2006)
Todd 2004   Todd, Malcolm *A Companion to Roman Britain* (Oxford)
Underhill 1999   Underhill, F.A. *For Her Good Estate: The Life of Elizabeth de Burgh* (New York)
VCH   *Victoria County History* (Published by Oxford University Press for the Institute of
                                     Historical Research)
VSBG   A.W. Wade Evans ed *Vitae Sanctorum Britanniae et Genealogiae* (Cardiff 1944).
Ward   J.C. Ward 'Elizabeth de Burgh and Usk Castle' *Mon Ant* 18 (2002), 13-22
Webb   J. and T.H. Webb *Memorials of the Civil War between King Charles Ist and the Parliament of
                                     England as it affected Herefordshire nd Adjacent counties* (2 vols, 1879)
Whittle   Whittle, E. *A Guide to Ancient and Historic Wales: Glamorgan and Gwent* (1992)
Williams 1970-1   Williams D.H. 'Goldcliff Priory' *Mon Ant* 3, part 2, (1970-71) 37-54
Williams 1976   Williams, Glanmor *The Welsh Church from Conquest to Reformation* (Cardiff, University of Wales
                                     Press)
Williams 1886   Williams, Stephen W. 'Architectural notes upon Usk church, Monmouthshire' *Arch Camb* 1886,
                                     90-93
Wood   Wood, Margaret *The English Medieval House* (1965)
Wrathmell   Wrathmell, Stuart 'The Earthworks of a post-medieval pottery industry at Gwehelog' *Medieval
                                     and Later Pottery in Wales* 3 (1980), 31-4

Chapter I Usk in Prehistory

1. Walker, E.A. 'The Mesolithic – the final hunter-gatherer-fisher societies of south-eastern Wales' *Gwent C.H. 1*, 39.
2. *Ibid.*, 41.
3. Burrow S. *Catalogue of the Mesolithic and Neolithic Collections in the National Museums and Galleries of Wales* (Cardiff 2003), 276. Savory, H.N. 'The southern Marches of Wales in the Neolithic and early Bronze Age' *Culture and Environment: Essays in Honour of Sir Cyril Fox* ed. I.Ll. Foster and L Alcock (1963), 32 n2 and fig 10, 1.
4. Peterson and Pollard 2004, 62.
5. *Ibid.*, 64.
6. Lynch, F., Aldhouse-Green, M. and Davies J.L. *Prehistoric Wales* (Stroud 2000), 51.
7. Mein, A.G. 'Trostrey Castle' *AW* 43 (2003), 107-10.
8. *Ibid.*, 150-51.
9. Marvell, A .'Usk' *AW* 28 (1988), 55.
10. Britnell, W.J. and Savory, H.N. *Gwernvale and Penywyrlod: Two Neolithic Long Cairns in the Black Mountains of Brecknock* (Cambrian Archaeological Monographs 2, 1984), 64.
11. Mein, A.G. 'Trostrey Castle' *AW* 41 (2001), 121.
12. *Ibid.*
13. Crampton, C.B. and Webley, D. 'A section through the Mynydd Troed long barrow, Brecknock' *BBCS* 22 (1966), 71-77.
14. Children and Nash, 34.
15. Cummings, V. and Whittle A. *Places of Special Virtue: Megaliths in the Neolithic Landscapes of Wales* (Oxbow, Oxford 2004), 183.
16. Peterson and Pollard 2004, 74.
17. Mein, A.G. 'Trostrey Castle' *AW* 40 (2000), 79.
18. Mein, A.G. 'Trostrey Castle' *AW* 39 (1999), 87.
19. Whittle 1992, 24; Children and Nash, 70-71.
20. Olding 2000, 46.
21. Children and Nash, 59-60.
22. Whittle 1992, 20.
23. Children and Nash, *The Prehistoric Sites of Monmouthshire* (Logaston Press, 1996), 62
24. Mein, A.G. 'Trostrey Castle' *AW* 41 (2001), 123.
25. Mein, A.G. 'Trostrey Castle' *AW* 40 (2000), 78.
26. *Ibid.*, 80.
27. Gwilt, A. 'Late Bronze Age Societies (1150-600 B.C.): Tools and weapons' *Gwent C.H. 1*, 111-139, Appendix I.
28. Babbidge, A.V. 'Reconnaissance excavations at Coed y Bwnydd, Bettws Newydd 1969-1971' *Mon Ant* 3, part 3 (1977), 159-178.
29. Probert 1976.
30. *Ibid.*
31. Leslie, J.V.L. 'The Camp, Tir y Mynach' *AW* 2 (1962), 5.
32. Mein, A.G. 'White Castle Farm' *AW* 30 (1990), 52.
33. Mein, A.G. 'Tregaer' *AW* 29 (1989), 48.
34. Olding 2000, 73.

Chapter II The Legionary Fortress

I must thank Maureen Manning for her invaluable help in preparing the illustrations which appear in this and the following chapter; Andrew Marvell for allowing me to use material from the plans originally published in Marvell 1996, and Evan Chapman for procuring photographs of the excavations.

1. W. Camden *Britannia* (London 1610), 636.
2. Claudius Ptolemy *Geographia* 2.3.24; J. Horsley *Britannia Romana* (London 1732), 320.
3. Rivet, A.L.F. & Smith, C., *The Place-Names of Roman Britain* (London 1979), 285.
4. .T. Watkin 'On the Roman Stations 'Burrium', 'Gobannium, and 'Blestium, of the Twelfth and Twentieth Iters of Antoninus', *Archaeol J* 35 (1878), 19-43.
5. Boon 1962; Grace Simpson *Britons and the Roman Army* (London 1964), 4.
6. V.E. Nash-Williams *The Roman Frontier in Wales* (Cardiff 1954), 80.
7. Tacitus *Annals* XII. 31-40; XIV. 29; *Agricola* XIV. Quoted and translated in Manning 1981, 24*ff*.
8. Manning and Scott 1989, 130-139.
9. The excavations are described in Manning 1981, Manning and Scott 1989, and Paul Courtney *Medieval and Later Usk (Report on the Excavations at Usk 1965-1976)* (Cardiff 1994).
10. Tacitus *Annals* XII. 32.
11. Manning 2004a, 63; Manning 2002, 39.
12. Manning 2002, 39.
13. Manning 2002, 39.
14. Jarrett 2002, 53.
15. For the fortress defences cf. Manning 1981, 64*ff*.
16. Marvell, 55.
17. Manning 1981, 198.
18. *Ibid.*, 103.
19. *Ibid.*, 196.
20. Manning and Scott 1989, 148.
21. Manning 1981, 108*ff*.
22. *Ibid.*, 114; Manning and Scott 1989, 3*ff*.
23. Manning and Scott 1989, 132.
24. *Ibid.*, 140*ff*.
25. *Ibid.*, 117*ff*.
26. *Ibid.*, 149.
27. *Ibid.*, 127*ff*.
28. *Ibid.*, 163*ff*.
29. *Ibid.*, 168*ff*.
30. *Agricola* 22.
31. Manning 1981, 177.
32. Manning and Scott 1989, 144.
33. *Ibid.*, 165.
34. *Ibid.;* 1989.
35. Manning and Scott 1989, 3*ff*.
36. *Ibid.*, 17, 30, 70, 75, 88.
37. *Ibid.*, 9*ff*.
38. *Ibid.*, 18, 53, 81, 93.

39. *Ibid.*, 53.
40. *Ibid.*, 93.
41. *Ibid.*, 32ff, 18*ff.*
42. *Ibid.*, 88*ff.*
43. *Ibid.*, 129*ff.*
44. *Ibid.*, 100*ff.*
45. *Ibid.*, 93.
46. *Ibid.* 9, 110.
47. *Ibid.*, 134.
48. Evans and Metcalf 1989, 28.
49. Marvell, 57.
50. *Ibid.*, 60.
51. Manning 2004a, 63.
52. *Ibid.*, 70.
53. Manning 1981, 47; Manning 2004a, 70.
54. Manning 1981, 52.
55. Evans and Metcalf 1989, 30.
56. Marvell 1996, 65.
57. *Ibid.*, 68.
58. Manning 1981, 195*ff.*
59. Manning and Scott 1989, 150.

Chapter III Later Roman Usk
1. For summaries of the Flavian military system in Wales cf. Davies 2004, 91ff; Manning 2001, 24*ff.*
2. Manning and Scott 1989, 4.
3. Manning, Price and Webster 1995, 319.
4. Manning 1981, 72.
5. *Ibid.*, 201.
6. *Ibid.*, 72.
7. Manning and Scott 1989, 173*ff.*
8. Marvell, 70.
9. *Ibid.*, 86.
10. Manning and Scott 1989, 180.
11. Marvell, 72.
12. Manning 1981, 47.
13. Marvell, 72.
14. Grimes 1930.
15. Boon and Hassall 1982, 59; Marvell, 73.
16. Boon and Hassall 1982, 51.
17. The Roman structures which post-date the fortress and fortlet remain unpublished and will be the subject of the final volume of the series devoted to the excavations of 1965-1976.
18. Manning 2004, 199.

Chapter IV Hospitals and Almshouses of Medieval Usk
1. Sweetinburgh, Sheila *The Role of the Hospital in Medieval England,* 2004
2. Cule, J. *The Diagnosis, Care and Treatment of Leprosy in Wales and the Marches in the Middle Ages,* Trans. British Soc. for the History of Pharmacy, 1970, 43-44.
3. Kissack, Keith *The Lordship, Parish and Borough of Monmouth,* 1996, 86-87.
4. *Valor Ecclesiasticus,* eds J. Caley and J. Hunter, 6 vols. London, Record Commission 1810-34, 367.
5. Young, A. *Tudor and Jacobean Tournaments,* 1987, 18-19.

6. Durant, Horatia *The Somerset Sequence,* 1976, 14.
7. Mein A.G. *Norman Usk, The Birth of a Town,* 1986, 43-45.
8. Cowley, F.G. *The Monastic Order in South Wales 1066-1340,* Cardiff, 1977, 204-206.
9. Mein, A.G. 'St Mary's Priory Church, Usk: Some Recent Work and Some New Theories', *Monmouthshire Antiquarian* vol.XVI, 2000, 70.
10. Cowley, F.G. *The Monastic Order in South Wales 1066-1340,* Cardiff, 1977, 204-206.
11. Latham R.E. *Revised Medieval Latin Word-List,* OUP, 1965, reprint 1973, xx, 324.
12. Sweetinburgh, Sheila *The Role of the Hospital in Medieval England,* 2004.
13. *CPR 1381-5,* 180.
14. *CCR 1385-9,* 149.
15. Mein A.G. 'St Mary's Priory Church, Usk: Some Recent Work and Some New Theories', *Monmouthshire Antiquarian* vol.XVI, 2000, 62,66.
16. Jones, Hartwell 'Celtic Britain and the Pilgrim Movement', *Y Cymmrodor* vol.23, 1912, 318.
17. Ward, J.C. 'The Estates of the Clare family 1066-1317', App iii, PhD thesis, London Univ., 1962, 347.
18. Cule, J. *The Diagnosis, Care and Treatment of Leprosy in Wales and the Marches in the Middle Ages,* Trans. British Soc. for the History of Pharmacy, 1970.
19. PRO S.C6/927/23.
20. PRO S.C6/927/16.
21. Courtney, P. *Medieval and Later Usk,* UWP, 1994, 101.
22. Clark, J.H. *Usk Past and Present,* 1891, 247.
23. NLW Bute M59/1.
24. Historical Monuments Commission, 7th Report (1879).
25. Bradney 3, pt.1.52.
26. Coxe, William *An Historical Tour in Monmouthshire,* 1801, 1, 133.
27. By letter 22/8/89.
28. GRO CD R & B/C.18.
29. Barrow, Jan *From Dawn Till Dusk; Usk, the story of its markets, trades and occupations,* 2004, 133-134.
30. Clark, J.H. *Usk Past and Present,* 1891, 247.
31. Bradney 2.8
32. Barrow, Jan *From Dawn Till Dusk; Usk, the story of its markets, trades and occupations,* 2004, 31-32.
33. Bradney 3.1.10-11.
34. Bradney 3.1.43-4.
35. Clark, J.H. *Usk Past and Present,* 1891, 131, 134-135, 151.
36. Bradney 3.1.29-30.
37. Clark, J.H. *Usk Past and Present,* 1891, 132-135.
38. Bradney 3.1.46.
39. Durant, Horatia *The Somerset Sequence,* 1976, 132-134.
40. Clark, J.H. *Usk Past and Present,* 1891, 135, 144.
41. Clark, J.H. *Usk Past and Present,* 1891, 138, 140
42. Clark, J.H. *Usk Past and Present,* 1891, 138.

Chapter V The Medieval Priory and its Community

1. Williams 1976, 563; Cowley, 38, 271; David Knowles and R N. Hadcock *Medieval Religious Houses: England and Wales* (London: Longman, rev. ed. 1971), 255, 267.
2. David Williams 'Usk Nunnery', *Mon. Ant.* Iv (1980), 44-5.
3. Mein 2000, 70.
4. S. Elkins *Holy Women of Twelfth-Century England* (Chapel Hill: University of North Carolina Press, 1988), 45-52; S. Thompson *Women Religious: the founding of English nunneries after the Norman conquest* (Oxford 1991); Brenda M. Bolton 'Daughters of Rome' in W.J. Sheils and Diana Wood, eds. *Women in the Church* (Studies in Church History xxvii, 1990); K.J.P. Lowe 'Female strategies for success in a male-ordered world: the Benedictine convent of Le Murate in Florence in the fifteenth and early sixteenth centuries' *idem*; also Cowley, 1977 52, for evidence of female recluses in south Wales, before and after the Conquest.
5. For an overview of the architecture see Newman 2000, 585-6.
6. Mein 2000, 70.
7. S.E. Rees 'The Priory Buildings' in D.H. Williams and K.E. Kissack, *Monmouth Priory* (Aberystwyth 2001), 41-64.
8. Manning 1981, 66 and Figure 14.
9. C.N. Maylan 'Excavations at St Mary's Priory, Usk, 1987', *Mon Antiq* IX (1993), 29-42.
10. *Ibid*, 32.
11. A.G.Mein Usk Priory: An Unrecorded Excavation, *Monm. Antiq.* IX (1993), 43-45.
12. S.W. Williams 'Architectural Notes upon Usk Church', *Arch. Camb.* XL (1886), 90-93.
13. Mein 2000, 68-73.
14. Newman, 586.
15. Roberta Gilchrist *Gender and Material Culture*, 90-91.
16. Mein 2000, 62.
17. Newman, 587.
18. Mein 2000, 67.
19. The detail in this section relies heavily on Eileen Power's pioneering study *Medieval English Nunneries: c.1275 to 1535* (Cambridge: Cambridge University Press, 1922); for more recent research see Gilchrist *Gender and Material Culture*, and Elkins *Holy Women*.
20. *Reg. J Peckham* (*RS*), III, 805-6, paraphrased in Williams 'Usk Nunnery'.
21. Power *Medieval English Nunneries*, 381-3.
22. *Gender and Material Culture*, 108, 110.
23. *Ibid*, 119-21.
24. Williams 'Usk Nunnery'.
25. *Holy Feast and Holy Fast* (Berkeley, Los Angeles and London: University of California Press, 1987), 270-3.
26. Caroline Walker Bynum *Jesus as Mother* (Berkeley, Los Angeles and London: 1982), 190; C.W. Atkinson *The Oldest Vocation: Christian motherhood in the Middle Ages* (Ithaca and London: Cornell University Press, 1991), 163.
27. TNA Prob.11/17 f 269.
28. Richard Marks *Image and Devotion in Late Medieval England* (Stroud 2004), 73.
29. Mein 2000, esp. 68-72.
30. The lives of a number of these women are edited and analysed in McNamara 1992. For more detailed discussion of Radegund's career see M. Gray 2002, 3-11.
31. McNamara, 77.
32. McNamara, 93.
33. Hanneka Mulder-Bakker *Sanctity and Motherhood: essays on holy mothers in the Middle Ages* (New York and London: Garland Publishing, 1995) 247-51.
34. The story is given in its fullest form in Jacobus de Voragine's *Legenda Aurea* (Jacobus de Voragine, trans. W.G. Ryan, *The Golden Legend: Readings on the Saints* (Princeton, New Jersey: Princeton University Press, 1993) and summarised in the Welsh *Buchedd Mair Fadlen* (D.J. Jones 'Buchedd Mair Fadlen a'r *Legenda Aurea*' *BBCS* 4 (1929), 325-39. see also K.L. Jansen 'Maria Magdalena: *Apostolorum Apostola*' Kienzle and Walker, 57-96.
35. Karen L. King 'Prophetic Power and Women's authority: the case of the *Gospel of Mary* (Magdalene)' in Kienzle and Walker, 21-41.
36. Jansen 'Maria Magdalena'.
37. John Mirk *Festial*, ed. Theodore Erbe (London: Early English Text Society, 1905), 203-8. The first part of Mirk's *Festial* is known to have been translated into Welsh. The surviving manuscript of the translation breaks off after the sermon for Pentecost, and the sermon for the feast of St Mary Magdalene is therefore missing. It is however possible that the manuscript is incomplete and that the whole work was at one time available in Welsh.
38. Mirk *Festial,* 204.
39. Cardiff Library MS 6. For the full text see G Hartwell Jones *Celtic Britain and the Pilgrim Movement* (London: Honourable Society of Cymmrodorion, 1912).
40. PCC 22 Spert, calendared in J. Hunt, 'Monmouthshire wills proved in the Prerogative Court of Canterbury, 1404-1560' (Cardiff University Diploma in Extra-mural Studies (Local History) dissertation, 1985), no. 61.
41. Paul Courtney suggests this was the modern Four Ash Street: Courtney 1994, 101.
42. John A.F. Thompson 'St Eiluned of Brecon and her cult' in Diana Wood, ed. *Martyrs and Martyrologies* (Oxford: Blackwell, 1993), 117-25.
43. *Valor Ecclesiasticus* iv, 365-6; M. Gray 'The Dispersal of Crown Property in Monmouthshire, 1500-1603' (unpublished University of Wales Ph.D. Thesis, 1984), 70-1.
44. David Verey *The Buildings of England: Gloucestershire. The Vale and the Forest of Dean* (Harmondsworth: Penguin, 1970), 95.
45. Gray 'Dispersal of Crown property', 84.

46. Mein 2000, 57-9.

47. Mein 2000, 61-2.

48. *VCH Somerset* vol ii, ed. William Page (London: Constable, 1911), 108, available online at http://www.british-history.ac.uk/report.asp?compid=40924 (consulted 29.09.07).

49. Peter Lord *The Visual Culture of Wales: Medieval Vision* (Cardiff: University of Wales Press, 2003). I am immensely grateful for Dr Morgan-Guy for providing me with a copy of the otherwise unpublished lecture.

50. BL MS 33725 ff 300-04.

51. I am grateful to Dr Andrea Tanner, formerly of the College of Heralds, for this point.

52. TNA E315/20/19, E321/7/13, 12/76, 17/39; cf E.A. Lewis and James Conway Davies *Records of the Court of Augmentations relating to Wales and Monmouthshire* (Cardiff: University of Wales Press, 1954), 134.

53. David Knowles *The Religious Orders in England, vol III: The Tudor Age* (Cambridge: Cambridge University Press, 1959, 412; Knowles & Hadcock *Medieval Religious Houses*, 267.

Chapter VI Welsh Space and Norman Invaders

1. Knight 1977. See also B.H. St J. O'Neil *Usk Castle* (privately printed 1938) and in *Arch Camb* 91, 1936, 376-8.

2. *ASC* (versions C and D), 137. *Vita Gundleii* c 13. (*VSBG*, 184-7).

3. *DB* folio 180b. Evans and Rhys 1893, 278. P. Courtney 'The Norman invasion of Gwent: a re-assessment' *Journal of Medieval History* 12 (1986), 297-313. Crouch 1985. M. Davies 'The coming of the Normans' *Gwent C.*H. I, 331-354. D. Crouch 'The transformation of Medieval Gwent', *Gwent County History* Vol 2 (2008) appeared as the present work was in proof stage, too late to take this important article fully into account.

4. *Monasticon* VI, 1076. *CChR 1257-1300,* 358-9. The charter mentions fitz Osbern in a grant by Richard Strongbow, confirmed by Henry II, but is not contemporary evidence.

5. Crouch 1985, 26. Orderic Vitalis IV, 22.

6. Evans and Rhys, 278-9. *By.T*, 27. Beverley Smith in *Gl C.H.* III, 6-7.

7. Evans and Rhys, 272 (Tref Rita), 274 (Llangwm).

8. Evans and Rhys 277-8. *Vita Gundleii* c 15, (V.S.B.G. 189-91.)

9. D. Crouch 'The transformation of Medieval Gwent' *op.cit,* 5. *DB.* i (Herefordshire) ff 162a, 185c. Crouch 1985, 28.

10. Ann Nerys Jones 'The Mynydd Carn prophecy: a re-assessment' *Cambrian Medieval Celtic Studies* 38 (1999), 73-92.

11. This had already been recognised in the nineteenth century: 'the extensive earthworks and dykes ... indicate that it must have been a strongly fortified post before the existing castle was erected', Anon, *Arch Camb* 1885, 345.

12. J.K. Knight *The Three Castles: Grosmont Castle, Skenfrith Castle, White Castle* (2nd, revised ed. Cadw, Cardiff 2000).

13. Williams 1970-71 .Conway Davies *Episcopal Acts Relating to Welsh Dioceses* 2, 618.

14. Orderic Vitalis V, 110. Giraldus Cambrensis *Itinerarium Kambriae* I, 4. J.E. Lloyd *History of Wales* II, 478 dated the seizure (and the first mention of Usk) to 1138, but David Crouch has shown that the date is 1136 (1985, 33 and n.54, 39). 'Morgan the Welshman' did homage to Earl Robert of Gloucester before Robert left for Normandy at the end of 1136. For *Wetuna* see D. Crouch 'The transformation of Medieval Gwent' *op.cit,* 25-26.

15. D. Walker 'Charters of the Earldom of Hereford '1095-1201' *Camden Miscellany* 22 (1964), no 49. Crouch 1985, 33-36. *CChR.*2, 358-9. *By.T*, 137. Orderic Vitalis VI, 518.

16. Walker *Charters* no 28. Crouch 1988, No. 7. *PR* XXI, 22. *By.T* sub anno 1158. O'Neill *Arch Camb* 1936, 376-8. D. Crouch 'The transformation of Gwent' *op.cit,* 30, 43-44, n.104.

17. David Williams 'Llantarnam Abbey' *Mon Ant* 2, part 3 (1967), 131-48. *PR* XXXIII, 59-60. *By.T* sub anno 1173

18. Giraldus Cambrensis *Itinerarium Kambriae* I, 5.

19. *PR* XXIV, 10; Taylor, 249-55.

20. Taylor.

21. Thurlby, 146-7.

22. My account of his career is based on Crouch 2002.

23. E. Besley in Kevin Booth 'Chepstow castle: excavation in the Great Gatehouse 1991' *Mon Ant* 9 (1993), 19-26.

24. D.H. Miles and M.J. Worthington 'List 94: Welsh dendrochronology – phase 2 *Vernacular Architecture* 29 (1998), 126-9. R. Avent and D. Miles 'The Main Gatehouse' in *Chepstow Castle.*

25. Crouch 2002, 80.

26. *Ibid.*, 87-8.

27. *Ibid.,* 93.

28. *Ibid.,* 120.

29. *Ibid.,* 136-7.

30. Knight 1987, 78-80, fig.15 p.86.

31. The South Tower still existed in 1800. Coxe *Historical Tour* vol 1, plate opp p.49, the earliest known plan of Usk Castle.

32. Drawbridge at the upper gate: PRO/NA Sc6/ 927/29. Priestley and Turner, 16.

33. PRO/NA SC6/927/5 m.1. Priestley and Turner, 13.

34. .K. Knight 'Excavations at Mongomery Castle I: The documentary evidence, structures and excavated features. *Arch Camb* 141 (1992), 111, 176-9.

35. O'Neil *Arch Camb* 1936, 376-8.

36. Knight 1977.

37. Avent 2003.

38. Jean Vallery-Radot 'Quelques donjons de Phillipe Auguste' *Bulletin Société Nationale des Antiquaries de la France* 119 (1964), 155-60.

39. J. Mesqui *Châteaux et Enceintes de la France*

Médiévale: de la defense à la résidence (Paris 1991), 137, fig 152. André Chatelain 'Recherche sur les châteaux de Phillipe Auguste' *Archéologie Médiévale* 21 (1991), 115-61; Avent 2006, 89 and fig. 71.]

40. Jean Vallery-Radot 'La genése des Châteaux de plan quadrangulaires' *Bulletin Societe Nationale des Antiquaries de la France* 120 (1965), 238-52.

41. The castle of the Louvre was contemporary with Philip Augustus's town walls of *c.*1190. The Great Tower was finished by November 1202, when it served as model for that at Dun le Roi (Cher). Erlande-Brandenberg. 601-2 Avent 2006 fig.67, p.86.

42. Denise Humbert 'Le Château de Dourdan' *Congres Archeol de France* 103 (1944), 236-45. Knight 1987, fig.17, p.88.

43. Jean Vallery-Radot 'Le donjon de Phillipe Auguste à Villeneuve-sur-Yonne et son Devis' *Château Gaillard 2: Colloque de Buderich* (Cologne 1967), 106-12.

44. T. McNeill 'Squaring circles: flooring round towers in Wales and Ireland' *Medieval Castle in Ireland and Wales*, 96-106. M. Pre 'Le château de Laval' *Congres Archeologique de France* 119e session (Maine) 1961, 353-372.

45. Roger of Wendover *Flowers of History* ed. H.G. Hewlett (*RS* 1889), III, 55-6.

46. Matthew Paris *Chronica Majora* ed. H.R. Luard (*RS* 1883), III, 249-52; Annals of Tewkesbury *Annales Monastici* I ed. H.R. Luard (*RS* 1864), 90.

Chapter VII The de Clares to the Herberts

1. PRO/NA S C 6/ 9216/30; Taylor 1947, 254-5. He originally thought that the 'new tower' might have been the projecting chamber block of the domestic range.

2. *Ibid.,* 255: '*in i can' emp' videlicet chocker'* — 'to the purchase of one dog, of the kind called cocker'; *OED*'s earliest citations for cocker — 'a breed of spaniels trained to start woodcocks, snipe and similar game' — are of 1811 and 1823.

3. Priestley and Turner, 11-20.

4. *CIPM* Vol 3, no 37, 14 October 1295.

5. Priestley and Turner, 13, 46.

6. Priestley and Turner, 13 and 48, n.19.

7. *Ibid.,* 13.

8. *Ibid.,* 15.

9. *Ibid.,* 15.

10. Bradney *Hundred of Usk*, 10.

11. Wood, 28, fig.10.

12. RCHME *Inventory: Herefordshire II, East* (1932), 29-31 and Plate 102. Wood, Frontispiece and Plate V.B.

13. Priestley and Turner, 15.

14. *Ibid.,* 15.

15. PRO/NA SC 6/927/27; Priestley and Turner, 15-16.

16. PRO/NA SC 6/927/29; Priestley and Turner, 16; Ward, 14-15.

17. BL Harleian Ms 1240 *(Liber Niger de Wigmore)*, 86-87.

18. G.A. Holmes 'A protest against the Despensers 1326' *Speculum* 30 (1955), 207-12; R.R. Davies *Lordship*

and Society in the March of Wales 1282-1400 (Oxford 1978), 279-81; Ward, 16-17.

19. *C. Anc.P.* 69 (3360), 102- 4; Williams 1970-1; 44. Ward , 17. 'Morbu' does not occur in dictionaries of medieval Latin, but is presumably from Latin *morbus*, an illness. It could be a nickname for some sort of sick bay.

20. Priestley and Turner, 18 and 49, n.37. *C. Anc.P.* 92 (4554), 139-40.

21. PRO/NA E.101/91/14; Priestley and Turner, 19.

22. PRO/NA SC 6/ 928/16; Priestley and Turner, 19.

23. Priestley and Turner, 49, n.39; J. Knight 'Newport Castle' *Mon Ant* 7 (1991), 26.

24. Ward, 20-21.

25. PRO/NA Exchequer Account Bundle 91, no. 14.

26. *CPR 1405-8*, 160. R.R. Davies 'Plague and Revolt' in *Gwent County History* Vol 2, ed. Ralph Griffiths, Joy Hopkins and Ray Howell (Cardiff, University of Wales Press 2008), 234.

27. PRO/NA SC6/928/22; Priestley and Turner, 20. PRO/NA SC6/928/19 quoted R.R. Davis *op.cit.*, 234

28. W.R.B. Robinson *Early Tudor Gwent, 1485-1547* (Welshpool 2002), 36-7.

29. Williams 1970-1, 47.

30. Thomas Herbert of Tintern *Herbertorum Prosapia* (Cardiff Central Library Ms 5.7)

31. NLW Bute Mss Box 3, Courtney *Medieval, Later Usk*, 99-100.

32. Thomas Churchyard *The Worthines of Wales* (1587, ed of 1776), 20, 55.

33. Bradney *Hundred of Usk*, 189, Coxe *Historical Tour* vol 1, 127.

34. G.H. Clark *Reminiscences of Monmouthshire*, 74.

Chapter VIII The Development of the Norman Town

1. R. Howell 'Roman survival, Welsh revival: The evidence of re-use of Roman remains' *Mon Ant* 17 (2001) 55-60.

2. Mein 1986

3. *Ibid.*, 84-8 and Table 1.

4. Cowley, F.G. 'Gilbert de Clare, earl of Gloucester (the Red Earl) and the Cistercians of south-east Wales' *Arch Camb* 156 (2007), 115-124.

5. Rees, 241-265.

6. Priestley and Turner.

7. Cowley 'Gilbert de Clare', 120-21

8. Underhill, 52-3.

9. Thompson, E.M. *Chronicon Adae De Usk, A.D. 1377-1421* (Oxford 1904)

10. Mein 1986, 100.

11. *Arch Camb* 88 1933, 347-8.

12. Mein 1986, 68.

13. *Ibid.*, 80.

14. Bradney *Hundred of Usk*, 23-33.

15. *Ibid.*, 26 and 31.

16. Mein 1986, 73.

17. Rees, 201.

18. Mein 1986, 72.

19. *Ibid.*, 66.

Chapter IX Adam Usk and Owain Glyndŵr

1. C. Given-Wilson is grateful to Mrs Rosemary Humphreys of Castle House, Usk, for showing me round on my visit to Usk.
2. *The Chronicle of Adam Usk 1377-1421*, ed. and trans. C. Given-Wilson, Clarendon Press, 1997, 86.
3. *Ibid.*, 192.
4. *Ibid.*, 272.
5. *Ibid.*, 84.
6. *Ibid.*, 98.
7. *Ibid.*, 158. On 13 May 1382, when the king confirmed to him a grant of 100s. a year from the issues of the lordship of Usk originally granted to him at the request of Philippa, countess of March, he was described as 'Adam Porter, clerk'. But he was never again referred to, or referred to himself, by this name, and it is very unlikely that it was his family name: it probably refers either to some minor office which he held at Oxford or to his status within the ecclesiastical hierarchy, for it would be another two years before he was ordained subdeacon: *CPR 1381-5*, 115, 307, and see Jeremy Catto, 'Masters, Patrons and the Careers of Graduates in Fifteenth-Century England', in *Concepts and Patterns of Service in the Later Middle Ages*, ed. A. Curry and E. Matthew (Woodbridge, 2000), 57.
8. *Ibid.*, 4.
9. *CPR 1381-5*, 307; *BRUO* ii. I937.
10. *Chronicle of Adam Usk*, 12.
11. The Register of John Waltham, *Bishop of Salisbury 1388-1395*, ed. T.C.B. Timmins (CYS, Woodbridge, 1994), 4; *Registrum Iohannis Trefnant Episcopi Herefordensis 1389-1404*, ed. W.W. Capes (CYS, London, 1916), 359.
12. *Chronicle of Adam Usk*, 152, 250.
13. Lambeth Palace Library, *Register of Thomas Arundel*, i, fo. 265v.
14. *GEC* viii, 448-9.
15. *Ibid.*, 40-48.
16. PRO E403/555, 22 Aug. For Overton, see *Reg. Arundel*, i, fo. 228r.
17. *Ibid.*, 114.
18. *GEC* viii, 459; *Chronicle of Adam Usk*, 146, 238-40.
19. *CPR 1391-6*, 636, 695; *CPR 1386-9*, 23, 28.
20. J.E. Lloyd, *Owen Glendower* (Oxford, 1931), 54, 151-52 (*Ann.OGD*).
21. *Chronicle of Adam Usk*, 160; Lloyd *op.cit*, 54; for Stafford revenues, see T.B. Pugh, *Henry V and the Southampton Plot* (Gloucester, 1988), 38, 46.
22. Walsingham, Thomas *Annals of Richard II and Henry IV* ed. H.T. Rilcy (London, 1866) 343; *CPR*, ii, 137-40.
23. CPR, ii, 294; Christopher Allmand *Henry V* (London, 1992), 26; Rhidian Griffiths, 'Prince Henry and the Exchequer', *Bulletin of the Board of Celtic Studies* 32 (1985) 203.
24. Lloyd *op.cit.*, 75-76; *DNB*, 1311.
25. Allmand *op.cit.*, 27; *PPC*, i, 229-32; *CPR*, ii, 50, 53.
26. *Eulogium Historiarum* ed. F.S. Haydon (London, 1858-

63), iii, 401; Lloyd *op.cit.*, 152 (*AnnOGD*).
27. *PPC*, i, 236.
28. *Chronicle of Adam Usk*, 176.
29. *Ibid.*, 174-6.
30. *Ibid.*, 178, 188.
31. The Pennal declaration is printed in *Welsh Records in Paris*, ed. T. Matthews (Carmarthen, 1910), 83-99.
32. *Chronicle of Adam Usk*, 212-16.
33. *Ibid.*, 239-40.
34. *Register of Robert Hallum*, 6-7 (no. 43); it was Gregory XII, who had succeeded Innocent VII in November 1406, who excommunicated him.
35. *Hierarchia Catholica Medii Aevi*, ed. C. Eubel (2 vols., Rome, 1898), i. 304 n.6. Usk is called 'Adamum Wesk'. The 'true' (Roman) bishop of Llandaff was Thomas Peverell, who was translated to Worcester on 4 July 1407.
36. *PPC*, i, 248-50; *Original Letters* II, i, 39-41.
37. *Chronicle of Adam Usk*, 212.
38. Lloyd *op.cit.*, 98, 152 (*Ann.OGD*); Walsingham *op.cit.*, 399-400; Walter Bower *Johannis de Fordon Scotichronicon cum supplementis et continuatione Walter Boweri* ed. Walter Goodall (Edinburgh, 1759), ii, 452. Before he died, Gruffydd endured six years of imprisonment in various castles, including Nottingham. Bower is wrong in calling Oldcastle Lord Cobham, as he did not acquire that title till 1409, when he married the heiress.
39. *Chronicle of Adam Usk*, 240.
40. *Ibid.*, 272.
41. A corrodian was someone who was granted a corrody (right of board and lodging) at a religious house, by the patron of the house or the king.
42. The original consists of four *cywydd* couplets, as follows (Morris-Jones, 'Adam Usk's epitaph', *Y Cymmrodor* xxxi (1921), 124, 127-33):

    Nole clode yi ethrode yar lleyn
    aduocade llawnhade llundeyn
    A barnour bede breynt apibe
    ty nev aro ty hauabe
    Seliff sunnoeir sinna se
    adam vske eva I kuske
    Deke kummode doctor kymmen
    liena loe i llawn o leue.

43. *Ibid.*, 112-34. C. Given-Wilson is grateful to the Revd R.L. Davies, vicar of Usk, for his help and guidance during my visit to the church.
44. *Chronicle of Adam Usk*, 134, 144.
45. *Ibid.*, 146-8
46. *Ibid.*, 160, 172.
47. *Ibid.*, 262.

Chapter X The Gwehelog pottery kiln and brickworks

1. The campaign of excavations by the Trostrey Excavation Group has run for some 20 years as a result of the co-operation and forbearance of Mr David Morgan of Trostrey Court Farm. Our visits to the kiln and brick-

works sites alongside Camp Wood, Gwehelog have been thanks to the interest in the site of the Humphreys family of Usk Castle, whose land runs out to the end of the ridge overlooking Llancayo and includes the fine Iron Age fort in Camp Wood.

2. Hughes; Wrathmell.
3. Courtney 1986-7.
4. *Ibid.*
5. Coxe *Historical Tour* vol 1, 162.
6. Gwent CRO Q/ PB1, 102.
7. Gwent CRO D. 271.47.
8. Bradney *Hundred of Usk*, 63.
9. P. Riden *Introduction* to the Facsimile edition of the Greenwood's Map of Monmouthshire of 1830 (South Wales Record Society 1985).
10. Bradney *Hundred of Raglan*, 49.
11. Gwent CRO Q/MB, 3, 89.
12. Gwent CRO D 43, 2994/5.
13. There are several possible roads and tracks that are locally known as Potters Lane in the area of Gwehelog and Trostrey. The one described by the late Mr James is the most direct route from the kilns at Camp Wood to Llancayo.
14. The history and archaeology of Trostrey has been the subject of articles in the *Gwent Local History Journal* Nos 65 (1988 with Frank Olding), 71 (1991), 78 (1995) and 86 (1999); Mein et al 1988.
15. Wrathmell, 14, fig.2; National Museum and Gallery of Wales Accession number 57, 115.

Chapter XI Religious Conflict and Religious Toleration in Usk

1. Pugh, 72; *Alumni Oxoniensis*, 1034.
2. *Certificate of the recusants within the diocese of Llandaph*, October 1577 quoted Griffith Davies 1934, 42. 'George Morysse, Mr of arte, resortyng ... to the sayd Roland Morgan, presented for not commyng to church, who dyd refuse his lyvings for that he would not subscribe'. Pugh, 109.
3. In the 1630 Survey of Usk 'saer' occurs frequently as an occupational name e.g. 'John Morris John, saer' (Bradney *Hundred of Usk*, 26)
4. Pugh, 79, 81.
5. *Ibid.*, 89, 91.
6. *Ibid.*, 95-6, 99, 102, 105. David John Morris and Walter John Morris of Usk 1620, but Monkswood 1624. There was often little practical distinction between 'yeoman' and 'gent'. John Pippin for example was 'yeoman' in 1622, but 'gent' the next year.
7. Bradney *Hundred of Usk*, 53. William Johns was vicar of Usk and Llanllowell in 1560; Griffith Davies, 39.
8. *Alumni Oxoniensis*, 519.
9. Bradney *Hundred of Usk*, 120. In 1630, Fortune occupied burgages in Puck Lane and in St Mary Street 'looking towards the church of Uske, called Church-garden', Bradney 27.
10. *Alumni Oxoniensis*, 762.

11. G.F. Nuttall 'The faith of Walter Cradock' *The Welsh Saints 1640-1660* (Cardiff 1957), 18-36.
12. BL Harleian Ms 163, f. 740; J. Eales *Puritans and Roundheads: The Harleys of Brampton Bryan and the Outbreak of the English Civil War* (Cambridge 1990), 106.
13. *A Letter from his Excellencies Quarters ... with a conference between his Excellency and the Marquess of Worcester ...* (London, Bernard Alsop, 21 August 1646) British Library, Thomason Tracts E 351 (13).
14. *AOI* August 15, 1645; 28 October 1646.
15. *CSPD 1657-8*, 363.
16. Bradney *Hundred of Usk*, 49-51 William ap John's widow was living at the Priory in 1555. (Bradney citing 'Mr Wakeman's Mss'). Her son, Thomas Jones of Usk Priory, died on 13 March 1589.
17. Webb, II, 91.
18. *Mercurius Aulicus* 23 November 1644, *Commons Journal* 26 March 1645, Webb II, 4 n.2, 101 and 113-14.
19. Gwent CRO D/ Pa 30.1. Parish register, Bryngwyn.
20. G.E. Aylmer 'Who was ruling in Herefordshire from 1641 to 1661?' *Transactions of the Woolhope Naturalists Field Club* 40 (1972), 373-387.
21. *AOI* Vol I, 780 (27 Sept.1645)
22. J.R.S. Phillips *The Justices of the Peace in Wales and Monmouthshire 1541-1689* (Cardiff 1975), 359.
23. *A Declaration of the Proceedings of Divers Knights and other Gentlemen in Glamorgan* (B.L. Thomason Tracts E 394 (5) Phillips *Civil War* II, 341-3). *A Full relation of the whole proceedings of the late rising and commotion in Wales, reported in letters to the Parliament and Sir Thomas Fairfax* (B.L. Thomason Tracts E 396 (9) Phillips II, 335-40); Knight 2005, 122.
24. Siddons.
25. *Alumni Oxoniensis*, 762.
26. John Kenyon *The Popish Plot* (1972) is the definitive account.
27. E.O.A. Whiteman *The Compton Census of 1676: A Critical Edition* (1986).
28. Knight 2005, 155-7.
29. J.K. Knight 'A nonconformity of the gentry? Catholic recusants in seventeenth century Abergavenny' *Mon Ant* 20 (2004), 145-152.
30. Foley Records I, 456-7; series XII, 912-31. Foley was unable to trace a Jesuit named John Pritchard (I, 633), but Lewis specifically mentions him in his deposition on entering the English College.
31. John Savage became Earl Rivers in 1640. He would have been about 32 at the time of the visit. His kinsmen, the Savages of Beeston and Clifton, were catholic recusants in the seventeenth century. S.J. Lander in *VCH Cheshire* vol 3 ed. C.R. Elrington (1980), 89.
32. One source claims that Lewis was a student at Middle Temple in 1632-5. This is confusion with a namesake from Abergavenny, the son of William Lewis, admitted in 1613. Another David Lewis, from Llandewi Skyrydd, was admitted in 1606. I am very grateful to Renae

Satterley, rare books librarian, Middle Temple, for this information.

33. Sean Kelsey 'Staging the trial of Charles I' *The Regicides and the Execution of Charles I* (ed Jason Peacey, London 2001), 78; *CSPD 1644*, 216.

34. *An Abstract of Several Examinations, and taken upon oath ... delivered unto the Honourable House of Commons ... by John Arnold and John Scudamore Esqs ...* (London J.C. For John Gain 1680).

35. David Lewis *A Narrative of the Imprisonment and Tryal of Mr David Lewis, priest of the Society of Jesus : written by himself ... to which is annexed his last SPEECH at the place of execution.*

37. Events after Lewis's return from London are recorded in a manuscript journal of 1780 by Henry Philips of Llantarnam, seemingly drawing on a lost prison diary by Lewis. Gwent CRO D. 3267. 114.

36. Lewis *Narrative* and *The Speech of Mr Henry Lewis, a Jesuit who was executed at Usk* (London 1679). A manuscript of the sermon, with what seems to be Lewis's signature, is in NLW (Baker Gabb Ms 723).

37. D. Hughes 'Galargerdd i'r Sant Dafydd Lewis' *Y Cylchgrawn Catholig* 2 (1994) 23; Olding 2006, 32.

38. This may have been a successor of John Rosser, cutler, of Old Market Street (Bradney *Hundred of Usk*, 33), a tenant of Sir Trevor Williams. I owe this suggestion to Mrs Jan Barrow. For a list of the pamphlets see Knight 2005, 203-4.

39. P. Bliss (ed) *Reliquiae Hearnianae* vol 2, 838-9; J.H. Clark *Reminiscences of Monmouthshire* (Usk 1908).

40. 'The Church in England in the 1640s' *Reactions to the English Civil War 1642-1649* ed. J. Morrill (1982), 91.

Chapter XII Some Buildings of Usk
1. PRO SC 6/927/1.
2. BL Harleian MS 6842, ff.292-302.
3. Newman *Buildings of Wales: Gwent Monmouthshire*, p.595. One is illustrated in Jan Barrow *From Dawn to Dusk* (2004), p.55.
4. Bradney *Hundred of Usk* I, 97.
5. *Ibid.*, 102.

Chapter XIII The 18th-century Market Town
1. PRO E179/148/97.
2. GRO Misc. MSS 519.
3. GRO D.896.050.051 1792.
4. Cadw, November 2007.
5. Peate, I. *The Welsh House* 1940, 179.
6. NLW Badminton Group II 10,718 Extracts from Rentals at Badminton.
7. NLW Badminton Group II 10, 720.
8. Davies, Twiston *Welsh life in the 18th century*, 113.
9. NLW Tred. 64/14.
10. Waters, Ivor *The Unfortunate Valentine Morris* 1964, 11-4.
11. GRO Usk Turnpike Minutes 1766-80.
12. Archer, M.S. *Welsh Post Towns pre 1840* 1970, 118.

13. Calendar of Chancery Rolls vol.iii, 449.
14. GRO D43.1554.
15. NLW Llangibby A51. f.252.
16. Michael, D.P.M. *Mapping of Monmouthshire* 1985, 72
17. Bradfield, Nancy *900 years of English costume* 1987.
18. Davies, E.T. *Monmouthshire Schools and Education up to 1870* 1957, 18.
19. Rickards, Robert *Church and Priory of St Mary*, Usk 1904.
20. Williams, A.C. (ed.) *John Wesley in Wales 1739-1790 Entries from his Journal and Diary* 1971.
21. Institute of Geological Sciences. Abergavenny Map Sheet 232 1" 1958.
22. Riden, P. *John Bedford and iron works at Cefn Cribwr* 1992, 10, 15.
23. John W.D. & Simcox A. *Pontypool and Usk Japanned Wares* 1966, 32.

Chapter XV Usk's Secret Army
1. For general information on this aspect of the Second World War, *With Britain in Mortal Danger* by John Warwickier, researcher and editor at the Auxiliary Unit Museum at Parham in Suffolk is a substantial book, and a mine of information. *Mercian Maquis* (Logaston Press) is a very readable story of the Auxiliary Units in Herefordshire and Worcestershire, but also covers the wider picture. A recently published novel *Resistance* by Owen Shears, which draws on the story of the Auxiliary Units, is a fictional account of units in the Olchon Valley between Abergavenny and Hereford following a successful German invasion of Britain in late 1944 after a defeat of the Allies in Normandy.

Chapter XVI Challenges to the Future of Usk
1. Lewis, David R. Early Victorian Usk Park Place Papers no. 10 1982.
2. Coxe *Historic Tour* vol.1 Town of Usk, 1801, New edition 1995.
3. Lewis *op.cit,* 110, 111.
4. Gwent CRO: Minutes of East Monmouthshire Joint Planning Committee.
5. County Development Plan (Part 1) County Area: Report of Survey and Analysis: 1954.
6. *Ibid.*, 446.
7. Gwent CRO CPC D-17/1.
8. Programmed for completion in the period 5-15 years after the plan's approval, *ie* in the 1960s.
9. Evidently, later found not to be required and the whole area was later developed as Priory Gardens housing estate.
10. Gwent CRO G32 R1 22.
11. Monmouth Borough Local Plan: adopted May 1997.
12. The subsequent planning application by Bovis Homes was refused by the county planning committee, was 'called in' and after a public inquiry was refused by the Welsh Assembly Government as it contravened the policy of not building on flood plains.

13. Monmouth Local Development Plan, 18.
14. Monmouth Local Development Plan, 54.
15. UDP, 60: paragraph 4.6.9.
16. At page 128 the adopted Unitary Development Plan states that the A472 Usk to Pontypool Road will become the responsibility of the Welsh Assembly Government. Correspondence between the author of this chapter and the county's Head of Planning has revealed that this statement is incorrect. The error will be rectified by an insert in all future copies of the UDP and the correction highlighted in the new Local Development Plan. This means that the county council will continue to be responsible for the A472 and for finding solutions to the traffic problems in Usk.
17. B. Tyson, Final Report on assessment of air quality in Usk, 2 April 2007.
18. a. The (Routes A472 and B4598 at Usk) (Prohibition of Vehicles) Orders 1995. b. The Gwent County Council (Various Roads, Caerleon and District) (Prohibition of Commercial Vehicles) Order 1985.
19. B. Tyson, specialist environmental health officer, Monmouthshire County Council. Draft report 7th March 2007, 2nd draft report 22nd March 2007, final report 2nd April 2007 Assessment of Air Quality in Usk. The documents are, as would be expected, highly technical.
20. Compiled from Tyson, final report *op. cit.*
21. The national increase in car use is expected to be 30% and there is no reason to expect that, given its social and economic character, the Usk area will be any different.
22. Surveys by the author: September 2007.
23. Challenged by several local councils in the High Court where the finding of a 'case to answer' caused the county council to withdraw the charging proposals.
24. The other being that Usk, unlike Caerleon, could not be supplied by sea. (W. Manning *Roman Wales* University of Wales Press, 2001.)
25. Jan Barrow *Llanbadoc: the history of a rural parish*, 1999, 15.
26. Planning Policy: Wales: March 2002, 139, supplemented by Technical Advice Note 15: Development and Flood Risk.
27. Monmouthshire: adopted Unitary Development Plan June 2006: Development on Flood Plains, 32.
28. *Ibid.* Policy C3 Special Landscape Areas: within these areas development will not be permitted if, taking into account its scale and nature, it would have a serious harmful effect on those characteristics of the area that have led to its designation, unless that harm is outweighed by benefits to the rural economy that could not be achieved by development on sites outside Special Landscape Areas and statutorily designated areas. Where development is acceptable in principle it must respect the high quality of the landscape and be sensitively integrated into it. (Adopted Unitary Development Plan, 146).
29. UDP Policy H9 (page 9) defines affordable housing as 'both low cost market and subsidised housing, irrespective of tenure, exclusive or shared ownership, or financial arrangements that will be available to people that cannot afford to occupy houses generally available on the open market'.
30. The other towns being Abergavenny, Chepstow, Monmouth and Caldicott.
31. The UDP quotes the Welsh Assembly Government's examples of expected need as:
a) existing residents needing separate accommodation in the area (newly married couples, people living in tied accommodation, or retirement);
b) people whose work provides important services and who need to live closer to the local community;
c) people who are not resident locally but have long standing links with the local community (eg. elderly people who need to move back to a village to be near relatives) and
d) people with the offer of a job in the locality who cannot take up the offer because of the lack of affordable housing.
32. Mark Lynas *Six Degrees: Our Future on a Hotter Planet* Harper Collins, 2007. This analysis postulates the possible effects of climate temperature increases, degree by degree, from one degree to six degrees Celsius over the next 50 years and beyond. It suggests that an average increase worldwide of between three and four degrees of warming would reduce the UK to an archipelago of tiny islands.
33. Monmouthshire Local Development Plan (LDP); Delivery Agreement as adopted.

Index